Methods and Methodologies for Language Teaching

Methods and Methodologies for Language Teaching

The Centrality of Context

Andy Curtis
Professor of TESOL, Anaheim University, USA

Applied Linguistics for the Language Classroom
Series Editor: Andy Curtis

BLOOMSBURY ACADEMIC
Bloomsbury Publishing Plc
50 Bedford Square, London, WC1B 3DP, UK
1385 Broadway, New York, NY 10018, USA
29 Earlsfort Terrace, Dublin 2, Ireland

BLOOMSBURY, BLOOMSBURY ACADEMIC and the Diana logo are trademarks of Bloomsbury Publishing Plc

First published by Palgrave Macmillan 2017
Reprinted by Bloomsbury Academic, 2024

Copyright © Andy Curtis 2017

The author has asserted their right under the Copyright, Designs and Patents Act, 1988, to be identified as the author of this work.

All rights reserved. No part of this publication may be reproduced or transmitted in any form or by any means, electronic or mechanical, including photocopying, recording, or any information storage or retrieval system, without prior permission in writing from the publishers.

Bloomsbury Publishing Plc does not have any control over, or responsibility for, any third-party websites referred to or in this book. All internet addresses given in this book were correct at the time of going to press. The author and publisher regret any inconvenience caused if addresses have changed or sites have ceased to exist, but can accept no responsibility for any such changes.

A catalogue record for this book is available from the British Library.

A catalogue record for this book is available from the Library of Congress.

ISBN 978–1–137–40735–1 paperback

To find out more about our authors and books visit www.bloomsbury.com and sign up for our newsletters.

Contents

Series Editor's Introduction   vi

Author's Introduction   x

Abbreviations   xiv

1	Five Thousand Years in Five Thousand Words	1
2	The Centrality of Context	20
3	Task-Based Language Teaching and Learning in Context	41
4	Communicative Language Teaching in Context	73
5	Content-Based Instruction and Content and Language Integrated Learning	103
6	The Direct Method and the Audio-Lingual Method	126
7	The Grammar Translation Method	147
8	Humanistic and Alternative Methods	159
9	Where Do We Go From Here?	194

Glossary   214

References   221

Index   240

Series Editor's Introduction

The purpose of this *Applied Linguistics for the Language Classroom (ALLC)* series is to help bridge what still appears to be a significant gap between the field of applied linguistics and the day-to-day classroom realities of many language teachers and learners. For example, Selivan recently wrote that 'Much applied linguistics research remains unapplied, is often misapplied, or is downright inapplicable' (2016, p. 25). This gap appears to have existed for some time, and has yet to be bridged. For example, in 1954, Pulgram published *Applied Linguistics in Language Teaching*, which was followed a few years later by Robert Lado's classic work *Linguistics Across Cultures: Applied Linguistics for Language Teachers* (1957). However, we are still seeing articles 60 years later helping language teachers to apply linguistic theory to language classrooms (Magrath, 2016).

Therefore, one of the features of this *ALLC* series that make it distinctive is our focus on helping to bridge the on-going gap between applied linguistics and language classrooms. Our envisaged readership for these books is busy classroom language teachers, including those entering the profession and those who have been in it for some time already. We also gave a lot of thought to what teachers completing a first degree in Education, teachers doing MA TESOL courses, and language teachers completing other professional qualifications would find most useful and helpful. One way of helping is to include a glossary at the back of each book in the *ALLC* series, and all of the words **in bold** are explained in more detail in the glossary.

Bearing such readers in mind, one of the ambitious goals of this *ALLC* series is to present language teachers with clear, concise and up-to-date overviews and summaries of what they need to know in key areas: Assessment; Methods and Methodologies;

Technology; Research Methods; and Phonetics, Phonology and Pronunciation. Attempting to do what much larger and weightier volumes have attempted, but doing so in volumes that are slimmer and more accessible, has been a challenge, but we believe these books make an original and creative contribution to the literature for language teachers.

Another distinctive feature of this *ALLC* series has been our International Advisory Board, made up of Professor Kathi Bailey and Professor David Nunan. These two outstanding figures in our field helped us to keep our target readers in mind and to stay focused on the classroom while keeping the connections to applied linguistics, so we can advance the building of the bridges between applied linguistics and language classrooms.

The subtitle of this *ALLC* volume, *Methods and Methodologies for Language Teaching*, is *The Centrality of Context*. That subtitle highlights one of the recurring themes of this book, which is that all methods and methodologies should be considered in relation to where they began, where they are being used now, and the times and distances in between. And in relation to time, in the first chapter, I summarize around 5000 years of language teaching and learning. When I refer to that number in my talks, attendees are often surprised, as our field has a much longer history than many language teachers and learners may realize. Also, although English is now the dominant second and foreign language of the world today, English language teaching was a relative newcomer within those 50 centuries of history.

Another recurring theme highlighted in Chapter 1 is the problem of 'methodological bandwagoning', in which 'we can find ourselves running from one new methodology to another – and sometimes back again – without stopping to ask whether this is really the best way to move language education forward' (p. 5). Because of the importance of context, the second chapter focuses on the Centrality of Context, based on the fact that 'Methods are not neutral' and 'Language teaching and learning do not occur in a vacuum', which means that 'where we do what we do is at least as important as how we do it' (p. 20).

One of the ways in which this book is different from what is already available is its non-chronological presentation of the methods and methodologies considered. In the traditional, timeline presentation, the first chapters are about the earliest and oldest methods, and the last chapters are about the newest and most recent methods. However, I have chosen to present the methods in the order of their prominence, so the first methodological chapter (3) is about Task-Based Language Teaching (TBLT). The reason why TBLT comes first is because it can be considered to be the dominant methodology currently, as reflected by the enormous amounts of research, writing, publishing and conference-presenting being done on TBLT, which is far more than that kind of work being done on any of the other methodologies at this time. It is important to note that 'prominence' is not the same as 'prevalence'. TBLT has been vigorously promoted in recent years, but it is not being used everywhere – nor should it be, as no methodology can claim to be the 'best' for all learners and all teachers, in all contexts and at all times.

Chapter 4 focuses on Communicative Language Teaching (CLT), out of which TBLT grew, and which has now been surpassed by TBLT in terms of prominence. New connections are considered, including CLT in relation to the growth of the tourism industry, and in relation to the privileging of one modality – speaking – leading to the privileging of one group of language users and teachers – native speakers.

Content-Based Instruction (CBI) and Content and Language Integrated Learning (CLIL) are the focus of Chapter 5. As with the other methodologies considered in this book, I start by highlighting the origins and some of the key features of the methodology. The readers are then taken inside the classroom, in this case, the CBI/CLIL classroom, after which the pros and cons of each methodology are considered. The assessment of learning outcomes should be one of the most important factors in deciding which methodologies to make use of, but it appears that this is often not the case. Therefore, to acknowledge the importance of assessment, there is a brief discussion of each methodology in relation to assessment of learning outcomes. Each chapter includes activities for the readers to engage in, and concludes with suggested readings for those who wish to learn more about and go deeper into any of the methodologies.

The same sequence is followed in Chapter 6, on the Direct Method (DM) and the Audio-Lingual Method (ALM), and in Chapter 7, on the Grammar Translation Method (GTM). It is worth pointing out here that GTM is usually the starting point for books on language teaching methods and methodologies, because GTM is considered to be the original, centuries-old language teaching methodology. However, although GTM is still used in a number of contexts, over the centuries it has fallen out of favour with those who decide which methodologies are currently 'in' and which are the methodological equivalent of *personae non gratae*.

In the penultimate chapter (8), I present concise overviews of four well-known but now relatively little-used methodologies, which are considered together, as they are all described as humanistic and alternative methods: Suggestopedia, Total Physical Response (TPR), Community Language Learning (CLL) and the Silent Way. In the ninth and final chapter, I look at where we are now methodologically, and where we might be headed. I conclude by reiterating the centrality of context, by highlighting the fact that methods still matter and that 'we still have a lot to learn about how languages are learned' (p. 195). I also try to lay to rest, once and for all, the idea that we are 'post methods'. We are, I believe, beyond that notion now – making us at least *post* post methods.

Andy Curtis

Author's Introduction

All of the books in this *ALLC* series start with a brief autobiographical introduction to the authors. The reason for this relates to the importance of context, as every learner and every teacher is a unique collection of experiences, which no other person on Earth has experienced in exactly the same way. That makes each person an individual context, different from the seven billion others around them.

My professional context started with a career in clinical medicine, specializing in biochemistry, working in hospitals in England. However, I became increasingly concerned about the way Western medical training, at that time, reduced people to patients, who were further reduced to a set of symptoms. I was also troubled by the compartmentalization of the body, separating the physiology from the psychology, based on the misguided but deeply held belief that flesh and blood had nothing to do with body and soul. There was also the entirely curative approach to healthcare, now known as Big Pharma, in which the person becomes ill and then is cured. This went against everything I was taught based on the 3000-year-old Indian preventative approach called Ayurvedic medicine, the whole and holistic point of which is to help people not get ill in the first place.

Following such a non-traditional path into language education – coming via clinical medicine rather than via a traditional literature or applied linguistics route – was difficult, but such a path allowed me to bring an organic perspective to the language classroom, which was new at that time, 25 years ago. For example, I saw language itself as a living, breathing entity, able to exhibit most or even all of the qualities and characteristics that constitute life, such as birth, growth, reproduction and death. By extension, then, language classrooms and language lessons were organic entities, changing from moment to moment, growing constantly in ways that could not be predicted or controlled.

Applying these biological and organic frames of reference to language teaching and learning helped me to see recurring patterns in the classroom, in terms of what the teachers and the learners were doing, which is how I became interested in language teaching methods and methodologies. This unusual career path, and the equally unusual perspective that comes with it, is reflected in the ways in which the methods and methodologies are presented in this book. For example, I often leave the literature of language education and go off into other areas that are not usually referred to in books on language teaching methods and methodologies. A good example of this can be seen in Chapter 4, on Communicative Language Teaching (CLT), in which I draw on the published research from the field of travel and tourism to help explain the rise of the 'native speaker myth' in English language teaching. There are also references to articles published in journals such as *Scientific American*, articles on mathematics education, women's history and semiotics, as well as articles published in newspapers, and other non-academic sources.

Unfortunately, I did not pay as much attention to my history teacher in high school as I should have done. As a result, it took me longer to realize the importance of having a historical understanding of whatever it is we are looking at today. But having understood the importance of knowing how we got to this point in order to know where we might be headed, I have gone further back than usual into the language education literature, more than a century, to the 1890s. This is partly to show that a significant amount of what is often put forward as being 'new' today is in fact old, and can be traced back to times long before now.

One of the things that I was keen to avoid was the duplication of other books on language teaching approaches and methods, such as Jack Richards and Theodore Rodgers' *Approaches and Methods in Language Teaching* (2014, third edition), or books on language teaching techniques and principles, such as Diane Larsen-Freeman and Marti Anderson's *Techniques and Principles in Language Teaching* (2011, third edition). Both of those books are included in the Suggested Readings at the end of Chapter 1, as they give detailed descriptions of the methods and methodologies covered in this book. Therefore, one of my goals was to look more critically at where these methods and methodologies came from, how they ended up being all over the place, and some of the consequences of the packaging, marketing and exporting of methodologies.

I was also interested in the rise and fall of methodologies, especially in relation to individuals who have been instrumental in promoting particular methodologies. Most of the time, when I read about methodologies, there are the family names of the most prominent proponents (with a year in parentheses), but few, if any, details about their lives. This may be because of the need to create the impression of scientific and/or academic objectivity through distancing the particular individuals, as though they were somehow 'incidental' in the rise (and sometimes the fall) of particular methods. That was not my experience in the medical sciences, where the lives of famous scientists, such as Steven Hawking, Albert Einstein and Marie Curie, are researched and written about in great detail, resulting in countless biographies and even Hollywood movies. This is not to suggest that movies should have been made about methodologists! But we do seem to have lost something by presenting methodologies as though they arose out of the ether; as though the lives of the individuals who proposed and promoted certain methodologies – who built entire professional lives and careers based on those methodologies – were not important.

Therefore, even if you are already familiar with the methodologies presented in this book, I hope that the approach I have taken will help you understand different aspects of the methodologies, such as their origins, their history and the lives of the individuals involved. And if you are new to these methodologies, I hope that this book will help you appreciate the importance of concepts such as contextual appropriateness and the use of principled and informed eclecticism, as you develop your own, unique teaching styles, over the years to come.

Andy Curtis

Abbreviations

ALLC	*Applied Linguistics for the Language Classroom*
ALM	Audio-Lingual Method
CALD	*Cambridge Advanced Learner's Dictionary*
CBI	Content-Based Instruction
CLIL	Content and Language Integrated Learning
CLL	Community Language Learning
CLT	Communicative Language Teaching
COLT	Community and Lesser Taught Languages
CoPs	Communities of Practice
DM	Direct Method
EAP	English for Academic Purposes
EFL	English as a Foreign Language
ELT	English Language Teaching
EMI	English as the Medium of Instruction
ESL	English as a Second Language
ESP	English for Specific Purposes
EVP	English for Vocational Purposes
GTM	Grammar Translation Method
ICC	Intercultural Communicative Competence
IELTS	International English Language Testing System
LEEP	Learning English for Examination Purposes
LSP	Languages for Specific Purposes
MODE	Macmillan Online Dictionary of English
NEST	Native English-Speaking Teacher
NNEST	Non-native English-Speaking Teachers
SALT	Suggestive Accelerated Learning and Teaching
SIOP	Sheltered Instruction Observation Protocol
SLA	Second Language Acquisition
STT	Student Talk Time

TBLA	task-based language assessment
TBLPA	task-based language performance assessment
TBLT	Task-Based Language Teaching
TBLTL	Task-Based Language Teaching and Learning
TOEFL	Test of English as a Foreign Language
TPR	Total Physical Response

CHAPTER 1

Five Thousand Years in Five Thousand Words

Before reading this chapter, consider the following six points. Think about whether you agree or disagree with them, and why. Whatever your response to the statements, regardless of whether you agree or disagree with them, they may help you read more thoughtfully and reflectively. These six statements also summarize some of the main learning points in this chapter.

- Language teaching and learning, including English Language Teaching (ELT), has a much longer history than many of us may realize.
- Language teaching methodologies have been with us for a very long time indeed, and show no signs of leaving us any time soon, in spite of claims that we are in a 'post-methods era'.
- Criticisms of methodologies are not new. Methodologies have always been criticized, and probably always will be. This does not mean we can or should do away with them.
- The development of methodologies in language education has not taken place along a nice, neat linear trajectory, in which each methodological era builds logically on the previous one. In our field, the methodological development has been circular – going in circles – and cyclical – coming and going. That development has often been chaotic, and it has been at least as much emotional, and based on feelings, as it has been rational, and based on data.
- Methodologies are at the interface of many different aspects of language teaching and learning, including knowledge, skills and understanding, as well as values,

beliefs and motivations. As a result, definitions and descriptions of methodologies can be highly complex. They can also be relatively straightforward and concise.
- Language teachers need to be able to articulate their bases for accepting certain language teaching methodologies and for rejecting others, based on a principled and **informed eclecticism**.

Introduction and Overview

It is not possible to compress 5000 years of history into 5000 words, but in this chapter, we will cover many of the main highlights of the first 50 centuries of language teaching. We will also consider some key questions, including: What is a 'language teaching method'? What is a 'language teaching methodology'? And: Where do these ideas come from? In the second part of this chapter, we look at several different definitions and descriptions of 'method' and 'methodology', including some of the classic definitions that have been central in shaping our understanding of these key concepts. After looking at areas of overlap in meaning, and the complexity of these concepts, we will then discuss the '**anti-methods**' and '**post-methods**' period. One of the recurring points in the chapter is the importance of language teachers today knowing something about the millennia of language education we have inherited, and within that, the centuries of English language teaching and learning that are the foundation of what we do today.

The First Five Thousand Years

Have you ever wondered what it would have been like to be a language teacher 100 years ago? Or a thousand? Or even 5000 years ago? Over the many years that I have been asking language teachers this question, they often look bemused and confused, partly because such questions seem so far removed, in time and space, from the immediate and pressing classroom concerns of today and tomorrow. Another reason for such puzzled looks is that many language teachers do not know that there is a documented history of language teaching stretching back thousands of years. Even those relatively few teachers who know that our field has such a history are not sure what is the point of knowing anything about that history.

The stories in the international media about adopted children spending years trying to find their biological parents show an extremely deep-seated desire to know where we have come from. Likewise, knowing our own professional history can also help us. For example, a character in one of the late Sir Terry Pratchett's (1948–2015) best-selling comic fantasy *Discworld* books says:

> It is important that we know where we come from, because if you do not know where you come from, then you don't know where you are, and if you don't know where you are, you don't know where you're going. And if you don't know where you're going, you're probably going wrong. (Pratchett, 2010, p. 477)

That idea also relates to the line in the song 'Any Road' by the Beatles guitarist George Harrison: 'If you don't know where you're going, any road will take you there.'

We do not necessarily 'go wrong' when we do not know our own history, but a strong case can be made that, if we want to know where we are now, and where we might be headed, we need to know how we got here. Some writers and researchers working in the field of language methodology have also highlighted the importance of teachers having some historical understanding of the field. For example, Diane Larsen-Freeman and Marti Anderson note in their *Techniques and Principles in Language Teaching*: 'we believe that educators should have a sense of the history of the field, not only of contemporary practices' (2011, p. xv). Larsen-Freeman and Anderson do not give reasons for that belief. Nor do they suggest how this 'sense of history' can be gained, other than implicitly, by presenting the methods along a historical timeline, but with relatively little, if any, actual discussion of the history of the field. Or, if there is such a discussion, it is usually confined to the last 50 years or so, as noted by Wheeler (2013).

This brings us to the question of how much documented, verifiable history there is regarding language teaching and learning. According to Claude Germain's book, *Évolution de l'Enseignement des Langues: 5000 Ans D'Histoire* (1993), there is up to 5000 years of such history. Germain starts with the Babylonians, who lived in the ancient lands of Mesopotamia, in the part of the world that we know today as Iran. This may have been the first time and place where language teaching formally took place, as a result of two cultural and linguistic groups, the Sumerians and the Akkadians, living side-by-side, borrowing liberally from each other's languages, competing and exchanging places, over long periods of time. Germain takes the reader on an epic journey, from Mesopotamia to ancient Egypt and ancient Greece; from there to the Middle Ages and the Renaissance, on into the nineteenth century, and finishing up in the twentieth.

In terms of ELT, Howatt's *A History of English Language Teaching* (1984) notes that documented ELT started in the 1400s. That is still more than 700 years of history, but compared with the teaching and learning of other languages, ELT was a relative latecomer. However, as we shall see in the following chapters, although ELT did not become established until several centuries after the teaching and learning of some other languages, the methods employed in ELT would come to dominate the language teaching and learning world.

There was a time, not so long ago, when some knowledge of the history of language teaching methodologies was considered an integral part of the education of future language teachers. However, the vocal anti-methods and post-methods critics (see below) have questioned whether such a detailed knowledge is necessary today – or even if it was ever needed.

But, because our field has a much longer, richer and deeper history than many language teachers may realize, just knowing that – even without knowing any of the details – can be potentially empowering, in a number of ways. One way is by helping us see where we are going, through understanding more about how we got here. Another is by helping us realize that although language education as a discipline may appear to be relatively new, compared with, for example, medicine or law, our field has a history that is as long and as rich, as wide and as deep as (m)any of the others. So, before we launch into chapters on the different methodologies, we should spend a little time briefly familiarizing ourselves with our own history.

One of the most thoroughly researched books ever written on the history of language teaching is Louis Kelly's *25 Centuries of Language Teaching*. The book covers the period from 500 BC to 1969, the year the book was first published, and includes a list of well over 1100 *primary* sources (pp. 409–455). However, in spite of such an achievement, Kelly's book appears to be largely unheard of by most of today's language teachers. That is a great pity, especially as Kelly made many observations that still apply, including the points that 'Nobody really knows what is new or old in present-day language teaching procedures' and 'much that is being claimed as revolutionary this century is merely a rethinking and renaming of early ideas and procedures' (1969, p. ix). This is an important point, because there is always someone, somewhere claiming to have discovered – and who now happens to be selling – some new, innovative and ground-breaking method that will revolutionize language teaching and learning (see Chapter 7).

This is not to agree with the position that 'there is nothing new under the sun'. But there does appear to have been a long, strong tendency in our field to jump from one 'methodological **bandwagon**' to another. As a result, as language teachers, we can find ourselves running from one new methodology to another – and sometimes back again – without stopping to ask whether this is really the best way to move language education forward. As Mark Clarke put it, in his article 'On Bandwagons, Tyranny and Commonsense': 'As a profession, we seem to have a strong propensity for bandwagons, an inclination to seek simple, final solutions for complex problems' (1982, p. 444). Dale Lange made the same point some years later, when he commented that, in relation to foreign language teaching, 'Unfortunately, the latest bandwagon "methodologies" come into prominence without much study or understanding, particularly those that appear easiest to apply in the classroom' (1990, p. 253). If we can finally and fully stop bandwagoning, we can stand still for a while and step back, so we can see where we are, how we got here, and where we may be headed.

The most recent example of this tendency to jump on whatever bandwagon happens to be rolling by could be **translanguaging**, which is defined by Canagarajah (2011) as 'the ability of multilingual speakers to shuttle between languages, treating the diverse languages that form their repertoire as an integrated system' (p. 401). This particular potential bandwagon gained momentum and picked up speed in 2014, with the publication of the book *Translanguaging: Language, Bilingualism and Education* (García & Wei, 2014). Two of the proponents of translanguaging, Lasagabaster and García, claim that it is 'a pedagogical strategy ... which fosters the dynamic and integrative use of bilingual students' languages in order to create a space in which the incorporation of both languages is seen as natural and teachers accept it as a legitimate pedagogical practice' (Lasagabaster & García 2014, p. 557).

In most of the many hundreds of language classes that I have taught and observed, all over the world, over the last 25 years, the students were constantly shuttling and scuttling between their first languages and the target language. The main distinguishing feature was the teacher's reaction. In my classes, and in many of those that I observed, the teacher was OK with the learners making such first language–target language moves. But in some of the more severe classes observed, use of the first language was not allowed. However, that position appears to have become increasingly uncommon, as the value of the learners' first language has been seen as an asset rather than as an interference.

Turning a noun into a verb, in this case, making 'languaging' out of 'language', does display a healthy linguistic creativity in terms of creating neologisms. Likewise, using 'codemeshing' (Canagarajah, 2011) instead of the long-established 'code-mixing' and 'code-switching' to describe how language users move between their languages is an effective way to create a (meta)language of translanguaging. Also, for those relatively few language teachers who still believe in the target-language-only myth, and who do not 'welcome other language structures into the classroom' (Hermann, 2015, p. 2), translanguaging can remind them of the value and importance of learners' first languages. And in terms of the politics of pedagogical practices, moving from a more compartmentalized model of bilingualism to a more open model may be helpful (Creese & Blackledge, 2010). But any claims that this is some sort of major breakthrough in the teaching and learning of second and foreign languages would be at best an overstatement, at worst an apparent attempt at rolling out the next bandwagon.

To return to Kelly, one of his more controversial claims is that 'The total corpus of ideas accessible to language teachers has not changed basically in 2,000 years' (p. 362). However, again, this should not be taken to mean that language teaching methodologies have not changed during that time. On the contrary, Kelly explains that 'What has been *in constant change* are the ways of building methods' from that total corpus of ideas, and that 'the part of the corpus that is accepted *varies from generation to generation* as does the form in which the ideas present themselves' (p. 362, emphases added). Kelly's reference to shifting generational acceptability and changing preferences helps to explain why the field of language teaching has suffered from this kind of 'bandwagoning'.

Some language teachers may be resistant to trying different methodologies that may be new to them, but not new to the field. This response is part of a normal and natural aversion to making mistakes, especially publicly, and particularly in front of one's peers, supervisors, managers and so on, and for teachers, in front of their learners. On this point, Kelly has some reassuring words: 'Very few inherently bad ideas have ever been put forward in language teaching' (p. 363). That may be another controversial claim, but given the breadth and depth of Kelly's work, it is worth considering such claims. We will look at this idea that there have been 'very few bad ideas' in some of the following chapters, especially Chapter 7, on **alternative** and **humanistic** methods.

One reason for many language teachers assuming that our field has only been around for the last half-century is the publication, in 1963, of Edward Anthony's brief but important paper 'Approach, Method, and Technique', with those three levels arranged within a hierarchy. As Anthony put it, 'techniques carry out a method which is consistent with an approach' (p. 64). Fifty years later, Anthony's paper is still being cited as a starting point. Another reason for this incorrect assumption that our field has a history of only 50 years or so are statements made in influential books, for example, Jack Richards' and Theodore Rodgers' *Approaches and Methods in Language Teaching* (1986, 2001, 2014). In that book, Richards and Rodgers state: 'The whole foundation of contemporary language teaching was developed during the early part of the twentieth century' (2001, p. 1). However, the foundations were laid long before the twentieth century, with contemporary language teaching being built on foundations laid centuries and even millennia ago, as noted by Wheeler (2013).

Anthony (1963) also observed that 'Over the years, teachers have adopted, adapted, invented and developed a bewildering variety of terms which describe the activities in which they engage and the beliefs which they hold' (p. 63). Although much has changed during the 50-plus years since Anthony's short paper was published, the 'bewildering variety of terms' has continued to grow and even multiply. For example, more than 40 years after Anthony's paper, Kumaravadivelu complained that a 'plethora of terms and labels such as approach, design, methods, practices, principles, procedures, strategies, tactics, techniques, and so on are used to describe various elements constituting language teaching' (2006, p. 83). As explained in the Introduction to this book, this is one of the reasons for writing this book, to help language teachers understand the ever-expanding number of terms and the activities they refer to, in the context of the teacher-readers' day-to-day classroom realities and practices.

One example of the longevity of Anthony's three-level definition is the fact that nearly 40 years after it was put forward, Brown described it as 'a definition that has quite admirably withstood the test of time' (2002, p. 9). However, Larsen-Freeman initially described Anthony's definition as 'too indeterminate for our purposes here' (1986, p. xi). But by the third edition of the same book, 25 years later, Larsen-Freeman and Anderson appeared to have changed their minds: 'Following Anthony in certain of the chapters we will introduce a particular method by showing how it is an example of a more general approach to language teaching' (2011, p. xvi). This shift demonstrates an important principle regarding the origins, history and development of language teaching methods and methodologies, in relation to the non-linear, circular, cyclical nature of such methods, but one which is not usually noted, and rarely commented on: What Goes Around, Comes Around. As noted above, that idea should not be taken to imply a belief that there is nothing new under the sun, but such shifts are compelling evidence to support Kelly's finding, cited above, that 'much that is being claimed as revolutionary this century is merely a rethinking and renaming of early ideas and procedures' (1969, p. ix).

Garon Wheeler (2013) starts his book *Language Teaching Through the Ages* by giving several compelling answers to the question 'Why should a language teacher be well-versed in the history of the field?' (p. 2). One reason is that 'Everything happening now in our profession has some cause, some root in the past, something that has led to that action, belief or technique' (p. 2). Wheeler gives many examples from his own language learning experiences, such as his discovery that the direct method (see Chapter 5) that his teachers were using in 1976 to teach Arabic in Morocco was not new, as Wheeler assumed it was, and that it had in fact been popular in the late 1800s. He also describes his surprise at finding that the so-called 'natural method', popularized by Stephen Krashen in the 1980s was not the cutting-edge breakthrough it appeared to be, as the basis of that method could be found 'in works from centuries ago' (p. 1). Wheeler also discovered that 'the umbrella term "natural method" is more than a hundred years old' (p. 1). Wheeler answers his question with another good reason for knowing some history: 'The more we know about the past of language teaching, the more memories we have upon which to base our actions. As a result, we can be wiser in our choices' (p. 2).

Wheeler's last point, regarding informed choices, is an essential part of teachers deciding which methodologies to use and when, where they have the freedom to make such choices. Those choices are based on the needs of the learners, the context, the resources available, and many other factors, as part of a principled and informed eclecticism, which was described by Mellow (2002) as 'a desirable, coherent, **pluralistic** approach to language teaching' (p. 1).

ACTIVITY 1.1

According to Kelly (1969), 'Very few inherently bad ideas have ever been put forward in language teaching.' Have you read or heard about or seen any 'bad ideas' in your language teaching and learning context? If so, what were some of the things that made them 'bad'?

The Multiple Meanings of 'Method' and 'Methodology'

Originally, Larsen-Freeman defined a language teaching method as a superordinate, 'comprising both "principles" and "techniques"' (1986, p. xi). The principles were based on five aspects of language teaching: the teacher, the learner, the teaching processes, the learning processes, and the target language and culture. Larsen-Freeman also explained that 'Taken together, the principles represent the theoretical framework of the method' (1986, p. xi), and that 'The techniques are the behavioral manifestations of the principles – in other words, the classroom activities and procedures derived from an application of the principles' (1986, p. xi). By that, Larsen-Freeman meant that what language teachers do in the classroom is the observable application of a set of principles. The principles themselves may not be stated explicitly, but by looking at what teachers do in the classroom – as we will do in the coming chapters – we can see how principles and practices can connect and inform each other.

Larsen-Freeman's definition is an example of how complex the notion of a method can be. First, there is the ternary set of the relationships between methods, principles and techniques, which is similar to – but not quite the same as – Anthony's triumvirate of technique, method and approach. This difference between Anthony's definition and Larsen-Freeman's definition supports Larsen-Freeman's point that the term 'method' is used by different researchers, authors and practitioners to mean different things (1986, p. xi). Definitions of 'method' in language education are further complicated by additional multiple relationships, such as those between the five aspects of language teaching identified by Larsen-Freeman, so that 'a particular technique may be compatible with more than one method' (1986, p. xii). This lack of a simple one-to-one relationship can be a frustrating complication, but one that reflects the overlap between different methods, and the relationships between notions of methods, approaches and techniques, and between principles, practices and pedagogy. A third trio was thrown into the mix by Richards and Rodgers (2001), who stated that 'any language teaching method can be described in terms of ... the levels of approach, design and procedure' (p. 32). In terms of a clear, concise and generally agreed-upon definition of method, the waters have been further muddied by attempts – well-meaning but nonetheless causing more confusion – to substitute alternative terms, such as 'pedagogy' instead of 'method' (Brown, 2002).

The different sets of relationships within and between the previous definitions of 'method', and the associated terms, can cause confusion. However, this is not the result of any of the authors' explanations, but because of complex sets of relationships between what language teachers do in the language classroom, how they do it, and why they do it that way, instead of some other way. Also, the relationships can be characterized as being chaotic, rather than **causal**, and circular or cyclical, rather than linear, in the same way that the history of our field is not linear. As Kelly (1969) put it, 'While one can ascribe a linear development to sciences, the development of an art is cyclical' (1969, p. 396). Many language teachers, when I ask them whether language teaching is more of an art or more of a science, respond by choosing the art option. A few brave souls raise their hands to choose the science option, and give the grammar of language as an example of science-like principles, and many choose a combination of both art and science, making it more of a craft (Lange, 1990). But most of the respondents choose the art option, which relates to Kelly's idea that 'the development of an art is cyclical'. That might also help to explain why the field of language teaching and learning methods tends to follows cycles, rather than the apparently more linear development of the sciences, although that too may just be an appearance of linearity, hiding the randomness and the messiness.

In language education, this methodological development is, in fact, a more messy process, which may help to explain why some methods appear to come and go, ebb and flow, while others appear to come and stay. It is even conceivable that some features of language teaching methods have always been with us, possibly for thousands of years, in some way, shape or form.

In a later edition of their book, Larsen-Freeman and Anderson (2011) expand upon their original three-part definition, by including a note on what is *not* a method: 'We are using the term "method" here not to mean a formulaic prescription, but a coherent set of principles linked to certain techniques and procedures' (p. xvi). Larsen-Freeman and Anderson also note the on-going challenges with using the term 'method': 'Admittedly, we have sometimes found it difficult to use the term "method" with more recent innovations' (p. xvi). At those times, they 'resorted to the term "methodological innovations"' (p. xvi), which shows that even the established experts in our field can be challenged by the plethora of terminologies and overlapping, multiple meanings.

In 2001, Rodgers stated that a language teaching method is 'a systematic set of teaching practices based on a particular theory of language and language learning' (p. 1). Although this is a relatively straightforward definition, it still needs some unpacking. For example, 'system' has more than a dozen meanings in English, including the somewhat tautological 'a way of doing things; a method' (*Cambridge Advanced Learner's Dictionary*, *CALD*), as well as 'a set of connected items or devices that operate together' (*CALD*). Although the latter is usually applied to, for example, computer systems, it can be modified to fit the language classroom, as a set of connected theories, beliefs and practices that operate together. Incorporating Rodgers' definition above, we have a set of connected theories, beliefs and practices about language, teaching and learning that operate together (in the classroom). Although there are a number of moving parts within Rodgers' definition, notions of connectedness and working together are central, and it is relatively succinct.

The use of techniques or principles based on hypotheses and/or theories was built into an early definition of 'method' from Richards and Rodgers: 'a coherent set of learning/

teaching principles rooted in clearly articulated theories of what language is and how it is learnt, which is implemented through specific types of classroom procedures' (1986, p. 468). In relation to language teachers' use of informed eclecticism in their choice of methods, where they have a choice, Richards and Rodgers highlight the importance of teachers being able to clearly articulate their understanding of theories, and/or their beliefs based on practice. More recently, Penny Ur (2013) defined a language teaching method as 'a set of principles and procedures based on a theory of language and language acquisition' (p. 468). Although Ur's definition raises the question of whose or which theory of language/acquisition is being used as the basis, it may also be a healthy sign that, as our field matures, our definitions may be becoming more concise.

However, as professionals who 'do language for a living', we may still be inclined towards the position taken by Lewis Carroll's Humpty Dumpty in *Through the Looking-Glass* (1872): '"When *I* use a word," Humpty Dumpty said, in rather a scornful tone, "it means just what I choose it to mean – neither more nor less"' (original emphasis, p. 205). Therefore, in spite of 'methodology' meaning simply 'the study of methods', Ur decided to use 'methodology' to mean 'a collection and combination of methods or procedures' (p. 468). Therefore, we have at least two distinct meanings of 'methodology' in language education now: 1. the study of methods used in language teaching and learning; and 2. a plural collective noun, referring to two or more language teaching methods.

Another aspect of the meaning of 'methodology' was added by Larsen-Freeman and Anderson (2011): 'A study of methods is also a means of socialization into professional thinking and discourse that language teachers require in order to "rename their experience", to participate in their profession, and to learn throughout their professional lives' (p. xi). The notion of professional socialization highlights a number of important reasons for the study of methods and methodologies in relation to three key roles and responsibilities of language teachers: as members of a community of professional practice; as reflective practitioners; and as lifelong learners. In terms of the importance of methodological studies, Larsen-Freeman and Anderson conclude that 'A study of methods is invaluable in teacher education' (p. xi).

> ### ACTIVITY 1.2
>
> How would you define the terms 'method' and 'methodology', and how would you use them to explain what you and your learners do in your language classes?

Confusingly and circuitously, Kumaravadivelu (2006) defined the term 'method' as referring to 'established methods conceptualized and constructed by experts in the field'. He distinguished method from methodology, using the latter to refer to 'what practicing teachers actually do in the classroom in order to achieve their stated or unstated teaching objectives' (2006, p. 86). In this book, I will use 'method' and 'methodology' to refer to what teachers and learners do in their language lessons and classes. But I will use 'method' when referring to a specific, named method, such as Grammar Translation or the Audio-Lingual Method, in the more singular sense, and when referring to specific aspects of a particular method. In contrast, I will use 'methodology' to refer more generally to the plurality of teachers' and learners' practices, including the theories, publications, policies and so on that surround a particular. These kinds of ideas about method and methodology stand in stark contrast to the position of the anti-methods and post-methods protagonists, whose views will be discussed in the following section.

The Anti-Methods and Post-Methods Era

The anti-methods movement, as the name implies, refers to a group of language educators who oppose the whole notion of 'method' as an inherently unhelpful and even destructive force in language teaching and learning. The post-methods movement is a more recent incarnation of the same belief. But as well as claiming that all methods are bad, the proponents also claim that we should be – or even that we are now – beyond the notion of methods, as though that were just a colonial or commonwealth phase that we were going through, and that we have now – or should have by now – grown out of.

For example, Phillipson (1992, 2000), Kumaravadivelu (2003) and Canagarajah (1999) have challenged the notion of 'methods' based on such claims. However, as with the history of language teaching and ELT, the anti-methods movement has a much longer history than Phillipson and his contemporaries appear to be aware of. For example, *Methods of Teaching Modern Languages: Papers on the value and on methods of modern language instruction* (Elliot et al.) was published more than 120 years ago, in 1893. In terms of history repeating itself, we find that in the 1890s there was the same kind of discontent with the current state of affairs regarding language teaching, and the same calls for change and innovation then, as we hear today.

This discontent is seen in the opening chapter of Elliot et al., titled 'Methods of teaching modern languages', based on the talk 'Modern Languages as a College Discipline', given by Professor Elliot in 1887: 'The fact of the matter is, that our whole system of modern language instruction needs overhauling' (Elliot et al., 1893, p. 7). Following up on Elliot's complaints about and disappointments with modern language teaching methods at that time, in the second chapter, Professor Calvin Thomas presented his paper on 'Observations upon methods in the teaching of modern languages' (Elliot et al., 1893, pp. 11–28). Thomas stated categorically: 'it is certain, that a good deal of language teaching that goes on in this country [the USA] is suffering severely because of laying too much stress upon matters of method' (1893, p. 11). These methodological complaints pre-date the current criticisms by more than a century, but more recent complaints about methods are presented as challenging modern or postmodern insights, which move the field forward in new and important directions. As his talk progressed, Thomas became even more vigorous in his condemnation of the focus on methods: 'Quite a large portion of the teaching fraternity are making of method, if not a fetish to worship, at least a hobby to ride' (Elliot et al., 1893, p. 11). And reiterating the point of history repeating itself, just over a century after Elliot et al., Lilia Bartolome published a paper in the *Harvard Educational Review* titled 'Beyond the methods fetish' (1994, pp. 173–194).

It does appear that those opposed to methods have felt more strongly than those in favour, who are often careful and cautious in their support of methods. For example, although not referring to language education specifically, Donaldo Macedo (1994) passionately called for 'anti-methods pedagogy that refuses to be enslaved by the rigidity of models and methodological paradigms' (p. 8). And a century after the 1880s presentations and publications of Elliot and Thomas, Stern (1983) – who *was* referring specifically to language education – criticized what he saw as 'a century old obsession' with methods that he decried as having 'been increasingly unproductive and misguided' (p. 251).

However, rather than espousing such impassioned pleas for the rejection of methods and methodologies, perhaps a more reasonable middle ground needs be found. In spite of the methods-as-fetish analogy (re-)employed by Bartolome, she does propose what is, in effect, a helpful compromise. Bartolome does this first by rejecting 'the "one size fits all" assumption [behind] a number of teaching methods currently in vogue, such as cooperative learning and whole language instruction' (pp. 175–176). She then states that 'it is important that educators not blindly reject teaching methods across the board, but that they reject *uncritical appropriation* of methods, materials, curricula, etc.' (p. 177, emphasis added). Bartolome's use of 'uncritical appropriation' can be contrasted with the notion of 'informed eclecticism', discussed above, in which language teachers need to be able to articulate their reasons for working with certain methods and rejecting others. Those reasons will be made up of many different components, including the knowledge, skills and experience of the teacher, aligned with the needs, wants and motivations of the learners.

> **ACTIVITY 1.3**
>
> What do you understand by 'a principled and informed eclecticism'? Is this a part of how you decide which language teaching methods to use with your students and which not to use?

Concluding Comments

Given the cyclical, circular, non-linear nature of language teaching and learning, it seems likely that 'fashions in language teaching methodology' (Adamson, 2005, p. 604) will continue to come and go. One possible consequence of those cycles may be that the relatively recent fashion for proclaiming a 'post-methods era' in language education will also pass, perhaps to be replaced with a new 'Renaissance' of methods and methodology. That Methodological Renaissance, in turn, may eventually pass, and so the cycle will continue. Some years ago, David Bell asked the question: 'Do [English language] teachers think that methods are dead?' (2007, pp. 135–143). Based on interviews with teachers, their discussion board postings, language teaching/learning autobiographies, and teaching journals, he concluded that the English language teachers in his study – like the thousands of language teachers I have met over the last 20 years – do not believe that methods are dead. What all of this means for language teachers today is that, whatever the historical anti-methods and more recent post-methods promoters may complain about and claim, language teaching methodologies have been with us for a very long time indeed, and show no real signs of leaving us any time soon.

Suggested Readings

Diane Larsen-Freeman and Marti Anderson's *Techniques and Principles in Language Teaching* (2011, third edition) is referred to many times throughout this book, and if you are looking for detailed descriptions of a variety of language teaching techniques, theirs is a very useful book.

Like Larsen-Freeman and Marti Anderson's book above, Jack Richards' and Theodore Rodgers' *Approaches and Methods in Language Teaching* (2014, third edition), which is also referred to many times in this book, is a more detailed (and more recent) description of a number of language teaching approaches and methods.

For those of you interested in knowing more about the history of our field, Garon Wheeler's *Language Teaching Through the Ages* (2013) is an excellent summary of thousands of years of language teaching and learning.

CHAPTER 2
The Centrality of Context

> *Before reading this chapter, consider the following questions:*
>
> - How would you describe your language teaching context?
> - How would your students describe their language learning context?
> - What are the relationships between the language teaching methods you use and your context?
> - What are some of the challenges and difficulties of teaching and learning in your context?
> - What are some of the benefits and rewards of teaching and learning in your context?

Introduction and Overview

Methods are not neutral. Language teaching and learning do not occur in a vacuum. These two statements reflect the importance of context and the fact that *where* we do what we do is at least as important as how we do it. According to Larsen-Freeman and Anderson (2011), 'a method is decontextualized' (p. xiii). In some ways, this is true, in the sense that it is possible to follow the steps of a particular method, in a predetermined way, in a variety of different settings. However, Larsen-Freeman and Anderson go on to explain that 'How a method is implemented in the classroom is not only going to be affected by who the teacher is, but also by who the students are, what they and the teachers expect as appropriate social roles, the institutional constraints and demands, and factors connected to the wider sociocultural context in which the instruction takes place' (p. xiii). These factors, and others, are presented and discussed in this chapter, so that methods are not seen as being decontextualized, but, on the contrary, as being inextricably bound to the place in which the teaching and learning are happening.

In the first part of the chapter, we will look at some of the many different meanings of 'context', in relation to language teaching and learning and in terms of 'internal' and 'external' contexts, starting with the definitions and descriptions in the 1980s and the 1990s. The second part of the chapter looks at the growing awareness of context, beyond the narrow linguistic definitions, in the 2000s, the 2010s and more recently. In part three, a case study of a particular context – students from Cape Verde in the USA – will be considered, to show how our developing definitions, descriptions and understandings of 'context' can be applied to a specific situation.

The Meanings of 'Context' (and the Context of Meaning)

The answer to the question 'What does "context" include?' may initially seem fairly simple and straightforward, perhaps even answerable with a single word: Everything! Or, if extended and clarified slightly: Everything in the Surrounding Environment. This simple 'everything' answer can also be given in response to the question: Where – in any given society or civilization – is culture? Again, a similarly simple answer would be: Everywhere! Or, if extended and clarified somewhat: Everywhere – *and nowhere in particular*. However, after thinking about our classrooms and schools, colleges and universities, we can see that our language teaching and learning contexts are complex, and constantly changing. This is partly because of the sheer number and the pervasiveness of the different factors and variables that influence what we do, how we do it, and why we choose to do it this way or that, and not some other way.

For these reasons, we need to spend some time thinking about what we mean – and what others mean – when we talk about our language teaching and learning contexts. As Roberts and Simonot wrote, 'it is worth trying to tease out what we mean by the different contexts' (1987, p. 134). They also drew on earlier work to point out that knowing our 'context' is not a simple matter: 'Levinson (1983) in an extensive tour around the notion of context concludes that we still have no clear idea of what it is' (p. 134). In their work on how language acquisition is accomplished, Roberts and Simonot also referred to one of the reasons for the creation of this *ALLC* book series: 'we are faced with the urgent need to relate SLA [Second Language Acquisition] to the actual contexts of situation in which adult learners have an opportunity to acquire, but with the difficult problem of deciding what that context is' (p. 135). Thirty years after the work of Roberts and Simonot (and many others), we are still working to do more to bridge this gap between SLA studies and the language classroom.

According to Douglas Harper, the word 'context' comes from the early fifteenth-century Latin word *contextus*, meaning 'a joining together', and *contextere*, meaning 'to weave together' (which is also the basis of words like 'texture' in English). Looking back at word origins is a natural tendency of many language teachers, especially those who are teaching vocabulary, and doing so can raise some relevant and revealing questions. For example, in your language learning and teaching context, what aspects of your environment are being woven together to create your context? It is also worth considering which aspects are within and which are beyond your control. For example, if you have the freedom, or permission, to display students' work on the walls of your classroom, that would be something within your control. However, if you are, for example, required to use a particular textbook, regardless of whether the contents of the book match the interests and abilities of your learners, then that would be something beyond your control.

The modern meaning of 'context' is given in the online *CALD* as 'the situation within which something exists or happens, and *that can help explain it*' (emphasis added). I have emphasized the last part of the definition because it helps to answer the following question: In relation to your language teaching methods, why do you do what you do, in the way that you do it? To put that in more concrete terms, if someone sees you teaching a language lesson using, for example, the Grammar Translation Method (GTM, see Chapter 7), and asks you why you are doing that, your answer should involve talking about the context in which the lesson is taking place. To expand this example, if you are using GTM in a context where the regional or national language examinations are focused on testing grammatical accuracy, then that aspect of your context is having a concrete impact on the main method you are using.

Another definition of 'context' will help to illustrate this point: 'the text or speech that comes *immediately before and after* a particular phrase or piece of text and helps to explain its meaning' (*CALD*, emphasis added). The first definition, above, is situational, whereas this definition is at the sentence level, but we can apply this second definition to our situation. If we do that, the emphasis added highlights the fact that whenever we see someone's language lesson (or our own), we are also seeing the culmination and manifestation of everything that came *before* that lesson. We may also catch glimpses of what will happen *after* the lesson, between the end of that lesson and the beginning of the next one, for example, if the teacher asks the learners to complete out-of-class work, consolidating that day's lesson and/or preparing for the next one.

We can now see two clear sets of meanings of 'context' emerging, which can be characterized as 'internal' and 'external'. The first relates to the choices a language user makes when deciding what to say or write, while the second relates to the external environment that surrounds the language users during their interactions. Applying this internal/external notion of context to language classrooms, we have multiple sets of 'internal contexts' in each class. Every learner and every teacher constitutes a unique collection of knowledge, skills and experiences that are drawn on to make decisions about what items of language to use (from the first language and/or the target language), so that the target language can be learned and taught most effectively and efficiently (assuming these are some of the goals of the lesson).

In relation to decision-making by the language user as one type of 'internal context', Rod Ellis and Celia Roberts (1987) explained that 'the construct of *context* is used by sociologists to explain why language users make the choices they do ... Both the linguistic context and the situational context affect choice' (p. 9). So, we need to bear in mind both external influences and internal decision-making processes when referring to our context. In the example above, in a context where the regional or national language examinations were focused on testing grammatical accuracy, then that aspect of the context could incline teachers and learners to make internal decisions about the grammatical correctness of the target language they produce.

One of the interesting aspects of much of the early work on the importance of context in language education is that while there are many references to the choices made by language users, especially language learners, there was little or no reference to the methodological choices made by language teachers. Although this kind of disconnect may seem strange now, it can still be seen today, and it is another one of the reasons for the creation of this *ALLC* book series: to help connect the published books and papers of applied linguists with the day-to-day classroom realities of language learners and teachers.

One reason for this disconnect is the tendency for professional academics to write for each other, such as applied linguists writing *about* language classrooms but writing *for* other applied linguists. A context-related example of this tendency is a definition that was cited throughout the 1980s and the 1990s and that can also still be seen today. In this classic definition, context is defined as 'a theoretical construct in the postulation of which the linguist abstracts from the actual situation and establishes as contextual all the factors which ... systematically determine the form, the appropriacy and the meaning of utterances' (Lyons, 1977, p. 572). As we can see from such definitions, the linguist is at the centre, rather than language teachers or learners, which is reflected in the abstract and theoretical way in which the definition of 'context' is worded and presented.

Lyons' definition relates to Adrian Holliday's (1994) work on appropriate methodologies and the social contexts in which they take place: 'methodologies are themselves ethnocentric constructs of professional-academic cultures' (p. 91). This statement by Holliday means that our ideas about our context are not 'neutral', because the relationships between context and culture mean that our notions of what is and what is not a context are shaped by our cultural values, our academic training, our professional experiences and so on. In terms of which methods persist and which decline, Jack Richards (1985), in his work on the context of language teaching, stated that 'Universities and academics likewise play a crucial role in influencing the fate of methods' (p. 39). As a result of all these 'behind-the-scenes' influences, when we read articles or listen to presentations on methodologies, we need to be aware that all methods have come from somewhere, and as such, they may not necessarily be appropriate in other countries, cultures or contexts, especially those that are far removed from where they began. An example of this notion of 'contextual appropriateness' was provided by Hu Guangwei, who reported on contextual influences on instructional practices in terms of ELT in secondary-level classrooms in China. Based on questionnaire data from 250 secondary school graduates in different parts of China, she concluded that 'what transpires in the foreign language classroom is inevitably shaped and constrained by contextual influences' (2005, p. 635).

Holliday also makes the argument that 'any methodology in English language education should be appropriate to the social context within which is to be used' (p .1). This point applies to education in general, and to language education in particular, and he goes on to explain that 'To achieve appropriacy, we must first investigate, try to understand, and then address, whichever social context we are working within' (p. 1). Drawing on the work of Leo van Lier (1988), Holliday distinguished between the 'macro context [which] includes the wider societal and institutional influences on what happens in the classroom' (p. 13), and the 'micro social context [which] consists of the socio-psychological aspects of group dynamics within the classroom' (p. 14). The example above, of using GTM in an environment in which grammatical accuracy is the focus of the local language exams, shows how the macro can affect the micro, and how the micro can reflect the macro.

Another example of the kind of language used by Lyons, above, which shows how we think about language learners, can be seen in Ellis' discussion of 'Variability and Social Context' (1987). Ellis noted that such variability includes: '(1) the educational background of the subjects; (2) the sex of the subjects; (3) the subjects' attitudes to different social groups; (4) the network of the subjects' social relationships' (p. 129). The repeated reference to 'subjects' reflects a scientific approach that was dominant for many years, and which can still be found today. In that approach, long-standing Western scientific paradigms were applied to language classrooms, as though they were laboratories and everyone in them was a 'human subject' in an experiment. Treating teachers and learners as experimental subjects, almost as though they were lab rats in a maze, reduced the educational process to little more than the satisfaction of basic biological drives, such as eating when hungry or excreting when full. Thankfully, such language is seen much less often these days.

Another challenging aspect of the discussions about the influence and importance of context is that the two different kinds of context – which I refer to as 'internal' and 'external', Ellis and Roberts (and others) call 'linguistic' and 'situational' (1987), and van Lier (1988) referred to as 'micro' and 'macro' – are often presented as though they were independent of each other. For example, Ellis and Roberts claimed that 'the route of [language] development is *impervious to context*. That is, there is general agreement that the order in which a set of morphemes are acquired ... *is not affected by the learning domain*' (1987, p. 12) (emphases added).

In the above statement we can see the long-held belief that the sequence of acquisition of grammatical and structural language features is fixed, and that the sequence is followed, *regardless of the external environment*. However, if a language teacher does not introduce a specific grammatical feature of the target language, or if the learner does not encounter it independently, then it will not be acquired at that time, in that order. In this way, the external environment is having a considerable impact on the acquisition sequence. This is an important difference between naturalistic, first language acquisition, and classroom-based second or foreign language learning environments, which relates to the traditional division of ESL (English as a Second Language) contexts versus EFL (English as a Foreign Language) contexts. In this particular **dichotomy**, if the English language learners and teachers are in an **English-dominant country**, that is, one in which English was the first language of the majority of the population, such as England, America or Canada, then it is labelled an ESL context. This was contrasted with contexts in which the majority of the population were not L1 users of English, which were labelled as ESL contexts.

An important point here is that such dichotomies, in this case, between different EFL and ESL contexts, are at best somewhat artificial, and at worst they are an unhelpful oversimplification that misrepresents continua as dichotomies. Every language lesson involves a number of the internal contextual factors meeting some of the external contextual factors, in interactions that are mediated by the languages and the cultures in the classroom, and in which the learners and the teachers are (at) the 'interface' between those factors, shaping and being shaped by the context. In her work on context and culture in language teaching, Claire Kramsch (1993) described a number of 'dubious dichotomies and deceptive symmetries' (pp. 2–9), including 'grammar versus communication' (pp. 4–5) and 'language versus literature' (pp. 7–8). In a section on 'the importance of context in language education' (pp. 9–14), Kramsch starts with some historical background: 'The polarities mentioned above can be traced to the age-old duality of language as text and language as context' (pp. 9–10). Kramsch also identified five factors and the contextual relationships between them: 'The notion of context is a relational one. In each of its five dimensions: linguistic, situational, interactional, as well as cultural and intertextual, it is shaped by the people in dialog with one another in a variety of roles and statuses' (1993, p. 67). And not only are the people who are communicating with each other shaping these five aspects of the context, but these contextual aspects are, in turn, shaping the people communicating, in a dynamic, multidirectional way, rather than in a more unidirectional manner. A good example of how these aspects of context interact can be seen by comparing a conversation between two **native users** of a language with a conversation between two people, both of whom are using a language that is a second or foreign language for them. In those two conversations, all five factors – linguistic, situational, interactional, cultural and intertextual – are at play in different ways, based on different sets of assumptions and expectations, commonalities and differences.

ACTIVITY 2.1

Having looked at a number of different definitions and descriptions of 'context', you can now try writing your own clear, concise definition or description – in 20 words or fewer – of what you understand by the term 'context'. If one of your language learners had come across the word for the first time, and asked you to please explain what 'context' means, what would you tell them?

In their work on discourse and context in language teaching, Marianne Celce-Murcia and Elite Olshtain (2000) focused on the situational and communicative aspects of context: 'Context entails the situation within which the communicative interaction takes place' (p. 11). They then contrasted discourse analysis of context with pragmatic analysis of context. Contextual discourse analysis is based on 'the linguistic and cognitive choices made relevant to the interaction at hand' (p. 11). Pragmatic analysis of context 'relates to the participants taking part in the interaction, the sociocultural background that is relevant, and *any physical-situational elements that may have some bearing on the exchange*' (p. 11, emphasis added). The last part of their definition/description covers a potentially very large number of elements.

In relation to discourse analysis, Celce-Murcia and Olshtain stated that 'The term "context" in discourse analysis refers to all the factors and elements that are nonlinguistic and nontextual but which affect spoken or written communicative interaction' (p. 11). Their point relates to Halliday's (1991) definition of context as 'the events that are going on around when people speak (and write)' (p. 5). Celce-Murcia and Olshtain also distinguish between 'context-embedded' and 'context-reduced' discourse, in which 'context-embedded' refers to discourse that depends 'primarily on contextual features found in the immediate environment', whereas 'context-reduced' refers to discourse that is 'relatively independent of context'... and which depends 'more on the features of the linguistic code and the forms of the discourse itself' (2000, p. 11). This distinction is not as clear as it might seem. For example, if a conversation between two people was taking place in a noisy environment, that would affect features such as the volume of the speech and the amount of repetition needed, so the speakers could hear and be heard above the noise. However, the words they use, the grammar, syntax and so on of what they say, would not be affected. In that sense, the discussion could be 'context-embedded', as it is affected by the environment, but also 'context-reduced', as *what* is said is not changed because of the context, although the *way* in which it is said is affected.

One of the recurring themes in the work on the importance of carefully considering and fully understanding our language teaching and learning contexts as much as possible is *interaction*. For example, Ellis and Roberts (1987) wrote that 'Context is, *more than any other particular set of non-linguistic features*, used to place or account for the nature of an interaction' (p. 19, emphasis added) – and in classrooms, that means student–student and teacher–student interaction. Ellis and Roberts went on to write that 'Context is created by the interaction itself. As such it consists of the particular beliefs and presuppositions that the interactants bring to the encounter' (1987, p. 19). Again, in the context of our classrooms, the interactants are learners and teachers, and the encounter is focused on language learning and teaching.

One of the most commonly referred-to lists of contextual factors in language teaching and learning was proposed by Stern in 1983. He identified six variables: (1) Sociocultural; (2) Historical/Political; (3) Educational; (4) Economic/Technological; (5) Linguistic; and (6) Geographic. These six factors are shown as a series of concentric circles, with 'national and international setting' at the outer edge of the circle, then 'regional factors', followed by the 'home environment and neighbourhood' and the 'school environment', and at the centre of the circle is language teaching. Stern's diagram shows visually that the six variables impact, to different degrees and in different ways, on the five different domains within which language teaching and learning take place, resulting in dozens of different possible permutations of variables in each context.

A different classification was presented by Duranti and Goodwin (1992), who proposed four types of context: 'a. setting (physical and interactional); b. behavioral environment (non verbal and kinetic); c. language (co-text and reflexive use of language); d. extrasituational (social, political, cultural)', with 'co-text' referring to 'the language material in any piece of discourse' (cited in Celce-Murcia and Olshtain, 2000, p. 12).

What we can see from these various attempts to describe the different kinds of context that are present in language teaching and learning situations is that *where* we do what we do is at least as important as *how* and *why* we do what we do, as the context shapes the how and the why in so many ways, some more subtle and implicit, others more obvious and explicit. For example, if English is being taught as a second or foreign language in England, the teacher will have access to a much wider range of naturally occurring materials in the environment, such as public advertising, newspapers, magazines, radio, television, music, movies and so on. Likewise, the learners in such a setting are surrounded by the target language in ways that they would not be in an environment in which the target language was only used during language lessons. However, as Internet access to material from everywhere is increasing, the availability of such materials may be one of the reasons for the traditional EFL/ESL division being less applicable now than before.

TASK 2.2

If you are reading this in a classroom, look around you (and if you are not in a classroom, visualize the one you were in most recently) and see if you can make a note of all of the 'physical-situational elements' (Celce-Murcia & Olshtain, above) that can have some effect on the language teaching and learning that occurs in the classroom.

Some things to notice include: lighting, whether the room is light or dark, with many windows or no windows; whether the walls are covered with students' work, posters and so on, or whether the walls are bare; how the furniture is arranged – in rows, in groups, in a U-shape and so on. What do you see that could affect the teaching and learning that take place there, and in what ways might these elements affect what happens?

It is important to note that the 'physical-situational elements' above only apply to the language classroom, as there will be other 'physical-situational elements' outside the classroom, depending on the context in which the language lessons are taking place.

Developments in Our Understanding of Context

Some of the key changes in our understanding of the importance of context that took place in the 1990s and in the new millennium were described by Mike Byram and Peter Grundy (2002), who wrote that 'Context and Culture in Language Teaching and Learning is a topic that has developed in many directions and with considerable vigour in the last 10 to 15 years' (p. 193). According to Byram and Grundy, one of the reasons for that vigorous development was 'the recognition of the social and political significance of language teaching [which] ... have led to a greater awareness of learners as social actors in specific relationships with the language they are learning' (p. 193).

A detailed discussion of the politics of language teaching is beyond the scope of this chapter, but it is no coincidence that as awareness of the importance of the external and environmental context has grown, so, too, has awareness of the politics of language education. For example, in their book on critical pedagogies and language learning, Norton and Toohey (2004) pointed out that each chapter in the book stressed the fact that 'identities and activities are historically constructed in diverse, dynamic, social, and political contexts and that politics will thus play a role' (p. 15). These ideas of language learners and language teachers as 'social actors' in 'diverse, dynamic contexts' affect the way we think about and talk about our contexts. At the end of this chapter, we will look at the specific example of the Cape Verdean community in a city in the USA, which will illustrate that statement made by Norton and Toohey (2004).

One important contextual factor can be the government of the time, and in relation to governmental influence on methodological development, an example of how national-level politics can have an impact is given by Richards: 'In 1902, for example, the French Minister of Education gave official approval to the Direct Method. It became the *only* approved method for teaching foreign language in France, and in the same year it also became the approved method in Germany' (1985, p. 39, emphasis added). We can see here how methodological decision-making at the national level – and at the international level – can impact on methodological decision-making at the individual level, in the classroom. In relation to concurrent changes taking place in language education, and how these affected the methods used, Byram and Grundy went on to note that 'methodologists have developed a more differentiated view of learners as human beings with feelings and identities which have to be taken into account by those who wish to help them to learn. *"Context" is thus as complex a concept as "culture"*, the latter being notoriously difficult to define' (2002, p. 193, emphasis added). Although this idea of 'learners as human beings' may seem obvious to most language teachers, it is in contrast to learners as experimental subjects, as discussed above in relation to the use of 'subjects', rather than 'teachers', 'learners' or 'students' (Ellis, 1987). This experimental view of teachers and learners, based on the classical scientific method, held sway for a long time.

Thinking of our teaching and learning contexts in relation to these factors – the internal and external variables – helps to explain why teaching and learning can be such a challenging, demanding and sometimes difficult endeavour. These difficulties may be especially prevalent in the case of *language* teaching and learning, because of the relationships between language and culture, and how Culture – which, as Byram and Grundy point out, is 'notoriously difficult to define' – is another critical aspect of context in the language classroom. In spite of the centrality of context being more recognized in recent years, Judith Shrum and Eileen Glisan (2010) still found that 'decontextualized mechanical practice has remained pervasive over the course of decades in language approaches used by teachers' (p. 59). But most experienced language teachers would agree that Culture and Context are inextricably bound, bringing together two essential but enormous aspects of our work as language teachers and learners, and making an already challenging endeavour all the more so. As Ian Tudor (1996) pointed out, 'classroom culture is a very complex concept, one that our profession is only starting to get to grips with' (p. 142). In the 20 years since we started to 'get to grips' with the idea of language classrooms as 'cultural centres', we have made some progress, but we are still learning about these language–culture–classroom relationships. (For more on this point, see, for example, Bishop & Berryman, 2006.)

Although the centrality of context is still being recognized, the complexities of context have long been recognized, for example, by Richards (1985), who stated that 'Language teaching is ... a complex issue, encompassing sociocultural, linguistic, psycholinguistic, as well as curricula and instructional dimensions' (p. 11). In relation to the external context, Richards also noted that 'The role English plays in a particular society, both pragmatically and symbolically, has an important influence both on language policies toward the teaching of English and on how the learning of English is viewed by members of a society' (p. 12). I would add that those societal roles played by English also greatly influence how languages are taught and learned in a particular context and culture. For example, in some contexts, such as Hong Kong, the English language was imposed as a consequence of the British Empire invading, conquering and enslaving the local population. This is different from, for example, the geographically neighbouring and culturally and linguistically closely related Mainland China, where English was not introduced via military might and colonial occupation in the same way. As a result, the pragmatic and symbolic roles of English were viewed, for a long time, very differently in these two contexts, which was reflected in differences in language policies regarding the teaching and learning of English in Hong Kong and in Mainland China.

Another important aspect of contexts is that they are not static, but are constantly changing, and in a state of continuous flux. Many of us have had the experience of teaching what is, *on paper*, the same lesson, on the same day, in the same place, but with very different results. For example, we might present a unit from a course book to a group of students in the morning, which can turn out to be a completely different lesson when we present, that afternoon, the same unit, from the same course book, to a group of students at the same language level in the same school, and even in the same classroom! Kramsch explained this flux in the following way: 'Because of the multiplicity of meanings inherent in any stretch of speech, contexts are not stable ... they are constantly changed and recreated by individual speakers and hearers, writers and readers' (1993, p. 67). This multiplicity of meanings and constantly changing contexts may be one of the important ways in which developing language skills is different from delivering content, as the raw material of what we do – Language – is itself constantly changing, in much the same way as any organic entity is constantly adapting to its environment. As Kramsch put it, 'Teaching a language is teaching how to shape the context of the "lesson" as an individual learning event and as a social encounter with regard to its setting' (1993, p. 67). That relates to Byram and Grundy's (2002) description above, of learners as 'social actors in specific relationships' (p. 193).

This idea of contexts being in a constant state of flux has been recognized in education in general, beyond language education specifically. For example, according to Edwards and Westgate (1994), 'Context is also seen much more dynamically – not as a set of factors or constraints already "there" at the outset of the talk, but as being brought into being, maintained, modified or challenged through the talk itself' (p. 23). And in relation to the importance of being clear about what we mean when we talk about context, Edwards and Westgate warned that the word and the idea can 'become an ill-defined dumping ground for assorted bits of social information of unspecified relevance' (p. 23).

These differences – between the morning and the afternoon classes – are largely because every teacher and every student is unique. As a result, no two lessons can ever be exactly the same – which is one of the joys and one of the challenges of being a teacher! But the differences between the two classes are also because of the constantly changing nature of the context. Here is how Ellis and Roberts expressed this idea: 'Context is, therefore, created in interaction partly on the basis of particular and individual choices by speakers at the local level and partly by those speakers being able to make inferences about each other on the basis of shared knowledge and assumptions about the world and how to accomplish things interactionally' (1987, p. 20). Applying Ellis and Roberts' statement to our language classrooms, I would rewrite the statement as follows: The classroom context is, therefore, created in interaction partly on the basis of particular and individual choices made in each moment of the lesson, by the learners and teachers, and partly by those learners and teachers being able to make inferences about each other on the basis of shared knowledge and assumptions about the world and how to accomplish things interactionally.

TASK 2.3

You may be familiar with teaching portfolios as part of language teachers' professional development, and/or as part of teaching **evaluations** or appraisals. The first section of such a portfolio (sometimes called a Teaching Philosophy) is a clear, concise statement of the teacher's beliefs about such key aspects as 'language', 'language teaching' and 'language learning', as well beliefs about, for example, how language teaching and learning can be achieved successfully. This statement of beliefs relates to the 'particular beliefs and presuppositions' (Ellis & Roberts, 1987, p. 19) that the teachers and the learners bring to the classroom.

To help you clarify some of your key beliefs and presuppositions, write your own personal definitions – no more than approximately 20 words for each – of these terms:

2.3.1: Language
2.3.2: Culture
2.3.3: Teaching
2.3.4: Learning

There are, of course, many more key terms that you could articulate and define for yourself. But the four above are some of the main concepts that all language teachers need to be clear about, because these will, directly and indirectly, shape everything you do as a teacher, as well as how and why – even where and when – you do it, in your particular context. If you are comfortable doing so, you could ask some colleagues to write their definitions, and then share your ideas with each other. You might be surprised by what you see, not only in your colleagues' definitions, but possibly also in your own.

A Specific Context

A useful, practical example of how to understand and articulate aspects of context in a language teaching and learning environment was presented by Inês Brito, Ambrizeth Lima and Elsa Auerbach (2004), who wrote about a course in Cape Verdean language, culture, and history (pp. 181–200). The country of Cape Verde is a collection of volcanic islands in the central Atlantic Ocean, located approximately 600 kilometres off the coast of Western Africa. It was colonized by Portuguese explorers/invaders in the fifteenth century, after which it became a centre for the Atlantic slave trade in the sixteenth and seventeenth centuries, eventually gaining independence from Portugal in 1975.

According to Brito, Lima and Auerbach, Cape Verdean students in the USA are 'all but invisible in educational literature and practice' (p. 181). To address this 'invisibility', they developed a high school course that 'integrated the teaching of Cape Verdean language, culture, and history, providing a context for students to gain academic skills through the medium of their first language' (p. 181), in a school in which approximately 30 per cent of the student population were from Cape Verde.

Brito, Lima and Auerbach start by stating that 'It is important to understand the historical and linguistic context in which the course was situated since they generated the context of the course. The community and institutional contexts, likewise, shaped students' engagement with it' (p. 183). Such statements are likely to apply to all contexts, but may be especially true in this case, because, as the authors explained, 'It is not possible to talk about the language education of Cape Verdean children without discussing issues of power, oppression, and resistance' (p. 183).

A useful five-part model of the context was put forward by Brito, Lima and Auerbach, starting with the historical context of the home country of the learners (in this case, Cape Verde), then the linguistic context. That was followed by the geographical location in which the course was taking place, which was Boston, Massachusetts, where the authors observed that 'Once in Boston, Cape Verdean families soon realize that finding a "better life" is not easy' (p. 184). The fourth layer or level of context was the institution, as, according to the authors, 'the institutional context, as well, has been shaped by ambivalence and struggle relating to Cape Verdean language, culture and identity' (p. 185). At the centre of the model is the classroom context, which the authors describe in terms of surrogate parenting, as 'The teachers in the Cape Verdean bilingual program understand that, at school, they are the students' educational parents' (p. 187).

Brito, Lima and Auerbach highlight the importance of making 'students' knowledge, attitudes, and experiences the starting point' (pp. 189–190) and of valuing 'students' skills, knowledge, and cultural expertise' (p. 192). This five-part model of context can be envisaged as a series of concentric circles, moving from the outer circle to the centre:
(i) historical; (ii) linguistic; (iii) geographical; (vi) institutional; and (v) classroom. This is a useful and practical way of thinking about our language teaching and learning contexts.

TASK 2.4

List some of the main features of each of these five aspects, in relation to your language learners' historical and linguistic contexts, together with your geographical, institutional and classroom contexts. Focus on features that distinguish your context from that of others.

2.4.1. historical
2.4.2. linguistic
2.4.3. geographical
2.4.4. institutional
2.4.5. classroom

Concluding Comments

The TESOL Press recently published a series of books under the title of *English Language Teaching in Context*. On the back cover of each is the tagline 'Context Is Everything' (Curtis, 2016b). The tagline may be challenged, as an overstatement, but the book series and the tagline are designed to draw attention to the importance of context, which is sometimes mentioned in books on methodology. However, relatively rarely is the centrality of context fully acknowledged. Therefore, one of the features of this book that distinguishes it from others on methodology is that all of the methods presented and described here are considered in terms of their relationship to the context in which they were developed, and the other contexts in which they have come to be used – sometimes far from where they began.

Suggested Readings

The nine books in the *ELT in Context* series (2016) include books on teaching English in Brazil, Cambodia, China, Colombia, Saudi Arabia and the USA, and teaching on the US–Mexico border. As each book is only about 50 pages, a great deal of local contextualized knowledge, skills and experience is condensed into relatively small packages.

Corwin Press (SAGE) is publishing a 'Complete Academic Language Mastery' series (2016), which includes titles such as *Culture in Context*, *Conversational Discourse in Context*, *Grammar and Syntax in Context* and *Vocabulary in Context*.

In *Language Teaching in Context* (2012), Beverly Derewianka and Pauline Jones look at language in terms of its different functions and purposes, including chapters on 'Language for Recounting What Happened', 'Language for Observing and Describing the World' and 'Language for Persuading Others'.

CHAPTER 3

Task-Based Language Teaching and Learning in Context

Before reading this chapter, consider the following questions:

- How would you define a 'task', in the general sense of the word?
- In the classroom, is a 'task' the same as an 'activity'? Are there differences between these two?
- What do you understand by the term 'task-based', in relation to language teaching and learning?
- Do you use Task-Based Language Teaching (TBLT) in your lessons?
- If so, why? Or, if not, why not?

Introduction and Overview

In the first part of this chapter, we look at some of the more general meanings of 'task', and highlight the need for us as language teachers to be clear, in our own minds, about what we mean when we refer to different methodologies, starting with 'task-based language teaching'. This starting point is necessary, as a number of studies have shown that language teachers may support or oppose a particular method – *even when they are not entirely clear what it is that they are supporting or opposing*. However, it is not only individual teachers who can find themselves in that position, as even ministries of education can also be found to be promoting – or even mandating – particular methodologies, while also appearing to be not entirely clear on what it is they are promoting or mandating. After considering more general meanings of 'task', we will then move on to more specific meanings in terms of Task-Based Language Teaching (TBLT) tasks, and I offer my own definition of such tasks in the context of the language lesson. In the third part of the chapter, readers are taken inside the TBLT classroom, to give them a sense of what the method looks like in the **real world** of language lessons, linking the theory and the practice of the method, using data from real classrooms, such as extracts from classroom transcripts. And although we refer to 'classrooms', we include within this term 'lessons', which may or not be taking place in traditional, physical, brick-and-mortar classrooms, and which may be happening, for example, in online environments.

Because TBLT has been, by far, the most researched, written-about and presented-on methodology in the last 30 years, the fourth part of the chapter briefly summarizes some of the main and most recent works on TBLT. The reason for this short section is so that teachers can be up to date in their knowledge and understanding of TBLT, if they choose to talk about TBLT with their colleagues, with parents, with administrators or with other stakeholders. This is an essential aspect of 'principled eclecticism', as noted in the previous chapters, which is referred to as a 'desirable, coherent, pluralistic approach to language teaching' (Mellow, 2002, p. 1), and which is one of the recurring themes in this book. Another reason for this short section is to show the influence of academic publications on classroom practice, as although it may be claimed that the latter is driving the former, it may be truer to say that academic trends are driving classroom practice considerably more than the other way around. The next part of the chapter looks at some of the pros and cons, strengths and weaknesses of TBLT, and the last part considers some aspects of **assessment** of TBLT **learning outcomes**.

From Tasks to TBLT: The Importance of Knowing What We Are Talking About

In the same way as the field of language teaching and learning methodologies was dominated by the rise of Communicative

Language Teaching (CLT) in the 1970s (see Chapter 4), the 1980s were similarly dominated by the rise of TBLT, or TBLT*L*, to include 'and Learning' at the end (see, for example, Kashif & Sajjad, 2015). TBLT is generally considered to be a subset and/or a logical extension, progression or outgrowth of CLT. That relationship raises the question of why the chapter on CLT was not presented before this chapter on TBLT, since the latter grew out of the former. The reason for this relates back to the note in the Introduction that the methodologies in this book are presented in order of prominence, and as TBLT has by now so far outstripped CLT, TBLT is presented first.

Interestingly, the *Macmillan Online Dictionary of English* (*MODE*) defines a 'task' as 'something that you have to do, often something that is difficult or unpleasant'. Such a definition can serve as a positive reminder of some of the challenges of being a language teacher and/or a language learner! These challenges can also be seen in the collocations provided in *MODE*, under adjectives frequently used with the word 'task', which include 'arduous, daunting, difficult, formidable, hopeless, impossible, onerous, thankless, unenviable, uphill'. The fact that all ten of the adjectives collocated with 'task' are negative – all the way from *daunting* and *difficult* to *hopeless*, and even *impossible!* – should also be an indication that to do TBLT well involves much more than simply putting learners in groups and giving them something to do. On a more positive note, the *MODE*'s list of the verbs frequently used with 'task' as the object includes 'accomplish, approach, attempt, begin, complete, face, perform, tackle, undertake'. None of these verbs suggests that TBLT is an easy option, but all of them are actions that effective language teachers and learners do regularly, as part of their daily work in classrooms.

In the same way as Sandra Savignon is seen as one of the pioneers of CLT (see Chapter 4), Michael Long (1985) is seen as one of the TBLT pioneers, along with N. S. Prabhu (1987). (See Greenwood, 1985, on Prabhu's Bangalore Project in South India, which began in 1979.) Long started with a similarly general definition of a task, but more positive than *MODE*'s, as 'a piece of work undertaken for oneself or for others, freely or for some reward ... the hundred and one things people do, at work, at play and in between' (1985, p. 89). The reference to 'freely or for some reward' reiterates the importance of the different kinds of motivation influencing the learners and the teachers, such as intrinsic or extrinsic, instrumental or integrative. (For more on these issues, see, for example, Dornyei & Schmidt's *Motivation and Second Language Acquisition*, 2001.) Examples of such general tasks given by Long include borrowing a book from the library, and making a hotel or airline reservation.

Although such an all-inclusive definition is extremely broad, it is a useful starting point, and it shows how non-specific notions, such as the completion of a task, can become highly specialized when applied to language teaching and learning. In terms of the importance of being clear about what we mean when we refer to key concepts such as 'task', Peter Skehan (1998) emphasized that 'it is necessary to address definitional issues [of TBLT] at the outset, since many different contemporary options give task a central role' (p. 286). Another reason for clearly defining what we mean by 'task' is that 'task-based' can mean many different things to many different people, as noted by Zheng and Borg (2014).

As teachers, we can sometimes fall into the trap of believing that something, such as TBLT, is 'good', even when the research shows that we may not fully understand what it is that we are assuming to be inherently 'good' (Littlewood, 2004). This assumption is partly the result of the pressures on language teachers to accept and embrace whatever the next set of methodological doctrines dictates, often as 'articles of faith'. This assumption and these pressures help to explain the outpouring of academic books, language textbooks and scholarly articles on TBLT. For example, in March 2017, Google Scholar showed more than *three million hits* for the search term 'task-based language teaching', and that number will most likely have grown by now. In fact, TBLT claims to be one of the few – and perhaps even the only – language teaching and learning methodology with so much research to support it (see 'Recent Developments in TBLT' below).

It is not only at the individual level that a clear understanding of TBLT appears to be conspicuous by its absence. As we saw in Chapter 2, governments and ministries of education can shape methodological trends at the national level – even if the government does not fully understand the methodology that they have chosen to mandate. For example, Xinmin Zheng and Simon Borg's (2014) study of TBLT for teaching English in secondary schools in China found that, although the Chinese Ministry of Education published TBTL guidelines in 2003, 'the curriculum does not define what precisely it understands a task to be, and how it might be distinct from other types of language learning activities' (p. 206). If even governments and ministries of education can promote a particular methodology without appearing to fully understand that methodology themselves, then busy language teachers can be forgiven for not being entirely clear on what it is they are attempting to employ in their classrooms. It is also important to note that, in the case of China, promoting a particular method directly impacts millions of teachers and learners of English. Beyond forgiving teachers for not always being clear, it is our responsibility as language teachers to ensure that we know what we mean when we think and talk, speak and write about 'TBLT', 'CLT' and all the other methodological acronyms that have been created for us over the last 50 years or so.

Some language teachers may be offended (and if so, my apologies!) by the notion that, methodologically speaking, sometimes 'we don't know what we're talking about'. However, I believe that this lack of understanding comes from inadequate teacher preparation and training programs, and a lack of on-going, in-service teacher professional development programs, which is one reason why books (and book series) like this one are needed – to help fill that gap. This lack of understanding was shown in a study of foreign language teachers in

New Zealand (East, 2012), which concluded that 'there was encouraging evidence of attempts by teachers to implement TBLT, though of concern was the finding *that a quarter of the participants in this study had minimal understandings of what TBLT was*' (Zheng and Borg, 2014, p. 208, emphasis added). The good news is that most of the teachers trying to implement TBLT in that study had more than a minimal understanding of it. But the fact that so many of them did not is the reason why the chapters in this book are designed to ensure that teachers are not trying to work with a methodology that they do not understand, and cannot clearly articulate. Using any of these methodologies effectively and engagingly is already a challenge – *even when they are fully understood* – so attempting to implement anything with minimal understanding of it appears to be setting ourselves up for failure.

ACTIVITY 3.1

Have you ever tried to employ a particular method in your language teaching without fully understanding it? If so, how did you find yourself in that position, and how successful – or not – were you in trying to use a method that you did not fully understand?

What Are TBLT Tasks?

Having established the need to know more fully what we mean – and what everybody else means – by 'task' and 'task-based', we can now move beyond Long's examples of 'the hundred and one things people do' (1985, p. 89) to some more specific meanings. But before we do that, having read many dozens of definitions of 'task' covering a period of 30 years or so, here is one of my favourites: 'A task is an activity in which a person engages in order to attain an objective, and which necessitates the use of language' (van den Branden, 2006, p. 5). As we can see, this definition is still rather general, and for some applied linguists, 'task' and 'activity' are not the same thing. For example, Zheng and Borg (2014) see 'activities' as referring to the kind of exercises 'normally found in textbooks' (p. 206). Thomas and Reinders (2012) distinguish between 'task', as 'the workplan that is given to the learners', and 'activity', as 'the communication that results from the performance of the task' (p. xvi). In that sense, a 'task' is what the learners are required to do, while the 'activity' is the language the learners use/produce while doing the task.

Based on van den Branden's definition, and the others I have read, my basic definition of a TBLT task is: *a series of connected activities, in which multiple language learners engage, in order to attain a language-oriented outcome, which is the successful, collaborative completion of a specific task.* Although it is possible to complete many general tasks individually, given the CLT origins of TBLT, my definition entails two or more learners completing the task by working together, 'which necessitates the use of language'. In the case of, for example, making a phone call, the call itself is usually preceded by some other activity, such as finding the phone number, and may be followed by some other activity, such as passing on a message, or making a note of the details learned during the call. Also, the call must involve at least two participants, and it may involve more than two if it is a conference call or phone meeting. This kind of definition raises the question of how 'successful completion' is assessed, which we will consider at the end of this chapter.

A 'task', in the TBLT sense of the word, was defined by Breen (1987) as a 'structured language learning endeavor, which has a particular objective, appropriate content, a specified working procedure and a range of outcomes' (p. 23). Breen's definition highlights the importance of **appropriateness** (see Chapter 4) as a seemingly straightforward concept, but which is, in fact, a rather messy notion (see, for example, Goodnough, 2008, on the messiness of educational research). Unfortunately, Breen then opened up the definition of 'task', 'implying ... that just about anything the learner does in a classroom qualifies as a task' (Nunan, 2004, p. 3), which, according to Breen (1987), can include everything 'from the simple and brief exercise type, to more complex and lengthy activities such as group problem solving or simulations and decision making' (p. 23). This led David Nunan to describe Breen's definition above as 'not particularly helpful' (2004, p. 3).

A decade later, by the end of the 1990s, greater clarity was possible in terms of what constituted a pedagogical task in the language classroom. According to Skehan (1998), a task in the TBLT lesson is recognizable as such because:

'meaning is primary
learners are not given other people's meaning to regurgitate
there is some sort of relationship to comparable real-world activities
task completion has some priority
the assessment of the task is in terms of outcome' (Skehan, 1998, cited in Nunan, 2004, p. 3).

The reference to regurgitating 'other people's meaning' is a criticism of, among other things, the production of language that has been memorized by the learners, who may not fully understand the meaning of the language they are producing This situation can lead to what can be thought of as *linguistic productivity without linguistic creativity*.

ACTIVITY 3.2

In 20 words or fewer, write your own brief definition or description of 'task', in the TBLT sense of the word. Share your definition/description with a colleague, and look for similarities and differences. Consider where these similarities and differences come from, that is, what is the basis for these similarities or differences.

In relation to the growth of TBLT in the 1980s and 1990s, Skehan (1998) noted that 'In the last twenty years or so, language teaching has changed to incorporate a higher proportion of meaning-based activities, in contrast to the era in which form was primary' (p. 268). By the new millennium, researchers and proponents of TBLT were continuing to be clearer on what a TBLT task is, as we can see in Rod Ellis' (2003) definition, which stated that a task 'requires learners to process language pragmatically in order to achieve an outcome that can be evaluated in terms of whether the correct or appropriate propositional content has been conveyed' (p. 16).

In the same way as CLT came to dominate language classrooms earlier, the new millennium also saw TBLT achieving a similar level of indisputability, as captured by William Littlewood's witty description in 2004: 'The task-based approach has achieved something of the status of a new orthodoxy: teachers in a wide range of settings are being told by curriculum leaders that this is how they should teach, and publishers almost everywhere are describing their new textbooks as task-based. Clearly, whatever a task-based approach means, it is a good thing' (p. 319). Littlewood's closing quip, that in terms of publishing 'whatever a task-based approach means, it is a good thing', makes an important point about the extent to which textbook publishers can drive the 'methodological market', and the extent to which they 'own' that market. This driving of methodological movements, based on maximizing textbook sales, adds to the pressures that teachers are already under to use certain methodologies, whether or not they fully understand them.

The focus on meaning was reiterated by Ellis (2003), who also stated that, in TBLT tasks, learners are required to give their 'primary attention to meaning and to make use of their own linguistic resources, although the design of the task may predispose them to use particular forms' (p. 16). These kinds of definitions tell us much about the assumptions made by the proponents of these methods, and about what the prerequisites are for the method to be employed, especially in contexts that may be markedly different from those in which they were originally created and developed. For example, Ellis' definition appears to assume and/or require that the learners have the necessary target language *to begin with*, in terms of 'their own linguistic resources'. If the learners had no linguistic resources in the target language, then they could not work on completing a task in that target language until they had developed those resources. However, there appears to be relatively little mention in the literature of such important factors as the target language competence levels needed for learners to engage in TBLT tasks.

Brooks and Donato (1994), drawing on the work of the Russian psychologist Lev Vygotsky (1896–1934), defined TBLT tasks as 'being internally constructed through the moment-to-moment verbal interactions of the learners during actual task performance' (p. 272). Although the focus is on speaking, with no mention of the other language modalities, Brooks and Donato's definition is an important reminder that the realities of any lesson, but perhaps especially a language lesson, are created *in the moment*, no matter how much planning and preparation have gone on beforehand. Another point that emerges in examining the definitions of 'task' is the recurring reference to somewhere referred to as 'the real world'. For example, 'A task is intended to result in language that bears a resemblance, direct or indirect, to the way language is used *in the real world*' (Ellis, 2003, p. 16, emphasis added).

This recurring reference in the literature to some seemingly far-away 'real world' is unfortunate, as it can give the impression that language classrooms, in spite of being filled with real people, such as teachers and learners, are somehow 'unreal'. The notion that language classrooms are not real can undermine the work that takes place there. This, in turn, can further lower the status of language teaching and learning, which is often already low down on the pecking order of subject studies, and does not need to be pushed down any further. Thankfully,

Nunan (2004) did clarify that by 'real-world tasks' he means the 'uses of language in the world beyond the classroom' (p. 1), although he appears to be one of the few to offer this important clarification.

Drawing on the work of Skehan (1998) and Ellis (2003) (and others), Nunan (2004, p. 4) proposed his own definition of a 'pedagogical task' as 'a piece of classroom work that involves learners in comprehending, manipulating, producing or interacting in the target language', thereby covering both the more receptive and the more productive language modalities. Nunan also included grammar in his definition, in terms of the learners' attention being focused 'on mobilizing their grammatical knowledge in order to express meaning'. But in relation to the balance between these two, he added that the purpose of the TBLT task should be 'to convey **meaning** rather than to manipulate **form**' (2004, p. 3). As an important concluding part of his definition, Nunan also emphasized the structured and the free-standing nature of TBLT tasks: 'The task should also have a sense of completeness, being able to stand alone as a communicative act in its own right, with a beginning, a middle and an end' (Nunan, 2004, p. 4). This comment reiterates Skehan's (1998) point above, that task completion should be one of the priorities.

ACTIVITY 3.3

In the section above, I refer to *linguistic productivity without linguistic creativity*. Have you come across instances of this kind of productivity without creativity in your and/or other teachers' language lessons? Maybe you have encountered this elsewhere, outside the classroom. You can also collect examples of the opposite, that is, *linguistic productivity that shows linguistic creativity*. Both kinds of examples can be used in language lessons, to show how language works, when it works well, and when it does not work so well.

Inside the TBLT Classroom

In *Doing Task-Based Teaching*, Dave Willis and Jane Willis (2007) note in their Introduction that 'Of course, where teaching goes on, learning does too – or so we hope' (p. xiv). In relation to causality, and whether or not teaching results in learning, or whether the learning that takes place is a result of the teaching, that is a more theoretical or philosophical discussion, which is not one of the goals of this book. But as we decide which methods to use in our language lessons each day, it is important to bear in mind such relationships, whether they be only **correlational** or more causal.

Willis and Willis (2007) present examples of TBLT tasks based on discussion of challenging and thought-provoking ideas, such as 'if you want to promote discussion of any controversial topic you can prepare students by offering a series of statements and ask learners as individuals to say how far they agree with each statement and to give reasons for their opinions' (p. 9). In one task, the students are first asked to respond to six statements, which include 'All drugs should be legalized' and 'It is pointless to send drug addicts to prison. In most cases this will simply reinforce the habit' (p. 10). Learners respond to such statements using a four-point Likert scale of 'strongly agree', 'agree', 'disagree' and 'strongly disagree'. (See Norman, 2010, for more on the use of Likert scales.)

In terms of contextual appropriateness, it is important to note that around 30 countries in the world today, such as Thailand, can impose the death penalty for importing, exporting or selling drugs, and in more than a dozen countries, such as China and Singapore, the death sentence for drug trafficking is mandatory. It is, therefore, highly unlikely that statements such as 'All drugs should be legalized' could be discussed openly in classes in those countries, and statements regarding sending addicts to prison may not even apply in those countries in which the death sentence for drug offences is mandatory. The fact that such statements should only be used in certain contexts is an important aspect of ensuring that tasks are appropriate for the context, and not assuming that all tasks are appropriate for all contexts. There is also no mention of the age of the learners, the target language competence levels needed to complete the task, or any other learner details, all of which need to be taken into account, as they could significantly impact the successful completion of such a task.

However, assuming that the learners are in an environment in which agreement with statements such as 'All drugs should be legalized' is possible, and assuming that the learners have the target language competence levels needed to engage in the activity, Willis and Willis present an activity sequence. The sequence starts with the teacher introducing the topic and highlighting one or two issues. In the second step, the teacher introduces the survey and asks for a brief statement of opinions, 'drawing attention to some of the lexis related to the topic' (2007, p. 10), which may be different from 'teaching vocabulary', as attention-drawing may be more implicit and indirect than vocabulary-teaching.

In steps three and four of the activity sequence, the learners write their individual responses to the six statements using the four-part Likert dis/agreement scale. They then work in groups, comparing and contrasting their opinions, and trying to reach agreement. After that, as a group, they decide on which of the four options, from 'strongly agree' to 'strongly disagree', they can agree on for each of the statements. Following a whole-class discussion, chaired by the teacher, the learners read a text on the issues, then compare the author's views with their own, and in the seventh and final step, the teacher chairs another whole-class discussion, in which learners compare the author's views with their own views. There is no indication of the class size for this task, or how much time would be needed to complete the seven steps. But it seems likely that such a task would need more than one lesson, as a whole-class discussion with larger classes generally takes more time than with smaller classes, if most of the students are to have the opportunity to express their thoughts, ideas and opinions. Two of the main points that emerge from an examination of such textbook TBLT tasks are: (i) that not all tasks are appropriate for all contexts, and (ii) that a whole range of factors need to be taken into account before recommending or using these kinds of TBLT tasks.

> ### ACTIVITY 3.4
>
> Are you in a teaching and learning context in which statements such as 'All drugs should be legalized' can be openly discussed, and agreed with? If so, how would you create a task, or a series of tasks, with your learners, based on a debate about the legalization of drugs, using such statements? If you are not working in a context in which statements such as 'All drugs should be legalized' can be openly discussed/agreed with, what would be a more suitable statement or topic for a debate in your context?

Drawing on the work of Willis (1996), Richards (2006) gives examples of six types of task that can be seen in CLT classrooms: listing, sorting and ordering, comparing, problem-solving, sharing personal experience, and creative tasks (Richards, 2006, pp. 31–32). In a sense, all tasks should involve some kind of creativity; otherwise learners' (and teachers') motivation levels may fall to problematically and prohibitively low levels. For a listing task, the example given is students drawing up 'a list of things they would pack if they were going on a beach vacation' (p. 31). For a sorting and ordering task, students work in pairs to make up a list of 'the most important characteristics of an ideal vacation' (p. 31), and for a comparing task, students compare and contrast advertisements for two different supermarkets. In a problem-solving task, students 'read a letter to an advice columnist and suggest a solution to the writer's problems' (p. 32), and for an experience-sharing task, students discuss their reactions to 'an ethical or moral dilemma' (p. 32). For the creative task, students 'prepare plans for redecorating a house' (p. 32).

I gave the problem-solving task described above to a group of five young adult students, in their early twenties, learning English in an upper-intermediate level English for Academic Purposes (EAP) class at a university in Ontario, Canada. As this lesson took place in December, and in a country in which Christmas is widely celebrated, the writer's problem, described in her letter to an advice columnist, was that she was unemployed and so she had very little money to buy Christmas presents for her family and friends. This part of the lesson was digitally recorded, with the student's permission, using a cellphone. T = Teacher; S1 = Student 1, etc.

S1: Why she has no money?
S2: 'Cause she is unemployed. Teacher just said. [S2 points to T; students laugh]
S3: She could make presents.
S4: What she could make?
S3: She could make … [long pause]
S4: She could make food.
S5: How to make food? [students laugh]
T: Yes, she could cook some food, make some dishes.
S1: Dishes? You mean likes cups and saucers? [students laugh]
S4: No. She could make food, and give to her family, her friends.
S1: She should have money. Everyone need money. You need money. [S1 points to T; students laugh]

As this point in the task, I intervened and re-focused the students on the original task, which was to give advice to the person who wrote to the columnist, rather than a discussion of the importance of money. However, it became clear from the students' comments that they would rather talk about having or not having money than give advice to the person who had no money. This was an important reminder of a point not usually mentioned in the mountains of literature on TBLT, which is that learners, depending on their target language competence levels and other factors, can create their own tasks that are different from the original task. Learners creating their own tasks, rather than working on the one given to them, may be an essential part of the definition of learner-centredness, but it is rarely mentioned in the voluminous writings on **learner-centredness** (see, for example, Tudor, 1996). This rarely referred-to part of the definition is that learner-centredness can involve the learners *not* doing what they have been asked to do, but doing instead something they have chosen to do. This learner behaviour raises some important questions about control and trust, which are considered in more detail in the section below, on the pros and cons of TBLT.

This aspect of learner-centredness, and the fact that I had to intervene to bring the students back on task, takes us back to Brooks and Donato's (1994) Vygotskian definition of TBLT tasks as 'being internally constructed through the moment-to-moment verbal interactions of the learners during actual task performance' (p. 272). And in terms of 'mobilizing' the learners' grammatical knowledge (Nunan, 2004, p. 4), in the lesson above, we reviewed the use of 'do' and 'did' as an auxiliary verb, to turn Student 1's 'Why she has no money?' into 'Why doesn't she have [any] money?' We also looked at 'cooking food' versus 'making food', which, as one of the students pointed out, might refer to farmers growing crops in fields, which could constitute 'making food'. And we discussed vocabulary items such as 'homemade' and 'dish/es', including the now somewhat dated use of 'dish' to mean 'sexually attractive', as in 'S/he is such a dish!'

This brief extract from the lesson transcript is also an important reminder of how little language needs to be produced by learners for there to be many opportunities for language teaching and learning – *if* the teacher knows how, or has been trained, to notice these opportunities. These five students, in the brief interaction above, produced a total of fewer than 70 words, which took only about one minute to produce, but which exemplified many structural features of the English language. These included the use of do/does/doesn't, 'to do' versus 'to make', and the use of articles, as well as 'cooking food' versus 'making food', the different meanings and functions of 'dish' and 'dishes', and more. Beyond grammar and vocabulary, the students also ended up having an engaging discussion about the importance and the value of money. They also discussed what it means to be 'wealthy', and other related topics, such as 'charitable giving', in terms of whether people who have money should give it – or be required to give a significant portion of it – to those who do not.

This is not to suggest that all of the aspects of English listed above should be taught in the same lesson. With training, development and experience, teachers can learn to effectively and efficiently identify, collect and store for later use samples of target language produced by learners. These samples can then be used to do more than simply *facilitate* learner-centred, communicative interaction, if such interaction is possible, depending on the factors discussed above. These samples can be used to explicitly *teach* English, so that the learner's knowledge of and ability to use the target language increases in quantity, and improves in quality.

ACTIVITY 3.5

Write a set of lesson-planning notes for a task in which your students would discuss their reactions to 'an ethical or moral dilemma'. What would that dilemma be, and how would you set up the discussion? Are there any particular or specific aspects of the target language that you would teach before the discussion, or that you would be paying particular attention to during the discussion?

Recent Developments in TBLT

There are two main reasons for this brief section. The first is to support the claim made above, that TBLT may be the language teaching methodology most published about in the history of our field. That kind of volume makes it difficult to look critically at TBLT, as most of the work published appears to support the idea that TBLT is the 'best' method. Another reason for this brief section is so that, if a language teacher is asked why they are using TBLT or what they know about TBLT, they are aware of some of the major works published on this particular methodology. This is not to imply that all or any of these works need to be read in their entirety, but an awareness of their existence, and of some of their main points, could help teachers articulate their reasons for using – or for *not* using – TBLT.

The *Task-Based Language Teaching* series started in 2009, with a collection of 20 articles (van den Branden, Bygate, & Norris), and is now up to the most recent book in the series, on TBLT for young learners in Japan (Shintani, 2016). That makes nine books, and more than 2500 pages, in a single book series, focused on a single methodology. The books in the series look at, for example, TBLT in New Zealand, where the entire country's language curriculum was revised and rebuilt around TBLT (East, 2012). It is worth noting that the book on New Zealand is titled *TBLT From the Teachers' Perspective*. If we say that we are committed to learner-centredness, it seems odd that there do not appear to be any books on TBLT *From the Learners' Perspective*. This focus on the teachers' perspective, while claiming a commitment to learner-centredness, may indicate a disconnect between what the research says that language teachers should do, that is, focus on learners, versus what the researchers themselves actually do, that is, focus on teachers.

One of the books in the nine-volume *TBLT* series is a collection of plenary talks presented at the Biennial International Conference on Task-Based Language Teaching between 2005 and 2013 (Bygate, 2015), which includes 'recommendations from influential researchers working within the TBLT paradigm over the last 30 years' (back cover). The authors and the chapters in that *TBLT* series make many significant contributions to advancing the research, publications and presentations on TBLT. However, what is not at all clear is how many of those thousands of pages advance the day-to-day classroom-based teaching and learning of languages. What is also not clear is who the audience is for the kinds of books in that TBLT series. Very few of the language teachers I have worked with over the last 20 years have the time to read such books. In that case, the TBLT series may be an example of books written *by* applied linguists *for* applied linguists, *about* language teaching, but *not for* language teachers.

Of the dozens of articles, book chapters and books on TBLT that have been published in recent years, one that merits particular attention comes from one of the earliest proponents of TBLT, Michael Long, as noted above. In *Second Language Acquisition and Task-Based Language Teaching* (2015), we can see how far TBLT has come in the 30 years since Long referred to 'the hundred and one things people do, at work, at play and in between' (1985, p. 89). Long (2015) starts by acknowledging that language teaching is 'notorious for methodological pendulum swings' (p. xi), in which we jump from one methodological bandwagon to another (see Chapter 2).

Long is critical of the fact that 'many of the very same textbook writers and commercial publishers who made large sums of money out of the structural, notional, functional, topical, and lexical movements of the past 30 years are now repeating the performance with tasks' (p. xi). The use of the term 'movement' is important here, as this word signals something more than a methodology or an approach – alluding to shared views of the world and similar belief systems. For example, the *MODE* defines 'movement', as a countable noun, to mean 'a group of people who share the same aim and work together to achieve it' and 'a change in someone's attitude, opinion, or behaviour, especially over a period of time'. When methods become movements, it is possible that they have, by then, taken on a life of their own. And as noted above, that status as a movement makes it difficult to view any methodology critically. Long is also critical of how methodologies can end up 'repackaged in a form acceptable to the powerful political and commercial interests that exert enormous influence on the way LT [Language Teaching] is conducted worldwide' (2015, p. 6) – as exemplified by 'the multimillionaire textbook writer sipping martinis a thousand miles away [from the classroom] on a beach in the Cayman Islands' (p. 13).

A key point here is that when approaches and methods such as TBLT, which were developed in contexts where they worked well, are then exported and shipped to other contexts, far removed from their origins, they might not be appropriate, so they might not work as well, or they might not work at all. However, one of the powerful reasons for this kind of packaging and exporting of methods to contexts where they may not be appropriate relates to the multibillion-dollar (US$) global business of language education. In such a business model, the more textbooks that can be sold within the one-size-fits-all model, the greater the profit margins.

Setting TBLT within the broader, global context of language teaching and learning, Long believes that 'Second language teaching and learning are more important in the twenty-first century than ever before and are more important than even many language teachers appreciate' (Long, 2015, p. 3). I would also add that second language teaching and learning are more important in the twenty-first century than even many applied linguists appreciate. The reason for this importance, according to Long, is because 'Second and foreign language teaching affect the educational life chances of millions of learners the world over' (p. 14). I would wholeheartedly agree with that statement, as it is, in my experience of working with language teachers all over the world, something that they are acutely aware of, and which is one of the reasons they became language teachers in the first place. It is reassuring to see that although Long is a strong advocate for and believer in the effectiveness of TBLT, he still acknowledges that TBLT is not necessarily 'the best approach to LT [Language Teaching], or even a good one. That is a judgment call' (2015, p. 14).

ACTIVITY 3.6

According to Long, 'Second language teaching and learning are more important in the twenty-first century than ever before.' Do you agree with this statement? If you agree, why do you think this is so? And if you disagree, how would you re-phrase the statement?

The Pros and Cons of TBLT

Some of the challenges of setting up TBLT tasks in the language classroom can be seen in the following exchange between a teacher and a group of beginner-level students, between nine and ten years old, learning English in a classroom in Turkey. The teacher is attempting to employ TBLT using games, with some difficulty:

T: Please speak in English.
S1: What are we going to do now? [said in Turkish]
T: Don't speak Turkish. Work in groups. Choose a card. Read and do it.
S2: Read the question.
S1: What is this? What is it in English? [said in Turkish]
S3: Sofa.
S4: Sofa. [said in Turkish]
T: In English please.

>Adapted from İlin, İnözü, & Yumru, 2007, p. 65)

İlin, İnözü and Yumru observed that 'During the game, as most of the students carried out the task in Turkish, the teacher very often stopped the discussions and asked them to speak in

English' (p. 64). The authors also observed that, during the TBLT lesson, 'the teacher had to focus more upon the process than on the product in language learning' (p. 64). The ubiquity of games and game-playing is one of the many areas of overlap between TBLT methods and CLT approaches (see Chapter 4). However, as the transcript of this small part of the lesson shows, we should not assume that games necessarily work more effectively with younger learners, such as children, than with older learners, such as teenagers and adult learners, especially if the older learners have higher levels of target language proficiency. In the extract above, if the learners had had higher competence levels of English, the teacher would have been able to set up the task more efficiently, and s/he would have been able to focus on production of the target language, rather than on the process. It is also likely that if the teacher had had more training in the use of TBLT, especially with young learners, s/he might have been able to employ the task more productively and more usefully.

One of the essential aspects of TBLT, CLT and a number of other approaches and methods is Control, specifically the teacher's control of the lesson or the class. This issue of Control is another one of those extremely important factors that appear to have received relatively little attention in the mountains of methodological literature. This lack of attention may be, at least in part, because 'control' has become negatively connoted, in the sense of 'to be under someone's control' or 'to take control of something'. One of the synonyms of 'control' is 'authority', which is also often negatively connoted. However, the general meaning of 'control' is 'the power to make decisions about something and decide what should happen' (*MODE*) and 'authority' is similarly defined as 'the power to make decisions or tell people what to do' (*MODE*). All teachers need to be effective classroom managers, and without some degree of control and authority, management is not possible. How, then, do 'control' and 'authority' relate to approaches and methods such as TBLT? This question relates to one of the conundrums or limitations of the learner-centred language teaching movement, and to the question of where this leaves the teacher: If the learner is to be at centre of the teaching, where should the teacher be?

This question may be part of what I refer to as the **facilitation** problem, in which some teachers may be reluctant to teach, preferring instead to 'facilitate'. By 'teaching' I mean the teacher working with the learners to develop their knowledge of the target language, including grammar, and other aspects of how the target language works. The focus in teaching is on helping the students learn things that they did not know before, whereas in facilitating the focus is on managing the interaction of the learners, with an emphasis on producing as much of the spoken target language as possible. Both are necessary, and the two are not mutually exclusive, but I have seen many English language lessons in many countries where there seemed to be a lot of facilitating of student interaction in small groups, but relatively little actual language teaching taking place.

If we connect factors such as the teacher's control and authority in the classroom with learner-centredness and the tendency or inclination to facilitate rather than to teach, we can see that one of the challenges of TBLT is that the teachers need to give control of the lesson to the learners. If the learners are mature and motivated, if they have the necessary target language competence levels to begin with, and if the other factors are favourable, then giving control of the lesson to the learners can significantly enhance the quality and the quantity of language learning. However, if the conditions necessary for successful task completion are not met, and if the teacher then relinquishes control, the plan for the lesson may quickly fall apart. Another important factor here is how well the teacher has **scaffolded** the learning, by setting up the task so that more support and guidance is provided by the teacher in the beginning, with that support being gradually withdrawn as the learners' language **competencies** and confidence levels grow.

In addition to control, another major factor is Trust. As we know, meaningful relationships – whether personal, professional, or both – cannot be built and sustained without trust. Therefore, most institutional contexts, including schools, colleges, universities and other educational institutions, can be categorized as high-trust/low-control versus low-trust/high-control (McNaught & Curtis, 2009), which is not a dichotomy but a **continuum**. Factoring in trust, we see that, in addition to all the other conditions that need to be met for TBLT to work well, there needs to be a considerable amount of trust between the teacher and the learners before control can be given by the teacher to the learners.

As Prabhu (1990) pointed out more than 25 years ago, there is 'no best method' (pp. 161–176) for teaching and learning languages, and yet we continue to focus on 'best practices' (see Chapter 4). Therefore, like all methods, TBLT has its strengths as well as its weaknesses, its advantages and disadvantages, its pros and its cons. One of TBLT's strengths, when it works well, is the potential for improvements in spoken English competence levels. As a Taiwanese learner of English reportedly said, referring to TBLT, 'The best thing is that I remember many new words and phrases for a longer time because I really use them for communicative purposes, not just for the exam. With more oral practice with my group members, I feel more conformable [sic] about speaking English' (Tang, Chiou, & Jarsaillon, 2015, p. 173). And as 'Miss Wu', a Chinese teacher of English in China, reported, 'If we can use task-based teaching in a proper way, I think it will give our students more opportunities to communicate in English and learn how to work socially with other learners' (Zheng & Borg, 2014, p. 213).

Perhaps the important part of Teacher Wu's comment is 'in a proper way', by which we can assume she means when TBLT is used effectively, that is, with most of the conditions for its success being met. This would include careful scaffolding, the learners being motivated and mature enough to take control of that part of the lesson, and the learners having the target language competence to work on the task. However, Teacher Wu also said that 'it is hard to control the large class. Moreover, it is time-consuming to carry out activities ... I have lots of content to cover' (p. 214). And in relation to class size, 'Miss Wu's colleague, 'Ms Ma', commented that 'The thing that I am worried about is that I am not able to monitor all of the performance in pairs or in groups ... I have fifty-one students in all ... I think the big challenge for me is how to organize more suitable activities for my students at different levels' (p. 217). This question of class size, in relation to the contextual appropriateness of a particular methodology, is discussed more in relation to CLT (Chapter 4).

In spite of the many thousands of pages and the hundreds of books, papers and articles published on TBLT over the last 30 years, Meghan Calvert and Younghee Sheen recently concluded that 'The creation, implementation, and evaluation of language learning tasks remain a challenge for many teachers, especially those with limited experience with using tasks in their teaching' (2015, p. 226). And in terms of the contextual appropriateness of TBLT, Scott Roy Douglas and Marcia Kim reported that 'Another drawback associated with TBLT is that it may be difficult to implement in differing teaching contexts' (2014, p. 6). Douglas and Kim went on to note that 'TBLT appears to be an approach that works well with students who are willing to take risks in their learning ... but may not be preferred by students who are familiar with more traditional approaches that involve direct grammar teaching and a structured curriculum' (2014, p. 6). This relates to the notion of students' preferred learning styles, which may clash with teachers' preferred teaching styles if, for example, the students prefer an explicit focus on grammar, while the teacher believes in CLT.

In considering contextual appropriateness more specifically, Douglas and Kim pointed out that 'Despite perceptions to the contrary, the Canadian context continues to have cultural norms and expectations that may not foster a receptive environment for TBLT' (Ogilvie & Dunn, 2010, p. 17). In terms of the positive features of TBLT, Douglas and Kim found that, for the teachers in their study, 'The most reported benefits of TBLT were its practicality, effectiveness, and learner-centeredness' (p. 13). But in terms of the limitations of TBLT, Douglas and Kim also found that 'The most prevalent drawbacks reported were a mismatch with student expectations, a lack of classroom time, and excessive instructor preparation' (p. 14). These three factors relate to the recurring themes of preferred learning styles, contextual constraints, and teacher training and professional development.

The last word in this pros and cons section will go to a teacher in Ogilvie and Dunn's (2010) study. The teacher's comment reiterates the opening points made in this chapter about the importance of teachers being able to articulate what they are doing, and to explain why they are doing it this way, and not some other way: 'Students feel a great sense of accomplishment, but you [instructors] have to weather a lot of anxiety and complaining and griping, and you have to be very clear on what they are learning from this, and why you are doing it this way' (Ogilvie & Dunn, 2010, p. 19).

ACTIVITY 3.7

As noted above, Douglas and Kim reported that 'Another drawback associated with TBLT is that it may be difficult to implement in differing teaching contexts.' Is your teaching and learning context amenable to and conducive to using TBLT? If so, in what ways is your context good for TBLT? If not, what are some of the obstacles to using TBLT in your context?

Assessment of TBLT Learning Outcomes

Most of the 250 or so methodological publications consulted in the writing of this book (see References) say little or nothing about assessment of learning outcomes. This is an all-too-common omission, yet it should be an important – or even essential – aspect of an informed and principled methodological eclecticism. In my experience, too often in teaching, assessment comes last, when it should be one of the key starting points. As a result, a common sequence in the designing and developing of language courses and programs is to start with the desired or required learning outcomes, then to select or develop materials, tasks and so on that will provide the necessary language input and opportunities for learners to develop their target language competencies.

Often, towards the end of the process, assessment comes to mind, in the form of questions such as 'How will we know what the students have learned?' assuming that the learning of something can be taken for granted (although in some cases, that can be an optimistic assumption). How will we know whether the students have learned *what was taught*? given that teaching cannot be assumed to automatically and causally result in learning. And, how will we know whether the students have learned *what they need and want to know*? in relation to their purposes for learning the target language.

Such questions open up a veritable Pandora's Box of questions about what it means to 'know' a language, about the complex and sometimes contradictory relationships between teaching and testing, and about the different kinds of assessment, such as summative, formative, diagnostic and so on, as well as questions about assessment *of* learning, assessment *as* learning, and assessment *for* learning. (See Chris Davison's 2004 and 2007 work for more on these different kinds and purposes of assessment.) Therefore, such topics require a more in-depth discussion (such as that in Liying Cheng's and Janna Fox's book, 2017, in this *ALLC* series) than can be entered into here.

What can be done here is to expand on the relatively rare and somewhat limited discussions of assessment of learning outcomes in relation to methodology. For example, Larsen-Freeman and Anderson (2011), in their chapter on TBLT, in response to their question 'How is evaluation accomplished?' answer: 'The teacher constantly evaluates students in light of task outcomes and the language they use' (p. 157). Although this is a useful starting point, it would be helpful to know more about assessment of learning outcomes, as an integral part of assessing the usefulness, appropriateness and so on of the methodologies being used. However, by the same token, we do not want to give the impression that something as complex as assessment can be covered in any depth in just a few pages. This concluding section at the end of each chapter is, therefore, a compromise. And while acknowledging that assessment of learning outcomes should be at the beginning of the educational design process, this section comes at the end of the chapter because we wanted to be clear on what we mean by 'TBLT', and to have a thorough understanding of the methodology, before we considered assessment of TBLT learning outcomes.

Assessment of TBLT learning outcomes has been an important segment of the burgeoning market of academic publications on TBLT, as discussed above (in 'Recent Developments in TBLT'). For example, Lyle Bachman reflected on what he referred to as 'TBLPA' (2002, pp. 453–476). Bachman concluded that 'The complexities of task-based language performance assessment (TBLPA) are leading language testers to reconsider many of the fundamental issues about what we want to assess, how we go about it and what sorts of evidence we need to provide in order to justify the ways in which we use our assessments' (p. 453). Bachman's comment shows that the influence of TBLT has been extensive enough to cause a re-visiting of some of the most basic assumptions in language assessment, which very few methods, apart from CLT, can claim to have done.

Bachman's reflections were part of a special issue of the journal *Language Testing*, on task-based language assessment (TBLA), which included papers on task-based assessment of oral proficiency (Elder, Iwashita, & McNamara, 2002), on assessment of listening (Brindley & Slatyer, 2002) and on assessing TBLT outcomes with learners of German (Byrnes, 2002) and with learners of Dutch (van den Branden, Depauw, & Gysen, 2002). There are also papers on test-takers' abilities in relation to task difficulty (Norris, Brown, Hudson & Bonk, 2002) and on design and analysis in task-based language assessment (Mislevy, Steinberg, & Almond, 2002), in which the authors drew on Brindley's early work (1994) in this area. Brindley defined TBLA as 'the process of evaluating, in relation to a set of explicitly stated criteria, the quality of the communicative performances elicited from learners as part of goal directed, meaning-focused language use requiring the integration of skills and knowledge' (1994, p. 74). Mislevy, Steinberg and Almond (2002) concluded that 'TBLA raises questions of just how to design complex tasks, evaluate students' performances and draw valid conclusions therefrom' (p. 477).

This interest in and outpouring of papers on TBLA has continued to the present day, and shows no signs of abating in the near future. For example, Yuko Goto Butler and Wei Zeng (2015) researched elementary school learners' interactional development, using task-based paired-assessment, with 24 fourth-grade students (aged 9–10) and 24 sixth-grade students (aged 11–12) in 'a large metropolitan city in China where TBLT has been part of the curriculum since 2001' (p. 297). Although the results of the study were inconclusive, Butler and Zeng did conclude that 'the paired-assessment format has gained increased attention for its potential to better observe students' interactional competence' (p. 297). But they also warned that 'we need to ensure that the students are developmentally ready to engage in communicative interactions in language tasks' (p. 316). That warning reiterates a recurring point in this chapter (and in some of the following chapters): that the learners need to be ready – not only maturationally, but also linguistically, culturally and in other ways ready – to engage in language learning using methodologies such as TBLT. Therefore, it cannot be assumed, simply because it has been decided that a method is 'good', that it will work well, in all places, at all times, with all teachers and learners.

Where does all this information leave busy classroom language teachers who are already using, or who may want to try using, TBLT in their language lessons? In her work on authentic assessment and designing performance-based tasks, Katherine Luongo-Orlando (2003) defined 'assessment' as 'the process of gathering information about student learning' (p. 6). Having skimmed and ploughed through some of the complexities of TBLA, it is a relief to return to the simplicity of definitions such as this, even though such simplicity lacks some of the necessary detail. Luongo-Orlando adds some of that detail by explaining that 'The data collected through the application of systematic and purposeful techniques forms the basis of evaluation of student achievement' (p. 6). And she distinguished between 'assessment' and 'evaluation', defining the latter as the process of *judging* the information gathered during the assessment process(es), on the basis of which decisions can be made about 'the quality of student performance' (p. 6).

Although Luongo-Orlando's book on designing performance-based tasks is not focused on language teaching and learning, she sets out a detailed, practical eight-step guide (pp. 8–17) to the creation and carrying out of assessment tasks, which can be applied to TBLT lessons and classes. Step One is 'Set focus goals and identify learning outcomes, purpose and audience' (p. 9), which should apply to any lesson, course or program, although the following steps are all task-based. For example, Step Two is 'Develop a performance task that will assess the learning outcomes' (p. 10), in which the teacher should 'contextualize the task' (p. 10) by connecting the in-class/during-lesson task to be assessed with out-of-class/after-lesson tasks that the learners will need to complete. (See the discussion of 'authenticity' in Chapter 4.) Step Three is 'Develop and implement a unit of study that will prepare students for the performance task' (p. 15), which reflects a particular approach to lesson, course and program planning, based on 'units', which will not be the case in every context. But the important point in Step Three is for the teacher to check that the learners have 'the prerequisite knowledge, skills, and attitudes needed for the performance task' (p. 15), which has emerged as one of the recurring points in this chapter.

In terms of developing tools for assessment, Step Four is 'Design scoring procedures and assessment tools that will be used to measure students' achievement on the performance task' (pp. 15–16). Luongo-Orlando lists approximately 20 such tools, from analytic (points-based), attitudinal (ratings) and holistic (generic) scales, to anecdotal notes and observation notes (based on teachers' observations of the learners), as well as teacher–student interviews and conferences (one-to-one, pair or small group) and self-, peer- and group-assessment. In Step Five, the performance task is introduced and administered, followed by Step Six, which is based on gathering evidence and scoring results (p. 16).

The notion of teachers as reflective practitioners has been well-established for many years in language education (see, for example, Farrell, 2009), which has led to the notion of students as reflective learners. Again, this notion would not necessarily apply in all contexts, but in those in which it does apply, Step 7 is 'Promote reflection and goal-setting in students' (p. 16). In the eighth and final step, teachers gather samples of students' work that will help them 'determine standards of performance for future assessments' by examining students' levels of achievement and overall performance (p. 16). How each of these steps is realized will be different in each context, but they do provide a way of applying some of the theories of TBLA to real-world language classrooms.

ACTIVITY 3.8

As noted above, Luongo-Orlando defines 'assessment' as 'the process of gathering information about student learning' (2003, p. 6). What kinds of information do you gather about your students' learning? How is the information analyzed and presented, and what is it used for? How is the information used to improve language teaching and learning in your context?

Concluding Comments

Whether or not we agree with the principles of TBLT or use the practices of TBLT in our language lessons, for better or worse, it has become something of a 'global method' for a 'global language'. However, the fact remains that it is only one of many possible methodologies, in spite of attempts by some of its proponents to present TBLT as *the* method, subsuming (and perhaps consuming) all other methods. At the beginning of this chapter, I highlighted the importance of 'principled eclecticism' as a 'desirable, coherent, pluralistic approach to language teaching' (Mellow, 2002, p. 1). All of these adjectives are positive, feel-good descriptors. But for 'principled eclecticism' to be possible, teachers, learners and other educational decision-makers need to be able to clearly and concisely articulate what they understand methodologies such as TBLT to be, and why they are being – or not being – used in a particular context. In the following chapter, we will continue to explore these themes, through a consideration of Communicative Language Teaching.

Suggested Readings

A good example of recent research on TBLT is Susan Benson's article 'Task-based language teaching: An empirical study of task transfer' in *Language Teaching Research* (2016, Volume 20, Issue 3, pages 341–365).

An example of the on-going interest in researching and writing about TBLT is Martin Bygate's article 'Sources, developments and directions of task-based language teaching' in the *Language Learning Journal* (2015, doi:10.1080/09571736.2015.1039566).

As noted above, Mike Long has been writing about TBLT for longer, and he has written more about TBLT, than almost anyone. Therefore, his 2015 book, *Second Language Acquisition and Task-Based Language Teaching*, at 400-plus pages, is one of the most thorough and detailed accounts of the research on TBLT.

CHAPTER 4

Communicative Language Teaching in Context

Before reading this chapter, consider the following questions:

- How would you define 'communication'?
- What do you understand by the term 'communicative competence'?
- Do you think 'effective communication' and/or 'communicative competence' is the same in your first language as it is in your other languages?
- If so, why? Or, if not, why not?

Introduction and Overview

In this chapter, definitions (including my own) and descriptions of Communicative Language Teaching (CLT) are first presented, compared and contrasted, so that the readers can fully understand what is meant by CLT. This is a necessary starting point, because CLT can mean different things to different people, depending in no small part on how we conceptualize and articulate essential terms such as 'communication', 'effective communication' and 'communicative competence'. In the second part of the chapter, the readers are taken inside the CLT classroom to give them a sense of what CLT looks like, linking the theory and the practice of CLT, using data from real classrooms, such as extracts from classroom transcripts.

The third part of the chapter considers the pros and cons of CLT, as all methodologies have their benefits and limitations, to help the readers decide whether CLT is or would be a good fit with their particular language teaching and learning context. In this chapter, I also discuss what I refer to as 'the dark side of CLT', as one of the features of this book that distinguishes it from other books on methodology is the fact that the methodologies presented here are critically considered. By that, I mean they are considered in relation to the historical, geopolitical, cultural, economic, post-colonial and other aspects that have shaped the methodology. These considerations are designed to be different from the presentation of each methodology in some 'neutral' way, as though such aspects were not essential influences, when they clearly are key. The last part of the chapter includes a brief discussion of how the learning outcomes with CLT can be assessed.

What Is Communicative Language Teaching and Where Did It Come From?

As we discussed in Chapter 1, 'method', 'approach', 'technique', and a range of other terms, have emerged over the years as different ways of describing what teachers and learners do during their language lessons together. Thinking about those concepts, for many of its proponents, CLT is not a methodology but an approach. For example, one of the original proponents of CLT, in the early 1970s, was Sandra Savignon (1972), who asked the question 'What's ahead?' (2007, p. 207). In answering her question, Savignon believed that 'CLT is properly viewed as an approach, or theory of intercultural communicative competence to be used in developing materials and methods appropriate to a given context of learning' (2007, p. 213), highlighting the importance of context.

One of the key words here is 'appropriate', as what is **appropriate** in one teaching and learning situation is not necessarily appropriate in another. As with a number of the recurring points made in this book, this statement may seem obvious and uncontroversial to many experienced classroom teachers; that is, 'this method works well there, but no so well over here', not only in relation to CLT, but applicable to all methodologies.

However, one of the most prominent themes that I repeatedly encountered when writing this book was how long the fields of education and language education can take to let go of things that are not working, or not true. For example, we are still talking about 'best practices' (see, for example, Waldrop and Bowdon's 2016 book, *Best Practices for Flipping the College Classroom*, which is part of an entire series of new *Best Practices* books), even though we know by now that there is *nothing* that is 'best' for all teachers and all learners, in all contexts at all times. But instead of talking about 'best fit', in terms of what is most appropriate for a particular situation (Curtis, 2016b), we continue to talk in terms of what is a 'best practice'. And even when we pluralize it, to make it 'best practices', it is still the word 'best' that the eye is drawn to and that the brain focuses on. Therefore, we may well have a natural tendency to think about 'best' in terms of 'better than all the rest', thereby relegating everything else to 'not (quite) as good', which I believe is unhelpful and untrue.

Richards and Rodgers (1986) concurred that CLT is not a methodology, but that it is 'best considered an approach rather than a method. Thus although a reasonable degree of theoretical consistency can be discerned at the levels of language and learning theory, at the levels of design and procedure there is much greater room for individual interpretation and variation than most methods permit' (p. 83). This 'room' has been one of the strengths of CLT, and a major reason for its popularity. But this 'room' has also been one of the limitations of CLT, as it has created situations in which almost anything that is not explicit grammar teaching, or anything that involves speaking, can be and has been referred to as 'CLT'. As Savignon put it, 'The widespread promotion of a jumble of materials and activities labeled "communicative" has understandably resulted in some uncertainty as to what are and are not essential features of CLT' (2007, p. 213).

An essential aspect of Savignon's (2007) definition above is the notion of 'communicative competence', which was first used by Savignon in 1972, in what she describes as her 'paradigm-challenging research' (Savignon, 2007, p. 209) on second language acquisition with adult learners. 'Communicative competence' is defined by Savignon as 'the ability of classroom language learners to interact with other speakers; this ability to make meaning was distinguished from their ability to recite dialogues or to perform on discrete-point tests of grammatical knowledge' (2007, p. 209). Savignon's work was very important in helping to shift the paradigms of language teaching from a focus on grammar to a focus on meaning, and from a focus on the teacher to a focus on the learner. However, such definitions also sowed the seeds of a 'schism' between grammar-focused and meaning-focused approaches, which polarized the discussions of language teaching and learning methodologies for the next 40 years, and which we are still living with today, although to a lesser extent now. This polarity has, I believe, been unfortunate, as it led to **dualistic, dichotomous** thinking, instead of seeing these different methodologies as being on a continuum. If we reject dichotomies and think instead in terms of continua, we can conceive of a purely grammatical focus, to the exclusion of all meaning, at one end of the continuum, and a purely communicative focus, to the exclusion of all grammar teaching, at the other end. But these ends of the continuum are theoretical constructs, which may be useful in more theoretical linguistics, but which are of limited use when applied to real-life classrooms. As we saw in Chapter 2, Kramsch (1993) identified 'grammar versus communication' (pp. 4–5) as one of the 'dubious dichotomies and deceptive symmetries' (pp. 2–9) that we should avoid.

Another limiting effect of definitions of 'communicative competence' like Savignon's above was the focus on speaking, which is one reason why we now refer to 'native speakers' of a language, rather than 'native users'. This notion of native *speaker* is so deeply ingrained in our vocabularies that when I use the term 'native user' in my published work and presentations, I am questioned and asked why I am not using 'native speaker', even though it is clear that the audience understands the term 'native user'. This prioritizing and privileging of speaking has put the other three main language modalities – listening, reading, writing – at something of a disadvantage. This privileging of speaking has been unfortunate, as all the modalities are necessary, and they all work together – we usually read while we are writing, listen while we are preparing to speak, and so on. As language teachers, language learners and language users, we know that we rarely use only one modality at a time. Yet I found, as the editor for this *ALLC* book series, that many of the world's leading experts on writing appear to know relatively little about reading, and vice versa. Likewise, many of the world's leading experts on speaking told me that they know relatively little about listening, and vice versa. This compartmentalization of language modalities is a good example of the ironies of the modern academic world – from where almost all of the writings on language teaching and learning methodologies have come. It is ironic, because the pressure to specialize leads to an intellectual narrowness that is the antithesis of a well-rounded education, which is supposed to be one of the primary purposes of universities.

Building on Savignon's work, Canale and Swain (1980) proposed a framework that, according to Savignon, 'would prove a pedagogical breakthrough in extending the description of language use and learning in terms of more than just sentence-level structure' (Savignon, 2007, p. 209). The three components of the structures were: (i) grammatical competence, or linguistic competence, 'in the restricted sense of the term as used by Chomsky' (p. 209); (ii) sociolinguistic competence, or 'rules of usage' (p. 209); and (3) strategic competence. Canale (1983) later identified discourse competence as 'a distinct fourth component' (p. 209). However, even though Canale and Swain started their list with 'grammatical competence', in its 'restricted' Chomskyian sense, the schism between the pro-grammar camp and the pro-communicative camp appeared to continue to grow over the following years.

Drawing on the work of the sociolinguist Margie Berns (1990), Savignon (2007) reiterated the importance of context: 'a definition of a communicative competence appropriate for a given group of learners should reflect sociocultural contexts of language use' (p. 211). Also, according to Sauvignon, Berns' summary of the core tenets of CLT was 'unambiguous and theoretically sound' (p. 211). In my experience, CLT became something of a methodological juggernaut, appearing to crush everything in its path for decades, until TBLT came along – to the extent that, in many cases, if you were not using CLT, you were quite simply a 'bad', 'unenlightened' or 'old-fashioned' language teacher. It is, then, perhaps another irony that one of Berns' eight defining features of communicative competence was 'No single methodology or fixed set of techniques is **prescribed**' (Savignon, 2007, p. 211), which appears to be exactly what CLT came to be in many contexts, that is, prescribed, required and mandated.

TASK 4.1

Before you continue reading, consider the following questions, and, if possible, share your answers with a colleague.

4.1.1: What are some of the main language teaching methodologies that you use in your language classrooms and lessons?
4.1.2: Why do you use these methodologies more than others?
4.1.3: In relation to the methodologies you do *not* use much, why do you tend not to use those methods?

To return to the question 'What is CLT?' and to look at some of its origins, according to Pham Hoa Hiep (2007), our 'current understandings of CLT can be traced back to Hymes (1972)' (p. 193). Hymes proposed that 'knowing a language involved more than knowing a set of grammatical, lexical, and phonological rules … learners need to develop communicative competence – the ability to use the language they are learning appropriately in a given social encounter' (p. 193). The work of Del Hymes (1927–2009) on communicative competence started in 1996, pre-dating the work of Savignon, and as a challenge to Noam Chomsky's *Syntactic Structures* (1957), which was initially hailed as a major breakthrough in our understanding of how language works. Taking these developments into account, we can see that although CLT is relatively new in some contexts, it has a history of more than 50 years.

As the quote above shows, Hymes also highlighted the importance of 'appropriateness': 'a child acquires knowledge of sentences not only as grammatical, but also as appropriate. He or she acquires competence as to when to speak, when not, and as to what to talk about with whom, when, where, in what manner' (1972, p. 277). Like Savignon's work, Hymes' was also seminal in developing CLT, but also like Savignon, his definitions and descriptions were problematic, again giving primacy to speaking and to speech, thereby elevating one language modality over the others. It is also possible that the focus on speaking and learning to speak may not have distinguished enough between how our first language is acquired, naturalistically, growing up surrounded by that language, and learning a second, foreign or other language through explicit and formalized instruction. (See the work of Stephen Krashen (1982) for more on language 'acquisition' versus 'learning'.)

In terms of the origins of CLT, according to Savignon (2007), 'The elaboration of what we know as CLT can be traced to concurrent 20th-century developments in linguistic theory and language learning curriculum design both in Europe and in North America' (p. 209). These European and North American origins of CLT may be an example of how an approach or a methodology that is developed in one set of contexts does not necessarily translate as well when exported to other contexts, far from its origins.

My own definition of CLT is that it became a methodology at the Fluency end of the Accuracy–Fluency Continuum, which is more volume-based or quantity-based than quality-based, in the sense that learners are encouraged to produce as much of the spoken target language as possible, with less of a concern for grammatical accuracy, and more of a concern for communicative effectiveness in the target language. This definition may be at odds with those that claim, for example, that CLT develops all modalities equally, and that CLT gives equal importance to accuracy and to fluency. However, that has not been my experience of CLT, nor has it been the experience of most of the other teachers I have worked with over the last 25 years.

> **TASK 4.2**
>
> Based on what you have read in this chapter so far and on what you may already know about CLT from your classroom teaching experience, consider the following questions. If possible, share your answers with a colleague.
>
> 4.2.1: Would CLT be appropriate in your classrooms and in your context?
> 4.2.2: If so, what is it about your classrooms and your context that would make CLT appropriate?
> 4.2.3: If not, what is it about your classrooms and your context that would make CLT inappropriate?

Inside the CLT Classroom

The CLT approach is generally characterized 'as an approach that emphasizes communication and speaking, meaningful input, contextualized grammar, and interactive activities through role play, pair work, group work, language games and songs' (Spiteri, 2010, p. 131). Here we can see that grammar has made something of a 'comeback' (see Chapter 7) within CLT in recent years, as long as it is taught in terms of how the grammatical correctness maximizes clarity of communication, or conversely, how the grammatical incorrectness may cause confusion and unintended ambiguity. The kinds of activities listed by Spiteri (2010) are based on the principles of CLT, which include what Saad Shawer (2013) refers to as 'negotiation of meaning, genuine classroom communication, communication through the target language, and extensive use of collaborative activities and authentic materials' (p. 413).

These principles raise a number of questions. For example, in relation to the existing competence levels of the language learners, how much target language do the learners need to know before they can function in class, working together, in the target language, while making use of **authentic materials?** Such materials are characterized by not having been produced for the purposes of language teaching and learning. For example, a daily newspaper in the target language can be used as authentic material in the language classroom, as it was not produced for the purposes of language teaching or learning. However, it is also important to note that in the drive for authenticity, which has characterized discussions of CLT for many years, it was eventually realized that some materials can be 'too authentic'. In that case, although the materials may be understandable to native users of the target language, they are too far beyond the current competence levels of the non-native language learners, making them potentially 'too authentic'.

Some of these same concerns come up in the descriptions of CLT curricula. For example, there is an emphasis in CLT on 'learning to communicate through interaction in the target language; the introduction of *authentic texts* into the classroom; the provision of opportunities for learners to focus, not only on language but also on the learning process itself ... and the linking of classroom language learning with language activities *outside the classroom*' (Hardman & A-Rahman, 2014, p. 261, emphases added). Having as an explicit outcome the goal of connecting the learning taking place *inside* the classroom with that taking place outside helps to dispel the myth that 'real life' occurs somewhere else, *outside* the classroom, giving the impression that what happens in the classroom is somehow 'unreal' (see Chapter 3). As language teachers and learners know, language classrooms can be as real as it gets, so what the writers who refer to 'real life' really mean is 'out-of-class', which is a valid distinction.

In relation to CLT syllabi, Shawer (2013) emphasizes the differences between notional-functional syllabi and structural-grammatical syllabi, in which 'A notion is a particular context in which people communicate, whereas a function involves the purposes for which people use language' (p. 434). For example, a role-play activity based on buying food from a local market, which would be the notion, involves a range of different functions, such as finding specific items, asking about the price, and paying. Another way of thinking about notional-functional is to think of the notion as the context in which the target language use takes place, and the function as the purpose for the language use. Notional-functional curricula are often contrasted with structural-grammatical curricula, which are based on presenting the target language according to the grammatical features of the language, rather than the place and purpose for its use. Again, as long as these distinctions are seen as points along a syllabus continuum, rather than as black–white dichotomies, it can be useful to distinguish between notions and functions, and between notional-functional and structural-grammatical syllabi.

Inside the CLT classroom, Muhammad Farooq (2015), working with university-level students in Saudi Arabia, advocates in-class activities that 'encourage learners to interact meaningfully in the target language' (p. 182). Drawing on the work of Celce-Murcia (1991), Farooq explained that the in-class activities could be grouped under four basic headings: 'structured activities (structured interview), performance activities (role play), participation activities (guided discussions), and observation activities (movies)' (p. 182). Farooq added that 'Other CLT activities may include information gap activities, jigsaw activities, communication games, discussion and debates, and prepared talks and oral presentations' (p. 182). These activities relate to some of the activities listed above by Spiteri (2010).

According to Tim Bowen, CLT language lessons make 'considerable if not extensive use of pair, group and mingling activities, with the emphasis on completing the task successfully through communication with others rather than on the accurate use of form' (no date). Bowen's description brings up the important distinction between accuracy, with a focus on grammatical correctness, and fluency, with an emphasis on producing a larger amount of the target language, even if it is not as grammatically correct as it could be. As I noted above, in relation to Kramsch's (1993) work, we need to be wary of, and avoid as much as possible, our natural tendencies to dichotomize, and I would add to her list of 'dubious dichotomies and deceptive symmetries' (pp. 2–9) the concept of accuracy versus fluency. Although these two essential aspects of language and communication are not the same, neither are they mutually exclusive, which means that they are, again, most helpfully seen and most usefully viewed as being towards opposite ends of the communicative continuum.

However, the differences between accuracy and fluency are, nonetheless, an important aspect of distinguishing some methods from others, and in my experience, they can be thought of, in some ways, as a difference between 'quality' and 'quantity' of language. Using that quality–quantity distinction, and connecting it to modality, traditional Grammar Translation lessons often appear to focus on producing smaller amounts of more grammatically correct written target language (Chapter 7). This can be contrasted with CLT lessons, which often appear to be focused on producing larger amounts of spoken target language, with less concern for grammatical correctness.

We can now look at some of the differences in the roles and responsibilities of teachers and learners in CLT classrooms, as these are some of the most distinguishing characteristics when comparing and contrasting different methods and approaches. Bowen notes that in CLT lessons, 'the teacher's role will be to facilitate and then to monitor, usually without interruption, and then to provide feedback on the success or otherwise of the communication and, possibly, on the linguistic performance of the learners in the form of post-activity error correction' (no date). As we can see, in CLT classrooms, one of the teacher's main roles, while the learners are engaged in their activities, can be to act as a kind of non-participant observer, in the ethnographic sense. However, while the teachers are circulating and moving around the classroom, from pair to pair and from group to group, the teachers in CLT lessons need to be listening and looking intently for samples of learners' spoken and written target language. Using these samples, teachers can then give corrective feedback on the target language forms produced that could be made more communicatively effective, and positive feedback on the forms that were effective. In both cases, teachers can explain what made these forms more or less communicatively effective, with the added benefit that they can do so without naming individual students. In that way, teachers can avoid the risk of embarrassing the learners who provided the target language samples that needed corrective feedback, thereby 'saving face' for those learners.

Also in relation to learners' and teachers' roles, Bowen predicted that there would be some degree of 'stepping back from the extremes of the totally communicative classroom, with its obsession about reducing teacher talking time to a minimum and maximizing the opportunities for communication'. The two three-part acronyms relevant here are TTT and STT, for 'Teacher Talk Time' and 'Student Talk Time', respectively. One premise of CLT lessons was that TTT should be kept to a minimum, so that STT could be maximized. However, this TTT/STT ratio appears to be based on a somewhat simplistic view of the language of language classrooms, as that language is often collaboratively, cooperatively co-constructed by the learners and the teacher jointly, depending on the target language competence levels of the learners. (See Chapter 8 for a discussion of how the Silent Way aims for near-zero TTT.)

In *Communicative Language Teaching Today* (2006), Jack Richards highlighted the focus on fluency, which he defined as 'natural language use occurring when a speaker engages in meaningful interaction and maintains comprehensible and ongoing communication despite limitations in his or her communicative competence' (p. 14). Richards contrasted accuracy tasks and fluency tasks, and gave an example of the latter: 'A group of students of mixed language ability carry out a role play in which they have to adopt specified roles and personalities provided for them on cue cards. These roles involve the drivers, witnesses, and the police at a collision between two cars. The language is entirely improvised by the students' (p. 15).

TASK 4.3

In the section below, details are given of an in-class activity based on the role-play above, involving a collision between two cars. Before you read what happened when I asked one of my classes to do this task, make some brief lesson-planning notes on how you would present and set up the same role-play; then you can compare what you would do with what I did.

This task was given to the same five young adult students as in the previous chapter, who were learning English in an EAP class at a university in Ontario, Canada. As in the previous lessons, the interaction was digitally audio-recorded, with the students' permission, using a cellphone. In the following discussion, the students are deciding on who will take on what roles. S1 = Student 1, etc.

S1: 'Who will be witness? Who will be driver?'
S2: 'I will be a police.'
S3: 'I will be a witness.'
S4: 'Can I be a witness?'
S1 to S4: 'OK. You be witness. I will be driver.'
S5: 'I will be other driver.'

This discussion of who would take on which roles went on for approximately five minutes, which was not my intention. But as I did not assign the roles to the students before the role-play activity began, they needed to talk about who would take on which role. Most importantly, the negotiation of roles was carried out in the target language, in this case, English. This negotiation relates to Richards' comment that 'Fluency is developed by creating classroom activities in which students must negotiate meaning, use communication strategies, correct misunderstandings, and work to avoid communication breakdowns' (2006, p. 14).

Once the members of the group had agreed on their roles, I intervened and spent a few minutes reminding the students of the use of the definite and indefinite articles, which had been covered in a previous lesson. For example, one student asked about the difference in meaning of '*a* witness/driver' compared with '*the* witness/driver'. I also explained why 'a police' is grammatically incorrect, whereas 'a witness' is correct.

After agreeing on their roles, and asking the teacher for some further clarification of the role-play task, the students proceeded with the task:

S1 to S5 [as the two drivers]: Why you hit me?
S5 to S1: I no hit you! You hit me! [students laugh]
S2 [as a police officer]: I am a police officer. You are both arrested. [students laugh]
S3:   I am a witness. *He* – pointing to S1 – hit *him* – pointing to S5.
S2:   OK. I will arrest *you* – pointing to S1.

At this point, Student 1 ran out of the classroom, pretending to flee the scene of the crime; the rest of the students started laughing loudly, and I ended the activity. Although the activity did not last as long as I had planned, and the students did not produce a large amount of the target language, the language they did produce led to a brief but useful revision of the use of 'did' as an auxiliary verb, in the questions and phrases 'Why *did* you hit me?' and 'I *did* not hit you.' There was also a discussion of 'specialized' vocabulary items and phrases, such as 'crime scene', 'scene of the crime' and 'You're *under* arrest.'

When I, as the teacher, pointed out that it is not usually necessary to say 'I am a police officer', as that is generally obvious because of the uniform worn by police officers, the students talked briefly about the different kinds of uniforms worn by the different kinds of police in their countries, for example, traffic police. And as the discussion took place in a Canadian context, some of the students asked questions about the Royal Canadian Mounted Police, showing how such discussions can take on a life of their own, in ways not envisaged when the lesson was planned, going off in unexpected but nonetheless target-language-producing directions.

One of the staples of the CLT lesson is information-gap activities, which, according to Richards (2006), 'refers to the fact that in real communication, people normally communicate in order to get information they do not possess' (p. 18). Richards gives an example of an activity that makes use of the information-gap principle: 'Students are divided into A-B pairs. The teacher has copied two sets of pictures. One set contains a picture of a group of people. The other set contains a similar picture but it contains a number of slight differences from the A-picture. Students must sit back to back and ask questions to try to find out how many differences there are' (p. 18). This back-to-back, facing-opposite-directions seating arrangement is known as 'tango seating', after the dance originating in Argentina and Uruguay. (See Kathleen Bailey (2005) for more on the use of tango seating in the language classroom.) If you look inside a CLT classroom, in addition to role-play of the kind above, you are likely to see the following kinds of activities:

(i) task-completion activities, such as puzzles and games;
(ii) information-gathering activities, such as surveys and interviews carried out by students;
(iii) opinion-sharing activities, in which students can compare and contrast their beliefs;
(iv) information-transfer activities, in which students 'take information that is presented in one form, and represent

it in a different form. For example, they may read instructions on how to get from A to B, and then draw a map showing the sequence' (Richards, 2006, p. 19);
(v) reasoning-gap activities, in which students derive new information from given information through inference, practical reasoning and so on. 'For example, working out a teacher's timetable on the basis of given class timetables' (Richards, 2006, p. 19).

TASK 4.4

Which of the CLT activities above have you used, or would you use, in your language classrooms and lessons? If you have used some of them before, which activities worked well with your learners? Which did not work so well, and why?

In relation to the ubiquity of puzzles and games in CLT lessons, Larsen-Freeman and Anderson (2011) believe that 'Games are important because they have certain features in common with real communicative events – there is a purpose to the exchange. Also, the speaker receives immediate feedback on whether or not she has successfully communicated' (p. 120). Another ubiquitous feature of CLT classrooms is that the students are arranged to work in small groups, rather than whole-class activities, as noted by Bowen, above. According to Larsen-Freeman and Anderson (2011) (and many others), having students work in small groups is because this 'maximizes the amount of communicative practice they receive' (p. 120). This may be true, but it should also be acknowledged that not all learners like spending most or all of their class-time working in pairs and small groups. However, the way CLT classrooms are often arranged does not usually allow for the learners – of whom there may a significant number – who may prefer to work individually.

The Pros and Cons of CLT

One of the most obvious features of CLT is, by definition, the focus on learning languages for the purposes of communication. As Larsen-Freeman and Anderson (2011) put it, 'Perhaps the greatest contribution of CLT is to ask teachers to look closely at what is involved in communication. If teachers intend students to use the target language, then they must truly understand more than grammar rules and target language vocabulary' (p. 128). This statement shows the assumption that students learning English wish to communicate in English, making CLT the logical choice. However, there are contexts in which English is not being learned for communication.

A major example of this non-communicative learning of English is the tens of millions of English language test-takers in China who are learning English *not* so that they can communicate in English, but so that they can pass national examinations, such as the College English Test (CET). Another national exam in China is the '*gaokao*', which, according to Tessa Wong (2015), is taken by more than nine million students in China each year, and which 'is seen as a make-or-break opportunity, especially for those from poorer families, in a country where a degree is essential for a good job' (p. 1).

Another largely non-communicative reason for learning English is the passing of standardized international examinations, such as the US-based Test of English as a Foreign Language (TOEFL), which, according to the TOEFL website, has been taken by 'more than 30 million people from all over the world' (ETS, no date). There is also the UK-based International English Language Testing System (IELTS), which, according to the British Council, was taken by more than two million test-takers in 12 months, between 2012 and 2013 (IELTS, no date). In my work (McNaught & Curtis, 2009), I have referred to this kind of English language learning as 'Learning English for Examination Purposes' or '**LEEP**' (pronounced 'leap'), and

I have also claimed that when a language is learned for such non-communicative purposes, it is no longer a language (McNaught & Curtis, 2009, p. 99).

If we revisit Larsen-Freeman and Anderson's statement, above – 'If teachers intend students to use the target language ...' – we can now ask questions about what the students will *do with* the target language they have learned – for what purposes, with whom and in what context. It should also be noted that, in relation to 'learner-centred language teaching', the teacher's intent is supposed to be of relatively minor importance compared with the learners' intent, in relation to what the learners want and need. But these conflicting wants and needs may be one of the reasons why we have, for the last 50 years or more, been discussing Communicative Language *Teaching*, thereby putting the focus on the teacher and on the teaching methodology, rather than Communicative Language *Learning*. Such a focus is another potential irony, given the espoused commitment in CLT to move away from teacher-centred teaching to learner-centred learning.

The question of purpose is addressed within the area of Languages for Specific Purposes (LSP), including English for Specific Purposes (ESP), but it turns out that for many millions of English language learners around the world, their purpose for learning English is not to communicate but to pass exams, without which their opportunities in life are severely curtailed and restricted, as reported by Wong (2015). This potential misalignment in the purposes for teaching English versus the purposes for learning English may be one of the reasons for some of the tensions around CLT, in relation to the assumptions made by its proponents conflicting with the needs and wants of the learners.

Another potential limitation of CLT is the level of language needed to be able to successfully complete some of the most common CLT activities, such as the activity with tango seating described above. Although such activities are often the mainstay of many CLT lessons, and are described in almost every text on CLT, it is not clear how learners can take part in such activities without already knowing enough of the target language to engage in meaningful communication. Therefore, CLT may not work as well with beginner-level learners, or with learners who may prefer to work individually, rather than in pairs and groups. However, these kinds of considerations appear to be rarely acknowledged in the mountains of literature promoting CLT.

For example, the detailed description and analysis of the lesson on which Larsen-Freeman and Anderson's chapter on CLT is based (2011, pp. 115–130) describes a class for 20 learners who are immigrants to Canada, who have lived in Canada for two years and who are at a high-intermediate level of English proficiency. They meet two evenings a week for two hours each class. In relation to the importance of employing methodologies that are appropriate within the context and appropriate for the learners. The teaching–learning situation described by Larsen-Freeman and Anderson raises a number of important issues in relation to the pros and cons of CLT. The first point relates to the fact that these learners are in Canada, and they are therefore in what is traditionally referred to as an 'ESL environment', meaning that the main language used in their surrounding environment is English. Second is the size of the class, which, at 20, would be considered relatively small in many or even most countries. And a third point is the competence levels of the learners, that is, high intermediate. Another possible factor is the age of the learners, which is not mentioned in Larsen-Freeman and Anderson's account. But based on the description of the lesson, they are likely to be adults. If so, as adult immigrants, they may be highly motivated to learn the language of their host country, as learning the language may be seen as an essential part of making a good life for themselves (and their families) in their new country.

These factors – the language environment (see Chapter 2), class size, competence levels, age and motivation – exert a tremendous influence on any language class, and may be some of the key caveats in claiming and realizing the potential benefits of CLT in an 'ESL' environment, with smaller classes and higher-level, highly motivated learners. The learners should also enjoy working in pairs and groups, and they should be OK with limited input on the structure of the target language they are learning, and willing 'to go with the flow'. Related to these factors, Richards (2006) stated that 'In planning a language course, decisions have to be made about the content of the course, including decisions about what vocabulary and grammar to teach at the beginning, intermediate, and advanced levels' (p. 6). However, as noted above, discussions about the language environment, class size, competence levels, age and motivation are conspicuous by their absence in an otherwise thorough and detailed 50-page booklet on CLT.

TASK 4.5

4.5.1: What are some of the characteristics of your learners, in terms of age, motivation, target language competence levels and so on, that have made, or would make, CLT an effective approach in your language lessons and classes?

4.5.2: What are some of the characteristics of your language learners that have made it, or would make it, difficult to use CLT approaches in your lessons and classes?

The 'Dark Side' of CLT

This discussion of the limitations of CLT will include what I have referred to as 'the dark side of CLT' (Curtis, 2016c) in the sense of something that is 'kept well hidden, especially because people would not approve if they knew about it' (*MODE*). For example, Shaofei Lu and Nancy Ares' (2015) article on 'western TESOL pedagogies in China' (pp. 112–128) argued that methodologies such as CLT in places such as China may not only be questionable, but may even be a form of 'oppression': 'Western TESOL pedagogies could be a new form of oppression or even colonization for local Chinese teachers and language policies because of the unequal power relations involved in globalization' (p. 122). According to Lu and Ares, 'even in less-developed regions of China where there is little social need for communicative competence in English, CLT is still promoted as the most advanced and scientific way of teaching English' (p. 116). This point relates to the earlier discussion of the purposes of learning English and the needs of English language learners. For example, learning English to pass an examination constitutes a valid and very specific purpose. But that may clash with the desires of English language teachers, if they wish to promote and aim for a degree of communicative competence in the learners that is not necessary and which may not be attainable, depending on the contextual constraints.

In their impassioned discussion of CLT as a form of oppression, Lu and Ares (2015) focus on this 'dark side of CLT'. Here, I am referring to the point at which the still highly contentious and emotional discussion about native-user English language teachers (referred to as NESTs, Native English-Speaking Teachers) and non-native-user English language teachers (NNESTs) meets the world of CLT: 'The global symbolic power of English puts Chinese people at a linguistic disadvantage in the hierarchical relationship with their English-speaking counterparts' (Lu and Ares, 2015, p. 116). I have highlighted above some aspects, such as the ages, language levels and motivations of the learners, as being conspicuous by their absence in the literature on CLT. However, even more conspicuously absent in the voluminous literature of the last half-century is the mention of the NEST–NNEST aspect of CLT. An examination of the NEST–NNEST debate is beyond the scope of this book. (See Mahboob, 2010, for more on this debate.) But a point that appears to have been almost deliberately avoided – or at best briefly glossed over – is the fact that CLT appears to have capitalized on the 'native speaker privilege' that Mahboob and others have been so understandably critical of and upset about. For example, Mahboob (2006) describes himself as an 'enraced TESOL professional … based on the analogy of *rage*' (p. 175).

The origins of the native-speaker privilege and CLT may be traced back to the long-accepted and well-documented avoidance of English grammar in England. For example, a study funded by the UK government in 2005 concluded that teaching grammar in schools in England was 'a waste of time' (*The Telegraph*, 17 January 2005) because 'it does not improve writing skills' (Lightfoot, 2005). The generation that I grew up with, and with whom I went to state-funded schools in England in the 1970s, studied with a curriculum in which English classes were entirely focused on literature, with little or no reference to the mechanics of the language and how it worked, apart from simplistic and superficial input on metaphors, analogies and other basic poetic devices. (See Chapter 7 for a discussion of the Grammar Translation Method.)

This unfortunate aspect of the British education system at that time produced generations of native users of English in the UK (and possibly elsewhere, such as the USA and Canada) who knew very little, if anything, about the structure of their first language. As a result, we knew much less about how the English language worked than many students learning English in other countries, in EFL settings. This lack of L1 knowledge might not have mattered so much except that, within those generations of native users of English who did not have the knowledge and the meta-language to talk about English much beyond 'noun', 'verb' and 'adjective', was an army of (mostly) young people wanting to travel the world. And teaching English was presented as the easiest way to fund that travel, which is sometimes referred to as 'The Backpacker Problem in ELT'. For example, Phil Wade (2015) asks: 'Are all NESTs unqualified backpackers?' (p. 1)

As far as I know, nobody in the field of language education, and nobody in the field of travel and tourism, has considered the possibility of a connection – not causal but perhaps correlational – between the rise of CLT and the growth of touristic travel.

However, as Douglas Pearce (1987) pointed out in his article on spatial patterns of package tourism in Europe (pp. 183–201), 'Package tours by air have been a significant factor in the expansion of international tourism in Europe since the 1960s.' And as we know, the 1960s were also the decade in which CLT started. Whether or not the timing of these two important, global educational and economic developments is purely coincidental is open to discussion and conjecture. But either way, CLT appears to have enabled large numbers of native users of English to turn up in language schools around the world, claiming to be 'English teachers', with their only 'qualification' being the fact that they happened to have been born and raised in England, or America, Canada, Australia and so on. (See Wade, 2015, for more on the particular problem within ELT.)

This situation can still be seen today, in online job ads by language schools that ask only that the applicant be a native speaker of English (Mahboob, 2006), which may have compounded the polarizing schism between the extreme grammarians (see Chapter 7) and the extreme **'communicarians'**. Another damaging effect of this focus on being a native user as the main or only qualification needed to teach English was that it may have helped to de-skill language teaching as a profession by creating a group of 'facilitators' with no teaching experience or qualifications. These facilitators (i) did not teach English, because (ii) they could not teach English, because (iii) they did not know English, in terms of how to explain, for example, why 'a witness' is acceptable but 'a police' is not. Without the necessary knowledge of the English language, such facilitators may resort instead to 'native speaker intuition', with unhelpful explanations along the lines of 'that's not how we say it, in England/English'.

These kinds of situations may be less common nowadays, but the important point here is that the global exporting of CLT to contexts where it may not have been appropriate resulted in, and was exacerbated by, a very large and special category of 'teacher' with little or no specialist knowledge of the subject matter they were supposed to be teaching. This may be unique to native-user language teachers, as nobody would be allowed to teach, for example, physics, biology or chemistry, history, mathematics, or any other subject *based mainly or solely on where they happen to have been born*. For example, before I was a language teacher I was a clinical biochemist and then a teacher of biology and chemistry. I was not qualified to teach biochemistry because my body (like everyone else's) is made up of chemicals, but because I had spent many years studying biology and chemistry, to the point that I knew enough about those subjects to help others learn about them.

It is possible that the focus on hiring unqualified and inexperienced native users of English, rather than hiring highly qualified and experienced non-native users, would have happened anyway, as part of the wholesale, post-colonial exporting of English as *a lingua franca* or *lingua mundi*. However, it does seem that CLT, with its focus on speaking, did unfairly and significantly advantage native speakers of English, which may have helped to create the de-professionalizing and damaging myth that anyone who can speak a language can teach it.

TASK 4.6

4.6.1: What are some of the main qualifications and experience required to work as a language teacher in your school, college or university?

4.6.2: Do these required qualifications and experience include requirements for knowing the target language to a particular level, such as advanced, near-native or native-like user?

4.6.3: If your teaching context included NESTs and NNESTs, what is the relationship between the two groups? How do they work together and support each other (if they do that)?

The Politics of CLT

According to Larsen-Freeman and Anderson (2011), 'Learning a language is a political act' (p. 165). Not only do I strongly agree with that position, but I would logically extend it to 'Teaching a language is therefore also a political act.' Perhaps more than any other language teaching and learning approach or method, CLT is where politics, economics and pedagogy have been colliding for many decades, and this collision looks set to continue. As Lu and Ares (2015) put it, 'In the case of CLT, the political relationships are highly intertwined with the economic relationships among nations in the context of globalization and are translated into educational policies *as if they were neutral constructs*' (p. 118, emphasis added). I have emphasized the last phrase because of the relationships between two mythical entities – 'neutral constructs' and 'neutral contexts'.

In Chapter 2, we considered the earlier and long-standing claims of some applied linguists (for example, Celce-Murcia & Olshtain, 2000) that some key features of language teaching and learning can be 'context independent'. However, I would counter-claim that nothing that is pedagogically significant is independent of the place in which the teaching and learning are taking place, because education does not occur in a vacuum. Therefore, I agree with the above comment by Lu and Ares, as policies that affect people cannot be context-dependent, because the people are an essential part of that context.

To be fair to those who have been promoting or 'pushing' – there can be a thin dividing line between these two – CLT all these years, some of the responsibility for these context–method mismatches must be shared by the countries in which CLT has been uncritically adopted. In relation to China – which is currently, by far, the world's largest ELT population – Lu and Ares (2015) found that 'Scholars in non-English speaking countries, such as China, tend to take Western pedagogies, such as CLT, as a much-desired remedy to solve the problems in English teaching practices in their countries

(Liao, 2004), *regardless of its limited efficacy in local contexts*' (p. 117, emphasis added). The accusatory tone of Lu and Ares' argument against CLT in China is clear, which is understandable, especially given the scale and scope of ELT in China, as discussed by Zhichang Xu (2013) in his research on **globalization**, culture and ELT materials in China (pp. 1–19). In terms of sharing the responsibility for the success or failure of approaches and methodologies, Lu and Ares add that 'many Chinese TESOL professionals still … cling tightly to CLT as that one dominant methodology that could solve all the problems of English teaching in China' (p. 119). (See Chapter 8 for a discussion of 'Methods as Medicine' and 'Methods as Messiah'.)

One of the most dramatic personal-professional examples of the potentially negative effects of attempting to implement CLT in China is given in Huhua Ouyang's narrative and anthropological account (2000) of what happened to one teacher, called Cheng, who was a keen and active proponent of CLT in China. Based on her story, Ouyang concluded that 'The CLT liberators, being in a privileged position, turned into oppressors by exploiting the trainees' submissiveness, passivity, dependence, and above all, total ignorance of the rules of the new game called CLT' (p. 408). Commenting on this much-cited case study of the rise and fall of Teacher Cheng, Lu and Ares also interpret the outcomes in terms of the clash between power and pedagogy: 'In Cheng's story, the symbolic power of Western pedagogies was exercised through the top-down training program's imposition of CLT upon the teacher trainees' (p. 120). It is important to note here that it was not the CLT methodology itself that was at fault, but the way in which its proponents presented CLT as some kind of 'liberatory pedagogy' (Freire, 1970). However, according to researchers such as Ouyang, Lu and Ares, promoting methods in CLT where it is contextually inappropriate is tantamount to a form of neo-colonialism.

In her research on the implementation of CLT and task-based language teaching (TBLT) in the Asia-Pacific region, Yuko Goto Butler (2011, pp. 36–57) found three main sets of challenges to 'implementing CLT and TBLT in Asian classrooms' (p. 36). These challenges were: '(a) conceptual constraints (e.g., conflicts with local values and misconceptions regarding CLT/TBLT); (b) classroom-level constraints (e.g., various student and teacher-related factors, classroom management practices, and resource availability); and (c) societal – institutional level constraints (e.g., curricula and examination systems)' (p. 36). Butler's three areas succinctly capture many of the challenges of successfully employing CLT (and TBLT; see Chapter 3) in contexts so far removed – geographically and historically, culturally and linguistically – from where the seeds of CLT were first sown and grown. Butler concludes with three possible ways of moving forward: '(a) employing more contextually feasible and flexible interpretations of CLT and TBLT, (b) implementing decentralized or innovative language-in-education policies, and (c) creating communities of learning outside of the classroom as well as in the classroom' (p. 36).

Butler's first point, about contextual feasibility, has already been discussed extensively in Chapter 2, and her second would require a relaxing of national- and regional-level controls of education, and language education in particular. Butler's third point is more feasible in ESL surroundings than in EFL settings, though such communities of learning are possible in both settings, especially with the growth of online communities of language teachers and learners who have Internet access. With access to such newer technologies, truly international communities can be created that cross geographical, spatial and temporal divides. However, it must be remembered that historical, cultural and linguistic differences are all still at play even in the Virtual World (and some might say, especially there).

> **TASK 4.7**
>
> 4.7.1: Which of the three main sets of challenges that Butler identified – conceptual, classroom-level and societal – are present in your school, college or university?
>
> 4.7.2: How are these challenges being met, or how could they be met and overcome?

Assessment of Learning Outcomes with CLT

One of the challenges of assessment of learning outcomes with methods such as CLT is the apparently self-evident outcomes, such as whether or not there were any 'communication breakdowns'. If there were none, then the outcomes might be judged as successful, and vice versa. However, effectiveness of communication is not an easily quantifiable or measurable construct, as it may depend on many different factors, such as where and when the communication broke down, how much effective communication there was before the communication broke down, who or what caused the breakdown, and so on. This assessment of communicative effectives relates to the notion of 'testing the untestable' (Curtis, 2013).

In Chapter 7, on the alternative and humanistic methods, we will see how methodologies can morph from one form to another, and another, with the re-formations and re-formulations being significantly different from the original. Similarly, one of the outgrowths of CLT was ICC, standing for Intercultural Communicative Competence, which was defined by Bennett and Bennett (2004) as 'the ability to communicate effectively in cross-cultural situations and to relate appropriately in a variety of cultural contexts' (p. 149). This morphing resembles the way in which TBLT (Chapter 3) grew out of CLT, but then took on a life of its own, eventually over-shadowing the source from whence it came, except that ICC still maintains its ties to CLT, via the overlapping concerns of communicativeness in both.

In relation to assessment of learning outcomes, an example of this was reported by Czura (2016), who collected survey data from 160 undergraduate pre-service teachers of English, to explore their perceptions of ICC, in three different departments at a university in Poland. Drawing on the work of the Danish ICC scholar Karen Risager (2005), Czura distinguishes between communicative competence as being 'related to the knowledge, skills and attitudes associated with the target language countries' and ICC as requiring 'a broader definition that embraces the knowledge, skills and attitudes necessary to participate in successful cross-cultural situations' (Czura, 2016, p. 85). Czura also notes that 'Unlike in the heyday of [sic] Communicative Approach, when the major goal of language teaching was developing native-like competence ... today teachers assist students in developing language skills as well as a number of non-linguistic competences that enable them ... to communicate appropriately in a variety of social contexts and situations' (p. 84). Czura's conclusion is a reminder of the mistaken but still on-going conflation of 'communicative competence' in the target language with perceptions of 'nativeness', in terms of having been born – or being assumed to have been born – in a country where the target language is the first and dominant language.

Concluding Comments

The section on the pros and cons of CLT appears to have focused significantly more on the 'cons' than the 'pros', so it is important to balance these two by highlighting the fact that many learners all over the world have learned (and are learning) multiple languages successfully, and becoming communicatively competent, up to a certain level, using approaches and methods based on CLT. (See, for example, Rebecca Belchamber's (2007) article on the advantages of CLT.) The key phrase here is *up to a certain level*, which refers to the focus on conversational-level speaking and listening skills, which can be advanced-level conversations about complex or controversial topics. But for these benefits of CLT to be fully realized, as noted above, certain prerequisites may be necessary. These include a more ESL-like environment, smaller classes and higher-level and highly motivated learners, who enjoy working in pairs and groups, who do not want or need much knowledge about the structure of the language and how it works, and who are more interested in developing their speaking and listening skills than their reading or writing abilities.

In more EFL-like environments, and in those in which there are large language classes, within more examination-driven education systems, and with learners who know relatively little of the target language, with a limited ability to use what little they know, and who may have lower levels of motivation, there may be other more appropriate and more effective methods and approaches. We will consider some of these other methods in the following chapters.

Suggested Readings

Tim Bowen writes about CLT in a 'onestopenglish' posting at www.onestopenglish.com/methodology/methodology/teaching-approaches/teaching-approaches-the-communicative-classroom/146489.article

Communicative Language Teaching Today. Jack Richards. 2006. This 50-page booklet on CLT is freely available online at http://citeseerx.ist.psu.edu/viewdoc/download?doi=10.1.1.618.3876&rep=rep1&type=pdf

CHAPTER 5

Content-Based Instruction and Content and Language Integrated Learning

Before you read this chapter, think about the following questions:

- What kind of content are your language lessons based on? How much adapting or 'localizing' of that content is possible?
- Depending on the kind of content you use, how do you try to integrate the content of your lessons and the language of your lessons?
- Are any of your language lessons based on content provided by your learners? If so, what kinds of content do your learners bring to class, and how do you make use of their content?
- Do you think it is possible to teach a language lesson without any content? If so, what would you use instead of content?

Introduction and Overview

In the first part of this chapter, we start by considering some of the different definitions and descriptions of 'content', in relation to Content-Based Instruction, known as CBI, and Content and Language Integrated Learning, referred to as CLIL. We also look briefly at an approach called 'Dogme ELT', based on the idea of not relying on the kind of typical and traditional content found in textbooks. After looking at some of the origins of CBI and CLIL – CBI came mainly from North America, with CLIL being the more European name for and version of CBI – we then compare and contrast some of the different kinds of CBI, and look at how it appears and is implemented in different contexts. We also revisit a theme identified in the chapter on TBLT (Chapter 3), which is how published papers in academic journals can colour the perception of and influence the adoption or the rejection of certain methodologies.

After taking a peek inside a CBI/CLIL lesson, in which the content is an animated movie, we then consider some of the pros and cons, the benefits and limitations of using CBI/CLIL methodologies in the language classroom. In the last part of the chapter, we discuss the importance of assessing learning outcomes, and explore some of the reasons why this is an area that is generally not as carefully considered, in relation to methodological decisions, as it should be.

The Meanings and Origins of CBI/CLIL

'Content' is one of those words, going back to Old French of the 1400s, that have multiple meanings (at least ten): as a verb, an adjective and a noun (roughly in that order of historical-linguistic development). Mostly, outside the world of methodologies, 'content' is usually used as a plural, as in 'contents', referring to 'the things that are inside something such as a box, bottle, or room' or 'the things that are written in a book, magazine, letter, document, etc.' (*MODE*). The first questions that come to my mind when I hear the phrase 'Content-Based Instruction' (CBI) or 'Content Integrated Language Learning' (CLIL) are these: Is it possible to teach anything without any content? Is there an opposite to CBI or CLIL, such as 'content-free teaching' or 'teaching without content'? On some level, any of the materials used in any language lesson or class can constitute 'content', but as we will see, 'content' has taken on a range of more specialized meanings within the world of CBI. It is also important to note here that, like CLT, CBI/CLIL can be considered to be an approach rather than a method. In that case, it is possible that CBI, with its focus on Instruction, may be seen as more of a method, compared with CLIL, with its emphasis on Integration, which may be seen as more of an approach.

The notion of 'content-free' teaching brings us to one of the most recent fashions to parade itself on the ELT catwalk, which is 'Dogme ELT'. This was taken from the Danish avant-garde film-making movement, started by the directors Lars von Trier and Thomas Vinterberg. They called their movement 'Dogme 95', as it started in 1995, plus the Danish word 'dogme', which means 'dogma' in English, to express their frustration with and rejection of the technological takeover of film-making at that time, such as special effects, computer-generated images (CGI) and so on. Scott Thornbury and Luke Meddings then adapted that idea for the ELT classroom, calling it 'Dogme ELT' (2003), which they defined as 'A teaching movement set up by a group of English teachers who challenge what they consider to be an over-reliance on materials and technical wizardry in current language teaching' (Meddings & Thornbury, 2010, p. 1). We will not explore the theories of Dogme ELT here, although it is a good example of one of the most recent trends and it is an attempt to move away from textbook-based ELT, towards an approach based on creating the lesson out of the environment itself and on the lives of the learners. Needless to say, this is also an example of an approach that is likely to be even more context-sensitive than others and it may also reflect, as CLT did (Chapter 4), political aspirations for democratizing the classroom, freeing everyone from what is seen by some as the tyranny of the textbook. (See Jobrack, 2011, for more on this idea.)

ACTIVITY 5.1

Is your language teaching mostly textbook-based? In your teaching and learning organization, what is the process for deciding which books will be used for your language courses?

In your experience, what have you found are some of the advantages and some of the limitations of using textbooks in language courses?

What are some of the alternatives to textbooks that you have tried (if any), and how do these compare with using textbooks?

To return to CBI, one of the most cited books in this area is by Donna Brinton, Marguerite Snow and Marjorie Wesche. It was published in 1989 but it is still being cited in papers on CBI nearly 30 years later. In *Content-Based Second Language Instruction* they presented three models of CBI: in theme-based courses, the language learning is 'organized around umbrella topics studied in depth' (Jansma, 1991, p. 713); 'sheltered courses' are taught by content-area specialists, with some training in language teaching and learning; and in 'adjunct courses', learners 'follow a content-area course with a support language course' (Jansma, 1991, p. 713).

We will look at these different types of CBI in more detail, but first it is necessary to delve a little further into the past, to a 45-page booklet, *Bilingualism and Minority-Language Children*, written by Jim Cummins and published in 1981, which laid the foundation for what was to become CBI. As Renner (1996) noted, 'Cummins' (1980, 1981) work was fundamental in providing the theoretical structure for considering the integration of language and content instruction' (p. 5). Similarly, some years later, in an article on 'The Grammar of History' (2004, pp. 67–93), Schleppegrell, Achugar and Oteíza described Cummins' work as being 'highly influential in the development of CBI' (p. 69). For more than 35 years, Cummins has been researching and writing about bilingualism, multilingualism and **minority language education**. (See, for example, his 2015 paper on the 'legacy of exclusion' in schools in South Africa.)

In between Cummins' 1981 booklet and Brinton, Snow and Wesche's 1989 book came Bernhard Mohan's *Language and Content* (1986). In this book, Mohan wrote: 'Language is not just a medium of communication but a medium of learning across the curriculum. The goal of *integration* is both language learning and content learning. Content-based classrooms are not merely places where a student learns a second language; they are places where a student gains an education' (p. 8, emphasis added). We can see a number of important things happening in Mohan's description, one of which is the beginnings of CBI becoming CLIL.

As we have seen in previous chapters, some methodologies can have quite modest beginnings (in this case, a 45-page booklet), but they can grow into methodological movements that take on a life of their own, to the extent that the methodological field is re-shaped in the image of the new method. We can also see some rather grandiose claims being made for CBI and CLIL, going beyond 'mere' language teaching and learning to 'an education'. This can be an important factor in the popularity of some methods over others, as some are more lauded than others. Also, in terms of the rise and fall of some methods, at different points along the timeline, the same method may have gone from being lauded to being vigorously challenged, to falling into disrepair and disrepute. (See Chapter 7, on Grammar Translation, and Chapter 8 on the alternative and humanistic methodologies.)

Another of the recurring themes in the methodologies considered in this book so far is the recent representation of language education in more globally important terms. For example, one of the most recent books on CBI, *Content-Based Foreign Language Teaching* (2016), edited by Laurent Cammarata, begins by stating that 'For millennia human beings have been compelled to learn languages for political, economic, social and personal reasons ... In the twenty-first century, however, the need has become critical' (Cammarata, Tedick, & Osborne, 2016, p. 1). The three authors of the introductory chapter go on to explain that 'A few reasons for the increase in demand for bi- and multilingualism include the rise in globalization of business and commerce, health and security matters that require international cooperation, the proliferation of international migration, and the huge impact that scientific advances and telecommunications have had on modern societies', such as the Internet and mobile technologies (p. 1). That echoes the statement made by Long (2015), in relation to TBLT (see Chapter 3), who wrote that 'Second language teaching and learning are more important in the twenty-first century than ever before' (p. 3). In terms of 'international migration', at the time of this writing, the Syrian refugee crisis is being passionately debated around the world (syrianrefugees.eu), and whatever the outcomes of these debates, there will be language teaching and learning implications, at the local, national and international levels, the implications of which we cannot yet know.

In terms of where CBI came from, like so many methodologies, in the case of CBI, building on Cummins' foundational work in Canada in the early 1980s, it appears to have taken off in the USA. For example, according to Schleppegrell, Achugar and Oteíza, 'CBI began to gain prominence in the 1980s in the United States when approaches were needed to promote simultaneous content and language learning for a growing number of English language learners (ELLs) in the schools' (2004, p. 68). In terms of what CBI is, Schleppegrell, Achugar and Oteíza describe it as follows: 'The basic notion behind CBI is that language should be taught in conjunction with the teaching of academic subject matter' (2004, p. 68). This is similar to other definitions, such as: 'Students in content-based instructional settings acquire subject matter knowledge and language simultaneously' (Musumeci, 1996, p. 321). As usual, this is not as simple or straightforward as it sounds, which is one of the recurring challenges of the methodologies presented in earlier chapters, that is, an apparent oversimplification in terms of thinking about how second and foreign languages are learned.

An example of this oversimplification may be Rodgers (2006). In his report on using CBI to teach Italian as second or foreign language, he defines CBI as 'the learning of language through the study of a content area, for example, history, geography, or science' (p. 373), in which 'the subject matter is the focus of classroom instruction; the acquisition of language is seen as *a natural consequence or by-product* of subject matter learning' (p. 373, emphasis added). These kinds of convenient assumptions about in-class language learning being a 'natural consequence' may be, at least in part, another example of the differences between acquiring a first language, as a child growing up and immersed in the L1 environment, and learning a second or foreign language, formally and later in life. If these differences are not fully recognized, this could result in potentially serious underestimation of the challenges of teaching and learning other languages.

> ## ACTIVITY 5.2
>
> According to Cammarata (2016), 'For millennia human beings have been compelled to learn languages for political, economic, social and personal reasons … *In the twenty-first century, however, the need has become critical*' (p. 1, emphasis added). Are you in a context in which language teaching and learning are felt to be essential, and of critical importance? If so, why are they felt to be so important?
>
> If you are not in a context in which language teaching and learning are felt to be so important, how would you describe the attitudes towards language teaching and learning where you are?

In relation to the different types of CBI and the importance of the relationships between context and content, 'CBI has been promoted – through theme-based ESL-EFL, sheltered classes, and adjunct courses – as a way of providing contexts for teaching language through a focus on grade-appropriate content' (Schleppegrell, Achugar, & Oteíza, 2004, p. 68). As with TBLT and CLT (Chapters 3 and 4), the importance of context is a recurring theme, as CBI is described as a methodology in which learners are presented with 'discipline-based material in a meaningful contextualized form in which the primary focus is on the acquisition of information' (Kasper, 1997, p. 310). There are many examples of such descriptions: for example, CBI as 'a way of providing a meaningful context for language instruction while at the same time providing a vehicle for reinforcing academic skills' (Curtain & Haas, 1995, p. 2), which relates to the development of higher-level academic skills in another language.

To return to the three traditional distinctions between different types of CBI, Brinton, Snow and Wesche (1989) described 'sheltered' CBI courses as those in which the course is taught in a second or foreign language 'by a content specialist to a group of learners who have been segregated or "sheltered" from native-language speakers' (p. 15). The use of 'sheltered' is perhaps an unfortunate term, as it suggests that non-native users, learning the target language, need to be in some way 'protected' from the native users of that language. However, the well-meaning idea is that non-native users of the language of instruction will not have to compete with native users while they are both trying to learn the same content. But one group are dealing mainly with understanding the content, while the other group are having to do both, that is, learn another language, and learn the content *through* that other language.

The 'sheltered' model of CBI gave rise to a patented product called 'SIOP'©, which stands for Sheltered Instruction Observation Protocol, and which was originally developed as a tool for teacher–researcher collaboration and professional development (Short & Echevarria, 1999). However, over the years, the observation protocol took on a life of its own, and became 'an instructional framework to help elementary and secondary teachers support English language learners (ELLs)' (Daniel & Conlin, 2015, p. 169), which researchers claim 'has led to positive results in language and literacy for ELLs in K–12 schools' (p. 171). Such claims have been vigorously challenged by James Crawford and Sharon Reyes (2015) in their book with the long and colourful title *The Trouble With SIOP®: How a Behaviorist Framework, Flawed Research, and Clever Marketing Have Come to Define – and Diminish – Sheltered Instruction*. According to Crawford and Reyes, 'in 2004, this taxpayer-funded pedagogy was privatized, trademarked, and acquired by Pearson, a British publishing conglomerate that describes itself as "the world's leading education company"' (p. 1), whose 'income from education alone was 7.3 billion [US dollars] in 2012' (p. 1). Whether or not the claims made about SIOP© being, according to Pearson, 'the only scientifically validated model of sheltered instruction' (Crawford & Reyes, 2015, p. 1) are to be believed, Crawford and Reyes highlight the enormous amounts of money that can be generated from the methodological marketplace in language education (see Chapter 8).

In the 'adjunct' version of CBI, two courses run side by side: one a language course, and one a content course. In this arrangement, 'language and subject/content are taught separately, but coordinated care is provided' (Satilmis, Yakup, Selim, & Aybarsha, 2015, p. 99). Theme-based and topic-based versions of CBI are perhaps the best known, as they form the mainstay of most generic content-based language textbooks on the market today. Common themes and topics include travel, food, holidays, entertainment, technology, festivals and celebrations, and so on. However, within CBI for ELT, because of the focus on academic language, the topics and themes are often related to English for Specific Purposes (ESP), such as English for Academic Purposes (EAP) and English for Vocational Purposes (EVP). For example, Mark Garner and Erik Borg (2005) took an 'ecological perspective' on CBI, based on Haugen's (1972) original work, which looked at the interaction between a specific language and its surroundings. In terms of appropriateness, Garner and Borg wrote that 'Within the broad domain of English for specific purposes, CBI has been advocated for a number of years as the most educationally appropriate approach' (2005, p. 120). And in relation to EAP, they stated that 'Context, *which is the organising idea of CBI*, is foregrounded in language ecology. At the same time, language ecology calls for a deeper understanding of the role of communication in language pedagogy, and particularly for English for academic purposes' (p. 120, emphasis added).

Garner and Borg (2005) also highlighted the influence of increasing numbers of students coming to English-dominant countries, such as the USA and the UK, to study at the tertiary level in universities, colleges and schools, and more recently at the secondary level, using English as the Medium of Instruction (EMI). In terms of what is meant by 'EAP', Hyland and Hamp-Lyons

(2002) defined EAP as referring to 'language research and instruction that focuses on the specific needs and practices of particular groups in academic contexts. It means grounding instruction in an understanding of the cognitive, social, and linguistic demands of specific academic disciplines' (p. 2).

Another recurring term and notion in CBI is 'immersion', which also reflects the history and origins of CBI. As Yuen Yi Lo, in Hong Kong, explained, CBI came out of the Canadian immersion programmes of the 1960s and the 1970s, when schools there 'attempted to facilitate the learning of French for Anglophone children' (2014b, p. 142). The results of the language immersion experiments of the 1960s and the 1970s were mixed, in that some students learned a great deal of the target language, as well as a good deal of content, but there were a significant number of students who did not learn much of either, as they did not have the language knowledge and skills to access the content well enough to learn it effectively. However, the CBI models of immersion and models based on using the target language as the medium of instruction were developed, and eventually morphed into Content Language Integrated Learning or CLIL. According to Do Coyle (2007), the term CLIL was adopted by a group called the European Network of Administrators, Researchers and Practitioners (EUROCLIC) in the mid-1990s. Coyle defined CLIL broadly as language teaching and learning in which 'the foreign language is used as a tool in the learning of a non-language subject' (p. 545). My own definition of CBI does not distinguish between CLIL and CBI, but considers the former to be a developmental progression of the latter. That is, CLIL is a methodology that is located towards the Content end of the Language–Content Continuum, but as all content is taught through some kind of language, and as all language contains some kind of content, movement along the continuum is constant. As a result, understanding the content is sometimes the priority, whereas at other times, understanding the language takes precedence.

ACTIVITY 5.3

Having read the various definitions and descriptions of CBI and CLIL above, write your own definition or description, and share it with a colleague. Look for similarities and differences in your definitions/descriptions, and talk about where these come from.

Inside the CBI/CLIL Classroom

Larsen-Freeman and Anderson (2011, pp. 134–139) give a detailed description of a CBI lesson – they do not use the term 'CLIL' – that took place at an international school in Taipei, Taiwan, with learners studying geography, using English as the medium of instruction. The students were sixth-grade (11 or 12 years old) users of Chinese, Japanese and Korean as first languages, and their levels of English proficiency are described as being at a 'low intermediate level' (p. 134).

In their analysis of the lesson, using the ten basic principles they derived, Larsen-Freeman and Anderson noted that the CBI lesson built on the previous experiences of the students, and that the teacher 'scaffolded' the language content, that is, the teacher helped the learners 'say what they want to say by building a complete utterance *together with the students*' (p. 138, emphasis added). They also observed that the students appeared to be highly motivated, based on which they concluded that 'Language is learned most effectively when it is used as a medium to convey content of interest to students' (p. 138), which included the learning of geographic vocabulary items, such as 'longitude' and 'latitude'. In terms of reading input and writing output, Larsen-Freeman and Anderson highlighted the importance of students learning 'the discourse organization of academic texts' (p. 139), supported by the use of 'graphic organizers'. Such organizers can help students develop 'the skills they need to learn academic content' (p. 139) using different kinds of visual mind maps or spider diagrams that show how different ideas are connected to each other.

Building on Larsen-Freeman and Anderson's work (2011), I presented a number of lessons during a film studies course to a group of students, between 16 and 17 years of age, at a community college in Ontario, Canada, who had chosen to take an elective course on Film Studies, as part of the college's English language requirement. Of the 24 learners in the class, all of whom were majoring in Engineering, and all of whom were from Mainland China, 22 were male and two were female. The level of most of the students, based on their most recent language assessment, was 'mid-intermediate'. I was allowed to present a number of lessons, as a guest teacher, using a CBI approach, during the course.

In one of the lessons, we had just watched a two-minute trailer for the animated movie *Kung Fu Panda II* (2011), which I showed using a DVD, in English and with no subtitles (Curtis, 2012). (Other language options were possible, such as the Mandarin Chinese version.) As a warm-up activity, I asked the students to tell me whether they had seen any movies over the weekend (as the class took place on a Monday morning), and if so, which ones, and what they had enjoyed or disliked about the movies they saw. About half of the class had seen one or more movies over the weekend (although none of them had gone to a movie theatre). I then showed the opening 30 seconds of the movie, which is the first part of a lengthy, scene-setting narration:

> 'Long ago, in ancient China, the Peacocks ruled over Gongmen City. They brought great joy and prosperity to the city, for they had invented "fireworks".
> But their son, Lord Shen, saw darker power in the fireworks.
> What had brought color and joy could also bring darkness and destruction.'

The following interaction, from the classroom transcript, took place immediately after the students had seen the opening 30-second narration. The interaction was video-recorded, with the students' permission, using an iPad. T = Teacher. S1 = Student 1, etc.

T: That was a very short clip, as I said it would be. Just 30 seconds. Remember, before showing it, I asked you to focus on two questions. What were the two questions?
S1: What do you see?
T: Good, and the second ...
S2: What do you hear?
S1: Ancient China ...
T: OK. What about ancient China?
S3: Imitating the dramatic voicing of the narrator: 'the peacocks ruled over Gongmen City'. [Students laugh]
T: That's a pretty good imitation of Michelle Yeoh.
S3: Who Michelle Yeoh?
T: The Chinese-Malaysian actress who was the voice of the narrator. [as I saw blank looks on the faces of the students, I found a picture of Yeoh, on Google Images, and showed it on the screen]
S4: I know her.
S5: *You know her*!? How *you* know *her*?! [Students laugh]
T: Good. Good use of *stressing* words to give extra *emphasis*, which we talked about last lesson.
S5: He don't know her. [Students laugh]
T: OK. We can talk about what it means to *know* someone later. But now, I need you to look at these words and tell me if you recognize any of them.
T shows a PowerPoint slide with film-related vocabulary including *backdrop, background music, backlighting, backstory, banned, B-movie* and other 'b words' related to movies and movie-making.

The students were then given five minutes to work, individually, in pairs, or in groups of three (but no more than three), using their phones, or other mobile technologies, to find examples of film-related 'b words' and what they meant. Each individual, pair or threesome was assigned one 'b word' or phrase to work on. After five minutes, many of the students asked for more time, so after another five minutes (ten, in total) I asked the students to share with the class what they had found during their brief Internet searches. As I made a point of calling on students who had not said much during the previous part of the lesson, the 'S' numbers here refer to different students from those above.

S6: Reading from the screen of her phone: 'backstory refers to the events that directly happened prior to the beginning of the story'.
T: That's right. And which site did you find that definition on?
S6: It's called 'filmsite dot org'.
T: [Finds that site on his laptop] OK. And you remember what we said about plagiarism [long pause] That if you write down the words of someone else, from somewhere else, you have to put inverted commas around it, and give the source details. Do you remember?
Students nod.
T: So, what do we mean when we say 'source details'.
S7: Where we found those words ...
S8: Who said them ...
T: ... Or who wrote them ... and it's important that you understand the meaning of the words you take from somewhere or someone else.
Students nod.
T: So, what does 'prior' mean?
S9: Before.
S10: Before what?
S9: Before what happened later. [Students laugh]
T: So, *without* looking at your phones – notice my emphasis of 'without' – what is a 'backstory'?
S11: The story behind the story. [Students laugh]
T: That sounds funny, but that's right. It's the part of story that happened *before* the part of the story we're seeing and hearing now.

Each of the two transcripts above only took approximately two minutes of the lesson (four minutes in total) out of a 50-minute lesson, which allowed time for pre-viewing discussion and post-viewing teaching and learning. Of the 45 main minutes of the lesson, approximately 15 were given to viewing and re-viewing carefully selected short scenes from the movie, of one or two minutes each, that gave visual examples of most of the ten different vocabulary items that related to movies and movie-making.

Referring to the ten basic principles developed by Larsen-Freeman and Anderson (2011), I can be seen/heard in the transcripts above 'scaffolding' the language content, by helping the learners say what they wanted to say, and working with them to help them build 'a complete utterance' (p. 138). Although the excerpts are brief, the video recording of the lesson also indicates that the students did appear to be motivated, engaged and interested in the content, partly because I chose a movie that was based on traditional Chinese stories and characters, but which was made and presented entirely in English. Also, about half of the 24 students asked if they could borrow my DVD so they could watch the whole movie. Instead, I arranged an optional movie night, at which I showed the complete film, with no language teaching input from me, which was attended by 18 of the 24 students. And in terms of graphic organizers, later in the lesson above, I was able to build on the board with the students a number of mind maps, showing some of the main themes in the movie, such as 'the triumph of the anti-hero'. These themes were then related to some of the main characters, which may have helped develop some of the academic thinking skills the students needed in some of their Engineering major courses, such as using graphs, charts and tables to present technical information to non-specialist audiences.

ACTIVITY 5.4

In one part of the lesson above, the students were asked to find content-related vocabulary items using Internet searches in class. Do you allow or encourage your students to find this kind of content in this way? What have you found to be – or what do you think would be – some of the opportunities and some of the problems of using this kind of technology in the language classroom?

The Pros and Cons of CBI/CLIL

As with CLT and TBLT, the positives of CBI/CLIL have been pushed hard, sometimes to the exclusion of any mention of the limitations of the methodology. This is disturbing and unhelpful, as all methods have their strengths and their weaknesses, their benefits and their limitations. Even though this could be counted as 'common sense', in the world of language teaching methodologies, such sense, at times, appears to be not all that common.

A few illustrative examples of this heavily skewed presentation of CBI/CLIL will be presented here, including Musumeci's (1996) paper, which appeared in *Applied Linguistics*. In that paper, according to Musucemi, the teachers of Italian were 'amazed' (p. 289) by 'the apparent ease with which students acquire knowledge of Italian social geography in Italian' (p. 290). Perhaps the key word here, apart from 'amazed' (which is not a word you would expect to find in a top academic journal), is 'apparent', as the learners were not asked specifically about how hard or how easy they found learning the target language to be. However, from the learners' perspective, according to Musucemi, the students reported 'enjoying the subject matter, the "academic" nature of the course, and – above all – the fact that it is taught entirely in Italian' (p. 290), which may or not be a common reaction to academic content being presented entirely in the target language.

This is not to suggest that such situations do not happen in language teaching and learning situations, but in my experience and those of my colleagues, these kinds of 'amazing' learning outcomes are more the exception than the rule, as such a perfect alignment of teaching and learning, of motivation and methodology, is very rare. However, Musucemi did note that some teachers expressed 'some frustration with one aspect of daily instruction', which was that they wished the students would 'contribute more to class discussions, that is, volunteer to speak more frequently and at greater length' (p. 290).

As noted in previous chapters, this is not a limitation specific to CBI/CLIL, but one common to all approaches and methodologies that are based on learners communicating in the target language, through which they will acquire the target language 'as a natural consequence or by-product' (Rodgers, 2006, p. 373) as a result of that interaction. If only language teaching and learning were that easy! If that were the case, it would not take so much time, effort and energy, as well as determination, commitment and sustained motivation, over such long periods.

Other examples of this kind of reporting regarding CBI and CLIL can be found in other top journals, such as *English for Specific Purposes*, in which Bailin Song (2006) reported that 'Numerous research studies demonstrate consistently that content-based second language teaching promotes both language acquisition and academic success' (p. 422). Song then cites more than a dozen articles, published over 15 years, between 1989 and 2004, in support of her claim. She continued: 'The literature on content-based instruction ... has documented many psychological and pedagogical benefits, e.g., high motivation, increased interest, reduced anxiety, the elimination of the artificial separation between language and content courses, and development of study skills' (p. 422). In all, around 20 published works are cited, all of which Song puts forward in support of the benefits of CBI/CLIL, with no mention of any its limitations.

As we saw in Chapter 3, on TBLT, the academic output surrounding a particular methodology can have a significant effect on its adoption and use, or its rejection, not only at the national level, but even at the international level. Fortunately, Song does provide a rare and much-needed insight into the underlying sources of this kind of reporting when she explains that 'Content-linked EAP or ESL programs often receive extra funding and administrative support, including tutoring and smaller class sizes. *To justify the extra funding support, administrators of the programs are often under pressure to provide evidence of students' superior academic performance* over time' (pp. 421–422, emphasis added). Of the more than 50 published papers, book chapters and books on CBI/CLIL that I read and reviewed for this chapter, this is one of the rare open and honest accounts of politics and pedagogy coming together in a correlational – possibly even a causal – relationship, in terms of how program funding can be influenced by published research. Here, the old expression 'Publish or Perish' refers not only to individual academics applying for contract renewal, tenure and/or promotion, but also to the potential perishing of entire programs.

Given the high-stakes nature of such studies, it is no surprise that Song writes, in her conclusion: 'This study provides further evidence that in addition to short-term merits, content-based language instruction has long-term benefits that impact students' future academic performance' (p. 435). She also added that 'Such a [CBI/CLIL] model merits continued institutional financial and administrative support' (p. 435). If the future of my language program depended on my published research, I too would focus mainly – or even only – on reporting the positives, as doing otherwise could put my program and other similar programs 'at risk'.

Another driving force behind the rise of CBI and CLIL has been the 'Increasing numbers of students whose first language is not English studying in English-medium universities worldwide' (Garner & Borg, 2005, p. 119). These students usually need university-level EMI language development, as well as preparation for the academic and disciplinary practices of their new departments and faculties. In terms of the benefits of CBI and CLIL, Garner and Borg (2005) drew on the work of more than a dozen journal articles, published over 25 years between 1979 and 2003, which see CBI and CLIL as 'the solution to a number of problems' (p. 120). These problems include 'the lack of authenticity in English teaching materials' (which was discussed in Chapter 3, on CLT) as well as 'the segregation of academic skills from their application ... the failure to prepare students to enter the academic community of their disciplines ... and the need to cater for the variety of discipline-related discourses and literacies' (p. 120).

As we can see from such lists, the benefits of CBI and CLIL are mainly in the areas of EAP and ESP. However, as a result of the specialist language needed by non-native users of English studying at English-medium universities, Garner and Borg (2005) also acknowledge that 'Teaching CBI puts new demands on teachers; they need to feel comfortable both teaching the theme that has been chosen, and relating the content of that theme to EAP-specific knowledge, such as genre analysis, without the guidance of a textbook' (p. 120). As with all of the methods considered in this book, my experience has been that the key to the successful use of these methods is initial teacher training and education, followed by on-going, career-long teacher professional development.

Another key factor in successful CBI and CLIL courses and programs is collaboration between language teachers and content teachers, 'with a team of language and content faculty working together to develop curricula' (Song, 2006, p. 421). It is important to add here that the two groups need to work together *as equal partners*, in which the language teaching is seen as equally important as the content. The make-or-break importance of this kind of collaboration has led to entire studies focused, not on the result of using CBI and CLIL, but on second language teachers and content subject teachers working together. An example of this kind of collaboration can be seen in Yuen Yi Lo's paper (2014a) about the contrasting beliefs and attitudes of these two parties in a Hong Kong context. Lo concluded that the two groups had 'significantly different beliefs about their roles concerning language teaching in CBI' and that, 'Even though they generally believe in the effectiveness of collaboration, they perceive some potential problems and are not fully committed to it' (p. 181). Lo (2014a) also identified other reasons for the growth of CBI and CLIL which are economic and geographic, rather than pedagogic: 'In countries where English is not the majority language but enjoys high socio-economic status (e.g., continental Europe and Asia), CBI is implemented to enhance the L2 proficiency of students, which will make them more competitive in the era of globalization' (pp. 182–183). These comments about language teaching and learning in a globalized world relate to those of other writers and researchers regarding other language methodologies, such as TBLT (Chapter 3).

One of the most unfortunate conclusions of Lo's extensive work in this area, but which concurs with my experience in the field, is that, in general, 'Language teachers are more willing to collaborate with content teachers than the other way around' (2014, p. 193). One of the reasons that Lo proposes for this seriously limiting one-sidedness is that content teachers 'may have a stronger sense of their own discipline and feel less ready for others to "intrude"' compared with English language teachers, as the subject in Hong Kong 'tends to be more open and less well-defined in nature ... since students are tested on their general language skills' (p. 193). Lo also suggests that differences in status may be another part of the problem, with language teachers and language teaching being perceived as having – or being assigned – lower status than content teachers and content teaching. Whatever the reasons for this disconnect between language teachers and content teachers, unless such barriers can be overcome and mutually respectful professional relationships established, the success of CBI and CLIL is likely to be limited. However, where such partnerships are possible, the likelihood of successful outcomes may be high.

ACTIVITY 5.5

In your teaching and learning organization, do content teachers and language teachers work together? If so, are these equal partnerships, based on mutual respect, or some other kinds of relationships, for example, more hierarchical?

If, in your teaching and learning organization, content teachers and language teachers do not work together, why is there not that kind of collaboration and cooperation?

Assessment of Learning Outcomes with CBI and CLIL

One of the challenges of estimating the effectiveness of any language teaching and learning methodology is the assessment of language learning outcomes. A substantial number of books and papers on language teaching and learning methods appear rather vague on this issue. For example, Larsen-Freeman and Anderson (2011), in their chapter on CBI, pose the question 'How is evaluation accomplished?', to which they answer 'Students are evaluated on their knowledge of content and their language ability' (p. 140). This lack of detail may be because the outcomes are to some extent self-evident, in the same sense that, for example, if CLT is the main methodology being used, and the learners can communicate with each other in the target language, with few breakdowns of communication, then the method has worked. Likewise, if the main methodology used was TBLT, and the learners are able to complete the task successfully, then the method may, by that fact, be considered to have been successful.

However, these somewhat self-fulfilling assessments rest on how 'effective communication' is defined, how 'successful task completion' is defined, and so on. Another complicating factor is *how* the methodology was employed. For example, it may be that the method itself was not used in the way that proponents or exponents of the method have described or prescribed. There may be various reasons for this, one of which is the recurring issue of adequate initial teacher training and education, which needs to be followed by on-going teacher professional development focused on how to use that particular method in class. Or, there may be other factors, such as the lack of materials, or being in more of an EFL-like environment, in which exposure to the target language is limited to the classroom, rather than more ESL-like environments, in which the learners are surrounded by, and even immersed in, the target language.

Our goal, then, in these notes at the end of each chapter, on assessment of learning outcomes, is not to provide in-depth explanations of how such outcomes can be assessed, as this is covered in detail in the language testing and assessment literature. (See, for example, the book by Liying Cheng and Janna Fox, 2017, in this *ALLC* book series.) What I am aiming to do here is to draw the readers' attention to the importance of considering assessment of learning outcomes as an integral part of deciding which methods to use and why, rather than the all-too-common situation of assessment concerns appearing as something of an after-thought.

In relation to CBI and CLIL, and the inseparability of language, content and context, Schleppegrell, Achugar and Oteíza (2004) noted that 'CBI can be enriched through an understanding that language and content are never separate, that content in school contexts is always presented and assessed through language' (p. 67). A detailed example of assessment of learning outcomes using CBI was given by Nancy Gaffield-Vile (1996), based on a course designed to prepare first-year university students in England, using Sociology as the main content heading. Sociology was chosen in part because it is interdisciplinary and in part because of examination preparation: 'A course in one of the social sciences is therefore a useful method of preparation for students intending to take the IELTS exam' (p. 109).

The assessment at the end of the academic year was based on 'two one-hour timed essays and two typewritten essays of 1,000–1,500 words in length' (p. 110), with continuous assessment exercises weighted at 20 per cent of the final, overall mark. There was also a 15-minute seminar presentation, on a set topic, and a final examination, which counted towards 70 per cent of the final overall mark. The exam consisted of '12–16 set questions on topics covered throughout the academic year, from which students must answer four' (p. 110). A final 10 per cent was also awarded 'for participation in class seminars and discussions' (p. 110).

None of the examination scores and none of the results of any of the assessments are presented by Gaffield-Vile, so it is difficult to judge the effectiveness of the testing and assessment procedures used. But she did conclude, anecdotally and personally, that 'It is my belief that students find content-based courses more motivating, once they have achieved a suitable language level, than skills-based courses alone, which can appear rather artificial and be de-motivating' (p. 114). Whether learners (and their teachers) find skills-based courses 'artificial and de-motivating' will, of course, depend on the individuals in the classroom. However, as with most methods and approaches, one of the claims made in favour of, in this case, CBI/CLIL is that it is more motivating than other methods and approaches, which will also depend on the individual learners and teachers.

Suggested Readings

A basic 50-page introduction to CBI, titled *Content-Based Instruction* (2013), was written by Margo DelliCarpini and published by the TESOL Press as part of their 'English Language Teacher Development' series (edited by Tom Farrell).

Content-Based Foreign Language Teaching: Curriculum and Pedagogy for Developing Advanced Thinking and Literacy Skills Paperback (Routledge, 2016), edited by Laurent Cammarata, is in four parts: 'Theoretical perspectives and empirical evidence'; 'Curriculum Development for the thinking-oriented foreign language classroom'; 'Critical pedagogy and the foreign language classroom'; and 'Exemplars of cognitively engaging curriculum planning for the foreign language classroom'.

Focus on Content Based Language Teaching, by Patsy Lightbown (2014, Oxford University Press) is a useful summary of some of the research on CBI/CLIL, with chapters on research on using CBLT with young learners (Chapter 3) and on using CBLT with adolescent learners (Chapter 4).

CHAPTER 6

The Direct Method and the Audio-Lingual Method

> *Before reading this chapter, spend some time thinking about the following questions:*
>
> - If you are familiar with the Direct Method (DM), how would you describe it, clearly and concisely, to someone who is unfamiliar with it?
> - If you are not familiar with the Direct Method, based on the name, what do you think you might see if you were to look into a classroom where the DM is being used?
> - As the name implies, the Audio-Lingual Method (ALM) is based on listening-and-repeating. How much target language learning, and to what degree of proficiency or competence, do you think may be possible with the ALM? Low, Medium or High, and why?

Introduction and Overview

This is the first chapter in this book in which we consider two methods together. One reason for this approach is the idea of current impact, in terms of how widespread the use of these methodologies appears to be these days, and how much they are being discussed in the current literature on language teaching and learning. Therefore, since the DM and the ALM are far less widely used now than they used to be, compared with, for example, TBLT, CLT and CBI, these two methodologies are considered together, and in less detail. Another reason for considering the DM and the ALM together is that both of these methodologies have as one of their fundamental principles the avoidance of, or even the prohibiting of, the first language of the learners. That prohibition was based on the assumption that the learner's first languages were a form of interference, which should be minimized, during a time when the first language was seen as some kind of confusing 'linguistic contamination'. In this chapter, we also look at how newer methods develop and grow as a result of disgruntlement with the existing methods, while reiterating the fact there is no one best method, as what works well in one context may not work in another.

In the second half of the chapter, we look at the Audio-Lingual Method, based on the principle of listen-and-repeat, and consider some of its pros and cons, strengths and weaknesses, including the idea of methodologies as fads or panaceas. We also touch on the anti-grammar method, with its similarities to the anti-methods movement. In the last part of this chapter, we briefly consider assessment of learning outcomes, and how newer technologies may be influencing those assessments.

What Is the Direct Method and Where Did It Come From?

As we saw in Chapter 1, language teaching and learning has a long history – much longer than many language teachers and learners may realize – going back thousands of years. This long history is in contrast to the three main methodologies presented so far – TBLT, CLT and CBI/CLIL – which have grown and become established in relatively recent decades. The Direct Method predates these three by up to a century, going back to at least the 1880s, as discussed by Susan Bayley in her *History of Education* paper on 'The Direct Method and Modern Language Teaching in England 1880–1918' (1998, pp. 35–57). As Bayley explains, in the 1880s and the 1890s, a '**Reform Movement**' attempted to 'revolutionize methods of modern language instruction by teaching them as living languages' (p. 35). Before then, in England and elsewhere, modern languages were 'taught like the classical, dead languages' (p. 35), such as Latin, based on grammatical, philological and literary analyses (see Chapter 7). However, in the 1880s, perhaps partly as a result of greater travel and scholarly exchanges between countries in Europe, 'a reaction had arisen to the stultifying methods used to teach French and German' (Bayley, p. 25), which were the main modern languages taught in schools in England at that time. French and German are still the main modern language taught in many schools in England today, more than 130 years later, which may reflect how long language education can sometimes take to change, in some contexts. Bayley (1998) concluded that, methodologically, 'The impact of the Reform movement on actual practice was muted but significant in the sense that it challenged teachers to rethink their methods', which led to 'the integration of oral work into day-to-day teaching and external examinations' (p. 56). This movement of modalities, from writing to speaking, was more important than may have been realized at the time, as without that shift, it is likely that the rise of CLT would not have occurred.

As a result of the Reform Movement, many slim volumes and discursive papers on DM were published in the early 1900s, mostly written by linguists from England travelling to France or to Germany. A noteworthy example was by Arthur Bovée, a teacher of French, who in 1913 visited language schools in Paris, after which he defined the teaching of French vocabulary using DM as 'the teaching of French words without having recourse to the **mother tongue**' (Bovée, 1919, p. 63). Like many of his contemporaries of the time, Bovée believed that 'it is more effective to teach vocabulary this way than by the [grammar] translation method' (p. 61). One of his reasons for reaching that conclusion was the belief in the greater effectiveness of sentences 'as opposed to single words' (p. 63).

The importance of moving beyond single words in language teaching and learning may seem obvious to us today, but this shift was seen as one of the major changes in moving away from Grammar Translation (see Chapter 7) and towards the

Direct Method. Although notions of language immersion as a way of learning languages had not yet been put forward as such, Bovée anticipated this interest in immersion during his time in Paris (in the days when only men learned other languages): 'The unifying element is the fact that the life of the pupil, from the moment he awakes in the morning to the time he retires at night, forms the background for the systematic development and logical connection of all the words studied' (p. 72). Also, in terms of the political reasons for some methods becoming established as *the* method, Bovée pointed out that in France DM was 'imposed by ministerial decree' (pp. 63–64). This kind of account, published as it was in one of the longest-established academic journals in the field, *The Modern Language Journal*, set the scene for a major 'sea change' of the kind that had not been seen for more than a century, from grammar translation to target-language-only teaching.

For the next 50 years or so, from the 1920s to the 1970s, the DM continued to emerge as the dominant 'new' paradigm in second and foreign language teaching. For example, Wilga Rivers (1919–2007), an influential professor of languages and literature at Harvard University, described the DM in glowing terms. She believed it 'provided an exciting and interesting way of learning the foreign language through activity', which was 'successful in releasing students from the inhibitions all too often associated with speaking a foreign tongue, particularly at the early stages' (Rivers, 1968, p. 20). However, following what we can now see as recurring patterns and repeating cycles of methodological fashion (Adamson, 2005) – new and fashionable, then old and unfashionable, then sometimes back in fashion again – by the 1960s DM was also being challenged, as CLT waited in the wings, ready to be hailed as The Next Big Thing. For example, in 1966, Dennis Hannan, in his work on what he referred to as 'common sense' and the DM in language teaching, pointed out that 'Educational techniques tend to swing from one extreme to another, and nowhere is this more apparent than in the area of foreign language teaching in schools and colleges' (p. 359). An important question to consider, 50 years after Hannan's observation, is whether such statements are still true today, and if so, to what extent and why. Or, if they are no longer true, what has changed? Another question is whether language education is, as Hannan claims, particularly susceptible to such '**pendulumic**' methodological swings, and if so, why.

> ### ACTIVITY 6.1
>
> Do you agree that language education is particularly susceptible to these kinds of 'pendulumic' methodological swings? If so, why do you think that is? If not, how would you describe the series and the cycles of methodological changes in language education?

Hannan's (1966) views are more personal and experiential, rather than data-based. For example, he wrote: 'It is my conviction that the direct method so much used and abused in the high schools may actually harm some students' (p. 359). The reason for such views at that time included a perceived lack of creative and intellectual engagement, so that the DM was seen as a methodology that 'bores and repels' (p. 360) the learners. There was also the DM's reliance on memorization and imitation, which was believed to 'deprive the learner of flexibility' (p. 360). In spite of this kind of opposition to the DM, Hannan did make some important general points about what he called the 'doctrinaire acceptance' of any language teaching method that 'fails to take into account differences in the age, temperament, ability and objectives of individual students' (p. 360).

In rejecting the one-size-fits-all approach (traces of which can still be seen in the world of language textbook publishing) and recognizing the uniqueness of every learner and every teacher, Hannan concluded with the important point that

'There can be no one perfect method in teaching because what will work with one age group will be ineffective with another and because there is no such thing as one standardized type of student' (p. 360). This is a point that Prabhu (1990) would make 25 years later; I would add that age is not the only distinguishing and differentiating factor, and Hannan himself recognized additional factors, such as temperament, which may relate to factors such as language learning aptitude, learner motivation (or lack thereof), and so on.

However, despite such early criticisms of DM in the 1960s, by the end of the 1990s, DM was being described within the TESOL world as a potential 'turning point' in relation to CLT (Celce-Murcia, Dörnyei, & Thurrell, 1997). In their critical appraisal of CLT, Celce-Murcia and her co-authors presented a more academic and gentler version of the cycles of fashion that I describe above, and that Hannan alluded to: 'L2 teaching methods and approaches tend to undergo a natural process of cyclical development' (p. 142). Celce-Murcia et al. describe the development cycles as following a particular and predictable sequence: 'A method or approach is first proposed (*often as a counterreaction to an earlier method or approach*), then accepted, applied and eventually criticized' (1998, p. 142, emphasis added). Although Celce-Murcia et al. put into parentheses the phrase I have italicized, I have added that emphasis because of the importance of new methods not developing independently, as part of some logical and systematic progression (as they are sometimes represented), but developing in opposition to the previous, existing and soon to become old and out-dated methods. Celce-Murcia et al. continue: 'The criticism may involve either the reform and revision or the complete rejection of the method or approach and perhaps its replacement with another' (p. 142). However, such a complete rejection is rare, as this would require all those who had put forward the previous method or approach to admit that they had been mistaken in suggesting that this was *the* language teaching and learning methodology.

In terms of circles and cycles, it is important to note that Celce-Murcia et al. believed that the DM, a 100-year-old method from the 1880s, had led to 'a significant shift ... in language teaching methodology', the scale and scope of which they described as 'comparable to the fundamental changes of the 1970s that resulted in the introduction and spread of CLT' (p. 142). However, this position was vigorously challenged by Scott Thornbury, who counter-argued that teachers have 'never abandoned a grammar-driven approach' and that there is 'little evidence that the alternatives, such as a task-based pedagogy ... have made a lasting impression on the current practice of ELT' (1998, p. 109). Things have, of course, changed since 1998, when Thornbury wrote this, and as we saw in Chapter 3, TBLT is now driving much of the research, publishing and language policy-making at a national level in some countries. But Thornbury proposed three reasons for this perceived lack of methodological change, one or more of which may well still apply today, in a number of contexts: 'the constraints imposed by grammatical syllabi; novice teachers' need for low-risk teaching strategies, and expectations of learners' (p. 110). Interestingly, outside of the world of language education, where the DM is no longer discussed much, in the business world, the DM may be enjoying something of a resurgence. For example, Mart (2013) described the DM as 'a good start to teach oral language' (p. 182).

ACTIVITY 6.2

As we saw above, according to Thornbury (1998), there are (at least) three reasons for a lack of methodological change: 'the constraints imposed by grammatical syllabi; novice teachers' need for low-risk teaching strategies, and expectations of learners'. Do any of these apply in your language teaching and learning context? If so, how do you adapt to (or overcome) such constraints?

Inside the DM Classroom, the Pros and Cons of the DM, and Assessment of Learning Outcomes

Larsen-Freeman and Anderson (2011) described a DM English language lesson, in Italy, with a group of 30 lower-level secondary school students, in what is known as a *scuola media*. The transcript below is taken from their description of the lesson (pp. 25–27), titled 'Looking at a Map'. The lesson starts with a reading passage, which is a description of the geography of the USA. The passage refers to a large map of the USA, which is displayed by the teacher at the front of the classroom. After the teacher has responded to the students' questions, for example, about the meaning of 'mountain range', the following exchange takes place.

T: Are we looking at a map of Italy?
Ss: No!
T: Remember to answer in full sentences.
Ss: No, we aren't looking at a map of Italy.
T: Are we looking at a map of United States?
Ss: Yes, we are looking at a map of United States.
T: Is Canada the country to the south of the United States?
Ss: No. Canada isn't the country to the south of the United States.
T: Are the Great Lakes in the North of the United States?
S: Yes. The Great Lakes are in the North.
T: Is the Rio Grande a river or a lake?
Ss: The Rio Grande is a river.
T: It's a river. Where is it?
Ss: It's between Mexico and the United States.
T: What colour is the Rio Grande on the map?
Ss: It's blue.
T: Points on the map, to a mountain range in the western USA.
T: What mountains are they?
Ss: They are the Rocky Mountains.

(based on Larsen-Freeman & Anderson, 2011, pp. 26–27)

In their analysis of the lesson, using the ten principles they derived, Larsen-Freeman and Anderson reiterate the point made by Bovée, in the early 1900s, as discussed above: 'Vocabulary is acquired more naturally if students use it in full sentences rather than memorizing wordlists' (p. 29). However, while it is true that putting a word in a sentence gives it a linguistic context, few native users of any target language speak in full and complete sentences all the time, unless they are engaged in highly formal and highly ritualized speech acts, such as making an official presentation to an audience of invited dignitaries. This use of complete sentences is, then, the kind of classroom language that has led a number of authors to refer to the classroom as being far removed from 'the real world' (see previous chapters).

This emphasis on the use of full sentences leaves us with a linguistic and pedagogical conundrum. As there are now far more non-native users of English in the world, native-user norms should no longer apply, and notions of such norms have been a contradiction in terms for some time now. Therefore, to criticize the kind of complete sentences produced by the learners – in response to explicit direction to do so by the teacher – because native users of English do not talk like that, is to counterproductively reinforce the out-dated notion of 'native-speaker norms'. However, if a user of any language only spoke in complete sentences, all the time, although they would be understood, they would probably be told that their speech sounded 'unnatural'. This 'unnaturalness' is the basis of some of the criticism of the DM, but this criticism only applies if the learner is trying to sounds like a native speaker. If the primary goal of the learner is to be understood, then speaking in full sentences all the time would not be a big problem.

A way out of this conundrum is to recognize, on the positive side, that DM can give some kind of context to vocabulary items by putting them in complete sentences, thereby making it more likely that such items will be understood and retained by the learners. This is in contrast to trying to memorize long lists of words, with little or no context, which appears to have been very common before the DM became popular. Such sentential vocabulary practice may also increase the likelihood that the items will be stored as part of the learners' active vocabulary, that is, words they can and will use, rather than their passive vocabulary, that is, words that the learners recognize and know the meaning of, but which they themselves would not use.

In terms of pros, there may also be benefits to using the DM with learners at lower levels of competence and/or confidence with the target language, in this case, English. One of the potential benefits is that the target language the learners produce is based largely on the language provided and modelled by the teacher. For example, although the likelihood of someone outside of a language classroom saying 'Are we looking at a map of Italy?' is almost zero, that rhetorical question from the teacher gave the students most of the language they needed to give the correct and sententially complete answer: 'No, we aren't looking at a map of Italy.' This same pattern of target-language-supply by the teacher, followed by minimal adjustments needed by the learners, is a common feature of the DM, as we see here:

'T: Are we looking at a map of United States?
Ss: Yes, we are looking at a map of United States.'

And here:

'T: Is Canada the country to the south of the United States?
Ss: No. Canada isn't the country to the south of the United States.'

In the first question–answer sequence above, all the learners have had to do is to make 'Are we' into 'No we aren't', and the rest of the sentence, which is the majority of the language produced, is the same, that is, 'looking at a map of Italy'. The same applies to the 'Are we looking' + 'Yes, we are' exchange. However, at lower competence/confidence levels, creating negations out of questions may be challenging, and it could be argued that being able to answer a question correctly, positively or negatively, is a fundamental language skill, without which even the most basic exchanges would be difficult.

From the earlier days of linguistic analyses and applied linguistics came the widely used acronym '**IRF**', with 'I' standing for 'Initiation' by the teacher, 'R' for the learner's 'Response' and 'F' for 'Feedback' from the teacher. We can see some elements of the classic IRF pattern in the DM classroom transcript above: as the teacher initiates the interaction, using simple Yes/No closed questions, the learners reply chorally, as a group, and the teacher, in some cases, gives some feedback – if asking the learners to answer in full sentences counts as 'teacher feedback'. On the negative side of the equation, we can also see that the interaction, and all of the language production, in the excerpt above is completely controlled by the teacher. However, there are parts of the lesson, not shown above, in which the learners ask questions about the meaning of particular vocabulary items, such as 'between', 'mountain range' and 'Appalachian' (a mountain range in the USA). In these parts of the lesson, the classroom interaction is being driven by the students' questions.

It is also worth mentioning the safety-in-numbers aspect of the whole class speaking together in this kind of call-and-response type of exchange, as learners who may be less competent/confident with the target language need not fear making a mistake individually, in front of the rest of the class, as they are all responding together. Other noteworthy features include the use of contractions – 'aren't', 'isn't' and the repeated use of 'it's' – which are examples of commonly used 'natural' spoken English. In relation to writing, although the DM may have come about, at least in part, as a move away from an exclusive focus on writing, using complete sentences orally may help when students need to produce written text in the target language. This is a potential positive, as long as the differences between spoken and written forms of the target language are made clear to the learners.

Before going on to explore the Audio-Lingual Method, we can briefly consider assessment of learning outcomes with the DM. Larsen-Freeman and Anderson (2011) stated that 'We did not actually see any formal evaluation in the class we observed' (p. 31), and after 25 years of sitting in language classrooms all over the world, that is not, in my experience, uncommon. However, Larsen-Freeman and Anderson add that, in the DM classes, 'students are asked to *use* the language, not to *demonstrate their knowledge about* the language' (p. 31, emphasis added). The possible examples they give are students being interviewed orally by the teacher, and students writing a paragraph based on 'something they have studied' (p. 31). Some of the main ways of assessing the DM outcomes are whether or not the learners can repeat and remember the words and phrases fed to them by the teacher and/or via the text. At a 'higher level', learning outcomes may be assessed by whether or not the learners can correctly manipulate the language forms, for example, making positive and negative statements out of questions. Also, as we have seen, other language features, such as asking questions correctly and incorporating contractions appropriately into their speech, can be used to assess some of the language learning outcomes.

ACTIVITY 6.3

Larsen-Freeman and Anderson (2011) make an important distinction between students being asked to 'use the language' and students being asked to demonstrate their 'knowledge about the language'. How would you explain the difference between knowing *about* a language, and *knowing* the language?

What Is the Audio-Lingual Method and Where Did It Come From?

In some ways, the Direct Method and the Audio-Lingual Method (ALM) are quite different. For example, Larsen-Freeman and

Anderson (2011) point out that the ALM 'drills students in the use of grammatical sentence patterns', whereas DM emphasizes 'vocabulary acquisition through its exposure to its use in situations' (p. 35). However, as the transcript from the DM lesson they observed clearly shows, there is a lot of 'listen-and-repeat' in the DM, which is also the basis of the ALM, as the name clearly indicates, that is, 'audio' for 'listen' and 'lingual' for 'speak' or 'say'.

The origins of the Audio-Lingual Method can be traced back to the work of Charles Fries (1887–1967) (1945, 1952, 1963). By the 1960s, it was being described in prestigious journals in the same way as we have seen with other methods presented. For example, Chastain and Woerdehoff (1968) wrote, in *The Modern Language Journal*, that 'In recent years there has been a decided shift in emphasis in the methodology for teaching modern foreign languages to the audiolingual approach' (p. 268). However, in another example of the ebb and flow of methods, Chastain and Woerdehoff describe the first part of what I call the 'Cycle of Dis/Content' in language teaching and learning, which was described above. This may be a natural, even healthy, cycle – as long as it does not lead to the problems of bandwagoning discussed in Chapter 1, that is, the indiscriminate rejection or acceptance of a methodology, without thorough and careful consideration, before jumping from one methodology to another.

Chastain and Woerdehoff (1968) begin on an anticipatory note: '*At its inception* the audiolingual method offered a revitalizing change in modern language instruction' (p. 268, emphasis added). They go on to explain that, as we have seen with other methods, 'The expectations of this newer instructional approach were reported glowingly' (p. 268). However, Chastain and Woerdehoff concluded that, in spite of such a glowing start, by that time, questions were being raised about 'the fundamental tenets supporting audio-lingual practices' (p. 268). Also in the 1960s, Hamilton asked whether the ALM in universities was a 'fad or panacea?' (1966, pp. 434–440). Again, in terms of how some methods come to be established as *the* method, Hamilton writes of how momentous the ALM in the USA was at that time:

'for the first time in the history of the world millions of dollars have been spent to show teachers and prospective teachers how to use a certain product, an oral-aural approach to the teaching of modern foreign languages in primary and secondary schools' (p. 434). Also, as it was the US Congress that appropriated those millions of dollars (which would be tens of millions today), and as the Modern Language Association of America was influential in establishing the ALM programs, 'in the minds of the masses' the ALM had acquired 'the stamp of approval of the MLA and the United States government' (Hamilton, 1966, p. 434). And again, we can see how powerful the influence of governments and academic organizations has been, and can still be today, in deciding officially that a method is *the* method.

Another important influence is the availability of new technologies, which today refers to Internet-based technologies. But in the 1960s, the cassette tape recorder was revolutionizing language classrooms, turning many of them into **language labs** – using the term 'laboratories' to give scientific credibility to the new approach and new technologies – with rows of tape recorders and headsets, and each language learner in his/her own little cubicle.

To go back to the beginning, before the seemingly inevitable methodological disenchantment set in, the work of Fries (1945, 1952, 1963) coincided with and was connected to the work of the behavioural psychologist B. F. Skinner (1904–1990) (1953). Skinner's experiments were based on the idea of 'conditioned responses', in which negative reinforcement, such as pain, was used to reduce instances of undesirable behaviour, and positive reinforcement, such as pleasure, was used to increase the likelihood of desirable behaviours. As result of these kinds of influences, and confluences, applied linguists such as Chastain and Woerdehoff (1968) wrote about the ALM in terms of audio-lingual habit theory, which had three basic characteristics: 'the study and manipulation of the structural patterns of the new language; the **inductive** presentation of new material; and the maintenance of the natural order of language learning' (p. 269).

By 'natural order', they meant that listening comprehension comes first, then speaking, then reading, and lastly, writing. However, this idea of a natural order may be another example of first language acquisition not being sufficiently distinguished from second and foreign language learning. Babies and children acquiring their first language do indeed follow the order of listening first (usually to their parents, siblings and other family members, initially); then comes speaking, often in the form of 'baby talk', followed by reading, with writing coming last. However, as we now know, there are many language learners, all over the world, whose second/foreign language learning is primarily for the purposes of passing international, standardized language exams. Historically, such exams focused on writing, as that may be the easiest modality to assess directly, followed by indirect measures of reading comprehension and listening comprehension, with assessment of speaking coming last. The reason for that is because speaking is the most labour-intensive, time-consuming and costly modality to assess, as it cannot be done *en masse*, and is usually done one-to-one or in pairs. Therefore, in the case of examination-driven language learning, the 'un-natural order' would be a reversal of the 'natural order', that is, first writing, then reading, then listening, and lastly, speaking. To their credit, Chastain and Woerdehoff (1968) accept in their discussion of the results of their experimental study that 'using all the senses in assimilating material being studied was superior to the natural order of presentation' (p. 279). They also concluded that '**deductive** presentation of material was superior to the inductive' and that 'drills stressing understanding were superior to **pattern practice**' (p. 279).

An explicit connection was made between the DM and the ALM by Thormann (1969), who connected the ALM to what he called the 'anti-grammar movement', which started in seventeenth-century France, with a 'striking awareness of the primacy of the direct method in language teaching' (p. 329). And in relation to the lack of agreement about the 'best' method (or 'best practice'), Thormann stated that 'It would probably be rash to assume that foreign language teachers could ever reach a unanimous opinion concerning the best method of instruction to be applied in the classroom' (p. 327). This is one of the things that may not have changed over the decades, and perhaps even over the centuries, although then, as now, there appear to have been similar pressures to accept *one* method as *the* method. As Thormann put it, in spite of disagreement about the effectiveness of the ALM in the previous 15 years, from the mid-1950s to the late 1960s, there emerged 'a general consensus, among the specialists at least, that the audio-lingual approach offered the best chance of success' (p. 327).

Therefore, on the one hand, we have the intellectual understanding that there is no 'best method' or 'best practice', but at the same time, there is the natural, emotional need for certainty and knowing that we are teaching and learning languages by the most effective and efficient means possible. Thormann (1969) even suggested that, for many of his fellow applied linguists of that time, the history of language teaching could be 'neatly divided into two parts' (p. 327) – before the ALM and after the ALM – such was the influence of the ALM at that time. Thormann concluded that the ALM and the anti-grammar movement 'could be another chapter ... in the evolution of the long history of language teaching' (p. 329).

ACTIVITY 6.4

Do you agree or disagree with Thormann (1969, p. 327) that 'It would probably be rash to assume that foreign language teachers could ever reach a unanimous opinion concerning the best method of instruction to be applied in the classroom'? Think about reasons for your agreement or disagreement.

What would be some of the benefits, and some of the problems, of language teachers reaching 'a unanimous opinion concerning the best method of instruction'?

Inside the ALM Classroom, the Pros and Cons of the ALM, and Assessment of Learning Outcomes

Larsen-Freeman and Anderson (2011) briefly observed an ALM class in Mali, West Africa, which had 34 students, who were 13 to 15 years old, and met five days a week, for one hour each time. This is an extract from the lesson transcript when the teacher is doing a 'backward build up drill' (p. 36), also known as an 'extension drill', in which the teacher starts at the end of the sentence and works backwards to the beginning:

'Teacher: Repeat after me: post office.
   Class: Post office.
Teacher: To the post office.
   Class: To the post office.
Teacher: Going to the post office.
   Class: Going to the post office.
Teacher: I'm going to the post office.
   Class: I'm going to the post office' (p. 36).

I have shown this extract to language teachers in many different countries, and the reaction is usually a negative one, of dismay, as one teacher put it: 'What's the point of that?' The understandable concern is that, in relation to assessment of learning outcomes, the students are 100% correct in their production of the target language, but that is because all they are doing is repeating, word for word, everything the teacher says, which is possible to do with no understanding at all on the part of the learners of what they are saying. As long as they have average short-term memory capacity, in terms of attention and retention spans, and can hear clearly what the teacher is saying, the learners can correctly reproduce what is said, with little or no understanding of what they are saying. However, with learners who are less competent with the target language, such forms of communication in the classroom – though they may be accused of being 'artificial' language – may help the learners build their confidence, and help them become familiar with hearing themselves producing the target language, orally, out loud. This kind of backward build up drill can also be used to show learners how rhythm, stress and intonation work at the phrasal and sentential levels. And it is worth noticing in the transcript above that the teacher is presenting and the students are practising 'natural' spoken forms of English, with the contraction 'I'm'. There is also, as noted above, the safety-in-numbers aspect of whole-class, choral repetition, which is not usually mentioned in the methodological literature.

Another example of language that may be called 'artificial' was also part of the English language lesson in Mali, when the teacher read out a two-person dialogue:

'Sally: Good morning, Bill.
Bill: Good morning, Sally.
Sally: How are you?
Bill: Fine, thanks. And you?
Sally: Fine. Where are you going?
Bill: I'm going to the post office.
Sally: I am too. Shall we go together?
Bill: Sure. Let's go' (p. 36).

Again, when I have shown this extract to language teachers in many different countries, their responses range from furrowed brows to bursts of laughter, because, as several of them have said, 'Nobody talks like that!' And as noted in previous chapters, this is the kind of dialogue that makes writers and researchers refer to the far-flung 'real world'. It is true that out of class, between fluent or native speakers of the target language, the sentences would not all be complete; for example, 'the post office', or even just 'post office', instead of the full sentence 'I'm going to the post office.' And the use of 'shall' has been, for some time now, far more limited than the use of 'will'. Added to this is the fact that both speakers happened to be going to the same post office, at the same time, with no prior arrangement to do so! More seriously, there is a complete lack of any form of negotiation, such as Bill asking Sally *why* she's going to the post office, or *which* post office, as there is often more than one, or either of them commenting with any surprise on the coincidence that they both happen to be going to the same place, at the same time.

These kinds of dialogue are, therefore, easy to dismiss as 'unreal' and 'unhelpful'. However, on closer inspection we can see that there is some 'real' target language in there, as fluent and native users do say, for example, 'Good morning + Name', 'How are you?', 'Fine, thanks. And you?' and 'Where are you going?' In fact, when I first came to live and work in Canada, some years ago, I was not used to strangers – such as the people who help you put your supermarket purchases in a shopping bag (which I was also not used to) – asking me 'How are you?' Consequently, it took me a while to realize that the 'correct' answer, in terms of what was expected, is 'Fine, thanks. And you?' Even today, many years later, I have to sometimes remind myself to give the correct reply, and under no circumstances, if interacting with someone I do not know, to actually answer the question with details of how I really am. So, for those who demand 'real' language in the language classroom, there are examples of that in these kinds of dialogue, as unlikely and as stilted they may seem or sound.

In recent years, having largely fallen out of favour for some decades, the ALM has been given a new lease of life, thanks to the Internet. For example, researchers at Microsoft Asia have reported on computer assisted audio-visual language learning (Wang, Qian, Scott, Chen, & Soong, 2012), which adds the visual element to the ALM that used to be provided by the teacher. Now, instead of a flesh-and-blood person, students may learn English by listening-and-repeating with 'a photorealistic person speaking English sentences extracted from the Internet' (p. 38). Such a computer-generated person is described as a 'talking head [that] generates karaoke-style short synthetic videos demonstrating oral English' (p. 38). Such technologies are in their relatively early stages, and it may be some years before they are commonplace in classrooms. But in the same way as the then-new technology of tape recorders was one of the main drivers of a major methodological shift towards the ALM, increasing Internet access is now doing for the ALM what the tape recorder did for the ALM before, by providing computerized digital models for students to listen to and then repeat.

> **ACTIVITY 6.5**
>
> What kinds of 'new technologies' do you use in your language lessons, and how do you make use of them?
>
> Do you make use of any 'old technologies' such as tape recorders, and if so, what do you use them for?

To a large extent, assessment of learning outcomes with ALM is based on the learners being able to repeat whatever it is they have heard. Beyond that, the greater their ability to *accurately* 'mimic' the sounds, words and sentences they have heard, in terms of, for example, rhythm, stress and intonation, the more successful the learning outcomes may be perceived to be. And beyond these two sets of parameters, if the learners can re-produce what they have heard, mimicked accurately, and produced correctly in response to an item of target language input, then that might be considered to be a higher level of 'success'. However, the question of appropriateness is more difficult. For example, if a learner of English meets someone for the first time, it is appropriate for the learner to say, as a somewhat formal greeting, 'Nice to meet you'. However, after that first meeting, it is often more appropriate to say something like 'Good to see you' or 'Good to see you *again*', as in most English-dominant contexts, 'Nice to meet you' is only used the first time people meet. Interestingly, even after longer periods of time, if one person were to greet another, after the two had met before, with 'Nice to meet you', the reply might well be something like 'We met before [pause] but you may not remember ...' However, methodologies such as the ALM do not accommodate or allow for such differences, which may be subtle, but which do nonetheless alter the meaning communicated in important ways, which can lead to communication breakdowns in even the most basic of introductory interactions.

Suggested Readings

In Diane Larsen-Freeman and Marti Anderson's *Techniques and Principles in Language Teaching* (2011), Chapter 3 (pp. 25–34) is on the DM, and Chapter 4 (pp. 35–50) is on the ALM.

In Jack Richards and Theodore Rodgers' *Approaches and Methods in Language Teaching* (2014), Chapter 4 (pp. 58–80) is on the ALM.

Many years ago, N. S. Prabhu published a paper in *TESOL Quarterly* titled 'There is No Best Method – Why?' (1990, Volume 24, Issue 2, pages 161–176). In answer to his question, the first reason he gives is: 'different methods are best for different contexts' (p. 161). As such, Prabhu's paper is an important historical point in the challenging of notions of what is considered to be methodologically best, regardless of context.

CHAPTER 7

The Grammar Translation Method

Before reading this chapter, consider the following questions:

- In your language classes and courses, do you teach the grammar of the target language? If so, what are some of the approaches, methods and techniques that you use to teach that grammar?
- How do you see, and how would you describe, the relationships between the forms and the functions of a language, that is, between how a language is structured and how a language is used to communicate specific messages?
- How much, if any, translation do you use between your learners' first language(s) and the target language? How do you decide what to translate, and when to translate?

Introduction and Overview

In all three editions of Richards and Rodgers' *Approaches and Methods in Language Teaching* (1986, 2001, 2014), the Grammar Translation Method (GTM) is given barely two pages out of 170 pages, 270 pages and 390 pages, respectively. These numbers show that, although the field of language teaching methodologies has grown considerably over the intervening 30 years or so since the first edition, the GTM has been seen as a consistently minor concern during that time. However, in all three editions of Larsen-Freeman's *Techniques and Principles in Language Teaching* (1986, 2000 and with Anderson in 2011), the first chapter is still about the GTM, reflecting the fact that, for many readers, the origins of language teaching and learning go back to the GTM. The difference in coverage between the two sets of books – Richards and Rodgers' and Larsen-Freeman's – can be accounted for by the fact that, even though the GTM may still be widely employed in a significant number of contexts, it is no longer being researched and reported on. This difference shows that 'popular' and 'widely used' are not necessarily the same thing, as the GTM may still be widely used in some places, but it is no longer popular, in the sense of being actively promoted by governments, researchers and textbook publishers.

The Grammar Translation Method

The Grammar Translation Method goes back centuries. According to Howatt (1984), 'The earliest grammar-translation course for the teaching of English was written in 1793 by Johann Christian Flick (1763–1821)' (p. 132). Howatt also noted, in his chapter on the GTM (pp. 130–146), that one reason for the 'prejudice against the teaching of English and modern languages' in England at that time was that 'girls were good at them' (p. 134). This became clear in 1862, when women were first allowed to take the Cambridge and Oxford Local Examinations, which were launched in 1858: 'from the outset they [the girls] proved they were better than the boys at French, German, and the more "expressive" aspects of English' (p. 134). This is important, because the gender differences between male and female language learners have been a growing area of research in recent years. For example, Selma Babayiğit, in her 2015 paper on language learning and gender differences in relation to writing, found that 'Girls outperformed boys on all dimensions, except organisation' (p. 33). However, it turns out that these differences were noted as far back as the mid-1800s in England, much to the consternation of some of the leading universities at the time, such as Cambridge and Oxford (Howatt, 1984).

Howatt reminds us that the GTM started out 'as a simple approach to language learning for young schoolchildren', which was 'grossly distorted in the collision of interests between the classicists and their modern language rivals' (p. 136). Such divisions may remind some readers of the on-going gaps between applied linguistics and everyday classroom language teaching. In each of the early GTM lessons, one or two grammar rules were introduced, together with a relatively short list of vocabulary items, and some practice examples that the students had to translate with the help of the teacher. In assessing such GTM lessons, Howatt stated: 'Boring, maybe, but hardly the horror story we are sometimes asked to believe' (p. 136). In fact, in Howatt's estimation, GTM 'was so ordinary that it is sometimes difficult to see what all the fuss was about' (p. 136).

Howatt's comment about 'all the fuss' reiterates a recurring point, made in previous chapters, about the rise and fall of language methodologies, in relation to what can happen to relatively straightforward ideas, presented in classrooms by experienced teachers working with motivated learners. Somewhere along the line, the methodological ideas become so big and so complicated that they form the basis of heated debates and deep divisions between those who oppose and those who support what, by then, have gone from being methods to becoming movements. There are many factors influencing such cycles, as we have seen with the other methodologies, but in relation to the GTM specifically, a major part of the problem was that the GTM 'contained seeds which eventually grew into a jungle of obscure rules, endless lists of gender classes and gender-class exceptions, self-conscious "literary" archaisms, snippets of philology' and other kinds of dense and impenetrable 'undergrowth', so that there ended up being 'a total loss of genuine feeling for living language' (Howatt, p. 136).

Another recurring point, discussed in previous chapters, is the non-linear progression of methodologies. However, that is sometimes how these methodologies are presented, or what is implied in the way they are presented, that is, as a gradual development along a line of improvement, with each new methodology being better than the last one, and with each new methodology being the *one* that will, finally, be *the* methodology. (See the discussion of bandwagoning in Chapter 1.) That linear improvement is not necessarily the case, and it was not so with the GTM, as Howatt pointed out, concluding his chapter by expressing sadness that 'all the excellent situational teaching between the sixteenth and the eighteenth centuries' (p. 144) was followed by GTM course books with such 'futile' exchanges as 'What bread has the baker? He has good bread' (p. 144). Howatt lays the blame for the unfortunate state of affairs at that time squarely on the shoulders of the university-based scholars, as 'Academicism laid a heavy hand on the teaching of languages in the nineteenth century' (p. 145) in England, France, Germany and elsewhere in Europe.

ACTIVITY 7.1

I have heard, in methodological talks and workshops, many different metaphors and analogies used to describe the grammar of a language. For example, 'grammar is the foundation of a language, which forms the basis on which all else is built', and 'grammar is like the scientific formulas of a language, which tell you which components can be combined, in what proportions, to produce predictable and reproducible results'. What metaphors or analogies would you use to describe the grammar of a language?

Added to the 'heavy hand of academicism' were the production and publication of many GTM-based language teaching and learning textbooks, and governmental adoption of certain methodologies. As we saw in Chapter 3 on TBLT, such governmental endorsement is an important factor, because when most governments endorse – or mandate – a method, usually only *one* method is officially mandated. As a result of these kinds of influence, the GTM grew, flourished and dominated, in spite of its limitations, for the next 150 years or so, from the early 1800s until the 1950s. For example, in the first and second semesters of the 1930–1931 school year, a group of 28 freshman students of French, at the Indiana State College Training School in the USA, were part of a study, carried out by Mary Olga Peters, a professor at Indiana State University, comparing the Direct Method (DM) and the GTM. The DM can be thought of as the opposite of the GTM, because there is no translation allowed in the DM, as 'meaning is to be conveyed directly in the target language through the use of demonstration and visual aids, with no recourse to the students' native languages' (Larsen-Freeman & Anderson, 2011, p. 25). (See Chapter 6 for details of the Direct Method.)

Peters presented her findings to the American Association of French Teachers in 1932, at Indiana University. She reported that during the GTM lessons, she observed the following: '(1) Studying a list of disconnected words (vocabulary); (2) Memorizing grammatical rules and exceptions; (3) Oral translation from the native tongue to the foreign tongue and vice versa; (4) Written translation; (5) Teaching of pronunciation; (6) Practice in reading aloud and listening to some spoken French' (1934, pp. 528–529). Based on an extensive battery of pre- and post-tests, Peters concluded that each method, the DM and the GTM, has its benefits and limitations, its pros and cons. As we have noted before, although this fact may seem self-evident to any teacher and any learner who has spent substantial amounts of time in language classrooms, the drive to adopt one methodology and reject the others can be surprisingly and overwhelmingly strong.

In favour of the GTM, the students' test scores were higher for translation, vocabulary and comprehension of written questions. For the DM, the students' test scores were higher for dictation, reading, pronunciation, aural comprehension and grammar. It is, then, perhaps ironic that the scores of the students who were taught with the DM, not the GTM, were higher on the grammar test. But one reason for this seemingly contradictory result is that the students in the DM classes were taught some grammar, but that it was not the explicit or main focus of the DM lessons. This was one of the problems of the experimental method in language education research, which also reigned supreme for more than a century. Methods cannot be isolated in this way, because most teachers will try different things until they find those that work with those particular learners in that particular setting. And in trying those different things, they will inevitably draw on different methodologies and approaches – even if they do not know the official names that have been given to those methodologies and approaches.

By the end of the 1990s, the GTM was, to use Howatt's (1984) wording, being blamed for a whole range of 'horrors'. For example, in a number of countries the low levels of language competence were being attributed to the use of the GTM, based on the assumption that the national exams encouraged the use of the GTM. Researching the situation in Japan, Watanabe (1996) translated (from Japanese to English) extracts from an official report by the *Gogaku Kyoiku Kenkyujo*, or Institute for Language Education. In the report, the following assumptions and claims were made: 'high-school teachers are forced to give priority to teaching English through GT to meet the demands imposed by various university entrance exams (1988: 47)' and 'Because translation is a time-consuming activity, teachers do not have enough time left to teach other skills, such as writing, listening and speaking. In fact, high-school teaching revolves around GT rather than the development of communication skills ... (1989: 49)' (Watanabe, 1996, p. 319). However, Watanabe found that there were a large number of factors contributing to the teachers' use of the GTM, including the teachers' personal beliefs, their educational backgrounds and their own prior language learning experiences, which showed the importance of teacher education (p. 332). Again, while this may not be news to experienced language teachers who are aware of their own practices and where these come from, the fact that many different factors account for the methods used continued to be a data-based and research-led endeavour for some time (see Chapter 2 on Context). Whatever the complex causes for low levels of target language competence, and whatever teachers' reasons for using the GTM, it was being blamed for many or even most of the problems and difficulties of teaching and learning second and foreign languages.

ACTIVITY 7.2

Why do you think the GTM came to be blamed for so many of the difficulties, challenges and problems of language teaching and learning? If the GTM is one of the causes of these problems, what are some of the other, non-GTM challenges in your context?

By the early years of the new millennium, the GTM was being described in these kinds of terms: 'The major focus of this method tended to be on reading and writing, with relatively little attention paid to speaking and listening. Vocabulary was typically taught in lists, and a high priority given to accuracy, and the ability to construct correct sentences' (Griffiths & Parr, 2001, p. 247). Another of the limitations of the GTM that had been recognized by that time was its teacher-centredness, and the fact that 'Consideration of what students might do to promote their own learning had little or no place in grammar-translation theory, which tended to assume that, if students simply followed the method, learning would result *as a matter of course*' (p. 247, emphasis added). The idea that learning follows as a matter of course is the same kind of convenient assumption that we saw with CBI/CLIL, in which 'the acquisition of language is seen as *a natural consequence or by-product* of subject matter learning' (Rodgers, 2006, p. 373, emphasis added). To be fair to the GTM, the same could be true of the assumptions and expectations of the proponents of many other methods, including CLT, in which one of the main ideas was that, by putting learners into groups and having them interact meaningfully, language learning would occur 'naturally', while the instructor merely facilitated.

However, it may be that in more recent years, the GTM has been making something of a comeback. For example, in 2010, a book was published about EFL reading instruction in high school classrooms in South Korea (Oak, 2010) with a focus on what Oak called the 'pedagogic life of the grammar translation method' (p. 1). Based on the observations, recordings and transcripts of 22 language lessons, Oak found that 'some teachers reviewed a considerable number of words and phrases, in addition to points of grammar' (p. 1). This finding reiterates the point made above, that the GTM may not be inherently 'bad', but it is limited. Therefore, if learners are only doing the first two of the six points observed by Peters (1934), that is, '(1) Studying a list of disconnected words (vocabulary); (2) Memorizing grammatical rules and exceptions' (p. 528), then that is indeed limiting. But her other observed points – oral translation, written translation, pronunciation practice, reading aloud practice, and speaking aloud – can all help with the learning of a second or foreign language.

Regarding the teacher-centredness of the GTM, although many learners in many contexts would find this kind of teacher-centredness constraining, there is the fact that every student represents a unique combination of different learning styles. As we now recognize that the range of learning styles in a class can be as wide as the number of learners in that class, we must accept that some learners may prefer a more teacher-centred teaching style, if that is what they are familiar with and comfortable with. Therefore, another potential irony is that, if we are being truly 'learner-centred', and some learners prefer a more teacher-centred methodology, such as the GTM, then we need to accept that fact, even if it conflicts with our particular beliefs about 'good' language teaching. The question, then, may not be whether or not to use the GTM, but what are the limitations of a particular method, and how can those limitations be overcome? One way of overcoming such limitations is to use more than one method, as part of a 'principled eclecticism', based on a 'coherent, pluralistic approach to language teaching' (Mellow, 2002, p. 1) (see Chapter 4), and not limit the learners to exposure to a single method.

In relation to the possibility of grammar instruction making a comeback, it may also be true that, in some contexts, GTM never left. Richards and Rodgers (2014) give four possible reasons for this long-time use of the GTM, in spite of its limitations, starting with a 'limited command of spoken English of language teachers' (p. 7), which relates to the fact that the GTM was at its height when language teaching and learning were focused on reading and writing. Another possible reason given by Richards and Rodgers (2014) for the continued use of the GTM by some teachers in some contexts is 'the fact this was the method their teachers used' (p. 7), thereby perpetuating certain methodological life cycles as they are passed on from one pedagogical generation to the next. Another reason given by Richards and Rodgers (2014) is that GTM can give teachers 'a sense of control and authority in the classroom' (p. 7), which may be especially important with large classes. As we will see in Chapter 8, on the alternative and humanistic methodologies, small class sizes are a key component in the use of such methodologies, but small class sizes are also a luxury that only certain economies can afford.

This economic factor was given by Jin and Cortazzi (2011) as another factor to explain why the GTM has persisted in some contexts, but withered away in many others. They concluded that traditional approaches to language teaching and learning 'have persisted longer in most developing parts of the world than in the more economically developed ones, due to the slower development of educational systems and language teacher training, cultural perceptions and different ways of change, limited learning resources and finances' (pp. 558–559, cited in Richards & Rodgers, 2014, p. 7). It is possible that the most effective way to teach and learn anything, but perhaps especially a second or foreign language, may be one-to-one and face-to-face (including such arrangements online). However, as class sizes increase, and the teacher–student ratios change so that there are fewer teachers teaching more learners, there may be pressure to use less effective methods both for economic reasons and to maintain teacher control of the class, as we discussed earlier in relation to TBLT (Chapter 3).

In terms of GTM never having left, and in relation to Oak's reference to the 'pedagogic life of the grammar translation method', Hussein Assalahi, working with English language learners in Saudi Arabia, asked: 'Why is the grammar-translation method still alive in the Arab world?' (2013, pp. 589–599). In relation to teachers' beliefs and their implications for EFL teacher education in that part of the world, and in answering his question, Assalahi noted that 'to date, there is no consensus among language educators about how best to teach grammar' (p. 590). He also considered the long-standing debate about whether the GTM should focus on the grammatical forms of the language, in relation to, for example, parts of speech and grammar rules, versus a focus on grammatical functions, for example, categories such as direct and indirect objects. This distinction relates to Kramsch's 'dubious dichotomies and deceptive symmetries' (1993, pp. 2–9) (see Chapter 2), which include 'grammar versus communication' (pp. 4–5), with these two being along a continuum, rather than a black–white dichotomy.

There is relatively little to say about assessment of learning outcomes with the GTM, as the assessment is based on the name, that is, the ability to translate from the learners' first language to the target language with the maximum amount of grammatical accuracy. In this assessment model, the more grammatical mistakes that are made in the translation, the lower the final test score, and vice versa. This ease of testing is one of the other reasons for the longevity of the GTM. As Larsen-Freeman and Anderson (2011) note, in their discussion of the GTM, 'Having the students get *the* correct answer is considered very important' (p. 20, emphasis added), with the focus on one right answer, thereby making marking relatively quick and easy. In relation to the language modalities, the focus of assessment of learning outcomes with the GTM is usually on writing. Traditionally, translation of a literary passage to or from the target language is carried out as the basis of the test or exam. In addition to writing, learners in GTM classes may also have their reading comprehension examined, in which the test-takers read a passage in the target language, and answer questions in the target language, by giving written responses, also in the target language.

One of the other reasons why there is relatively little to say about the GTM today is because, as Richards and Rodgers (2014) put it, the GTM is a method 'for which there is no theory. There is no literature that offers a rationale or justification for it or that attempts to relate it to issues in linguistics, psychology or educational theory' (p. 7). This statement highlights the importance of theory in the acceptance or rejection of a methodology, and as we saw in the academic publications regarding TBLT (Chapter 3), the stronger the academic support for a method, the more widespread will be its use. However, academic support is a relatively recent criterion for acceptance of a particular methodology, mostly within the last 50 years or so, compared with the centuries over which the GTM has been used. In relation to the ways in which methodologies grow based on the profile of the proponents, by which high-profile supporters of a particular methodology can encourage its widespread adoption, and vice versa, Richards and Rodgers (2014) conclude that the GTM today 'has no advocates' (p. 7). Although the GTM did have its advocates, they have long since passed, and with them the belief that the GTM should be employed as a separate and distinctive methodology, rather than being a component of all approaches and methodologies.

Suggested Readings

Although the GTM is no longer being actively promoted as a desirable methodology, some comparative research is still being carried out. For example, Hina Durrani (2016) reports on the attitudes of undergraduates at a university in Pakistan towards the GTM and CLT (*Advances in Language and Literary Studies*, Volume 7, Issue 4, pages 167–172). Interestingly, Durrani found that 'the students had a positive attitude towards GTM and their attitude was less favorable towards CLT' (p. 167).

In Diane Larsen-Freeman and Marti Anderson's *Techniques and Principles in Language Teaching* (2011), Chapter 2 (pp. 13–23) is on the GTM.

Pawel Scheffler (2013) reported on a study in which secondary school Polish learners of English (in Poland) were asked to 'evaluate two consciousness-raising activities they had performed: a grammar-translation task and a communicative language exchange' (p. 255). According to Scheffler, 'The results show that the learners considered translating sentences from Polish into English to be as useful and interesting as communicatively oriented consciousness raising' (p. 255) (*Language Awareness*, Volume 22, Issue 3, pages 255–269).

CHAPTER 8

Humanistic and Alternative Methods

Before you read this chapter, consider the following questions:

- What do you understand by the terms 'humanistic methods' and 'alternative methods'?
- If you are familiar with the idea of 'alternative methods', what are they alternatives to, and why are alternatives necessary?
- Have you ever used such methods to teach English? If so, were these methods effective, for you and/or your students?

Introduction and Overview

In this penultimate chapter, we will look at four well-known but now relatively little-used methodologies, which are grouped together, as they are all considered to be humanistic and alternative. In the first part of this chapter, we will look at Suggestopedia, which is sometimes referred to as Desuggestopedia, and which is based on the theories of Georgi Lozanov (1926–2012). This section is longer than the others, which partly reflects the fact that more studies on Suggestopedia appear to have been published than on the other humanistic and alternative methods, and because a number of original concepts are introduced in this first part of the chapter, including: the *Mystique of Methods*; *Methods and Magic*; the *Methods Marketplace*; and *Methods as Messiah*. Total Physical Response, or TPR, based on the work of James Asher, is examined in the second part of this chapter, where *Niche Methods* and *Methods for Specific Purposes* are discussed. And in the third part, we consider Community Language Learning, or CLL, proposed by Charles Curran (1913–1978), in relation to *Methods as Medicine* and *The Men Behind the Methods*. In the last part of the chapter, we consider the Silent Way (about which there is relatively little to say), based on the theories of Caleb Gattegno (1911–1998).

Because each method is now relatively rarely reported on, the origins, principles and practices, as well as the pros and cons of each method, together with a note on assessment of learning outcomes, are considered together, for each method, rather than separately. It is also important to acknowledge that, within the ebb and flow, the rise and fall, the in and out of methodologies, some of those that have, by now, fallen into disuse, disregard and perhaps disrepair may one day make a comeback.

In terms of definitions, in this chapter I am using the most general meaning of 'humanistic', that is, 'a belief system based on the principle that people's spiritual and emotional needs can be satisfied *without following a god or religion*' (*CALD*, emphasis added). The last part of the definition may turn out to be somewhat ironic, as many of the humanistic methods we will look at in this chapter appear to have required some sort of 'blind faith' on the part of the teachers and the learners. And for 'alternative', in the context of this chapter, I found the following definition most applicable: 'Alternative things are considered to be unusual and often have a small but enthusiastic group of people who support them' (*CALD*).

Suggestopedia

After a book published by Georgi Lozanov, originally in Bulgarian, in 1971, titled *Suggestology*, and a couple of articles (Lozanov, 1975a, 1975b), Suggestopedia started to be noticed by the international academic community in 1978, with the publication of Lozanov's *Suggestology and Outlines of Suggestopedy*. This was the first of his works to be translated into English. Lozanov (1926–2012) is described as 'a Bulgarian psychiatrist-psychotherapist, brain physiologist and an educator ... creator of the science Suggestology and its application in pedagogy – Suggestopedia', which is described as 'the pedagogy operating on the level of the reserves of mind' (lozanov.org). Lozanov was also, according to the website, the creator and director of the State Suggestology Research Institute in Sofia, Bulgaria (from 1966 to 1984), the Centre for Suggestology and Development of Personality at the Sofia University, The International Centre for Desuggestology in Vienna, Austria, and The International Centre for Teacher Training in Voralberg, Austria. The site also notes that Lozanov was 'detained under home arrest for the period 1980–1989 until the political changes in Bulgaria'. During those ten years, the world heard little from Lozanov, as the goal of the Bulgarian government appears to have been to ensure that Bulgaria retained control of the Suggestopedia. Therefore, one of the things that make Suggestopedia interesting – or 'Desuggestopedia', as it was later re-labelled by Lozanov – apart from what it is and how it is done, is how it shows the ways in which the life cycle of one particular methodology can be tied so closely to the life cycle of one particular individual.

ACTIVITY 8.1

Have you heard of Suggestology, Suggestopedia and Desuggestopedia before? If so, how would you explain them to a colleague who has not previously come across these terms?

If these terms are new to you, what do you think they mean, based on their word forms?

In *Suggestology and Outlines of Suggestopedy*, Lozanov explained that 'Suggestopedy started purely as a psychological experiment aimed at increasing memory capacities in the educational process' (1978, p. 5). He noted that 'Suggestopedy, as an experimental method of suggestology, has revealed new laws and patterns of human memory' (p. 6). Lozanov's explanations of the benefits of Suggestopedia include statements such as: 'As a universal form of communication and inner re-adaptation related mainly to paraconscious psychical activity and containing the informative algorhythmical[sic]-re-programming aspects activating man's mental and emotional potentials, the desuggestive-suggestive liberating-stimulating mechanisms have proved to be of exceptional importance for understanding the activity of the individual' (1978, p. 11). Although, at around 40 words, that is not an especially long sentence, it seems much longer, and requires several re-readings, which is one of the problems of methodologies that, accidentally or deliberately, make it so difficult for others to understand the principles of what they are proposing.

In the same year as *Outlines of Suggestology and Suggestopedy* appeared, Allyn Prichard and Jean Taylor summarized the principles and practices of Suggestopedia more succinctly and more understandably: 'Lozanov's entire instructional technology is focused on freeing the hyperlearning reserve; that is, he believes that humans are capable of learning much faster than we ever thought possible if instructional procedures include use of the power of suggestion' (1978, p. 81). This notion of a 'hyperlearning reserve' appears to have come from the idea that humans use as little as 10 per cent of their brain, making the possibilities limitless if the other 90 per cent could be tapped into (Sidis, 1919). However, that figure of 10 per cent has been largely discredited by now, with current neurological thinking being that up to 100 per cent of the brain's potential may be used every day by most of us (Boyd, 2008).

According to Prichard and Taylor (1978), there are four basic principles of Suggestopedia, starting with: 'The student is enveloped by inaccurate beliefs concerning his ability to learn. Sources found everywhere in his environment generate these beliefs' (p. 82). These sources include the students' low self-esteem, which can be inadvertently reinforced by negative non-verbal communication from the teacher. The second principle states that 'The teacher has at his or her command several tools to counteract the effect of negative suggestion and to create a positive atmosphere which promotes higher learning rates than the teacher previously thought were possible' (p. 83). The tools include positive verbal and non-verbal feedback from the teacher, as well as the use of drama, mental relaxation and breathing exercises, and music, which are used 'in combination to help the student feel good about himself and to feel relaxed and comfortable in the classroom' (p. 83). (Interestingly, although the teacher may be male or female, the student is always referred to using the male pronoun only.)

The third principle is based on three 'barriers to suggestion', which are called the 'critical-logical', the 'intuitive-emotional' and the 'ethical-moral' barriers (p. 83). As the names imply, these barriers arise within the students when they are faced with suggestions that contradict their sense of what is versus what should be, suggestions that cause them to feel insecure or uncomfortable, and suggestions that contradict their ethical worldview, respectively. The teacher should, then, consciously and carefully avoid doing or saying anything that would cause these barriers to go up within the students' minds. (See Dhority (1991) for a discussion of how Lozanov's work relates to Krashen's work on the affective filter.) The fourth principle relates to how the teacher 'orchestrates suggestion so that it will have a positive impact upon the student's expectancy of himself and of the learning process' (p. 83). These expectations include the suggestion that the student 'can learn much more than he thought he could' and that 'learning is more pleasant than he thought it could ever be'. This orchestration of suggestions should also have a 'positive impact on the student's motivation to participate whole-heartedly and freely in the scheduled classroom activities' (p. 83).

This kind of focus may reflect Lozanov's own experiences as a language teacher and/or as a language learner growing up in Bulgaria in the 1930s and 1940s, which would have included World War II (1939–1945). It is not possible to know what effects such experiences have on an individual, not least because each person is affected differently. But it is likely that such experiences cannot *not* shape an individual's understanding of the world, resulting, in this case, in Lozanov's concern for students' positive self-esteem, and his belief that learning can be and should be a positive experience. This belief may be taken for granted, as a guiding principle, by many language teaching professionals around the world, but the fact remains that for many teachers and learners, perhaps including those such as Lozanov, it may not be a positive experience. It may, for example, be an experience in which the self-esteem of the individuals involved – which may include the teacher's, too – is greatly challenged.

Another interesting aspect of Suggestopedia is the fact that, although it started to become popular at around the same time as CLT (see Chapter 4) and notions of learner-centred teaching were taking hold, Suggestopedia is, in fact, extremely teacher-centred, as Bancroft (1982) noted: 'In accordance with yoga, both Sophrology and Suggestology stress the importance of the personality of the therapist or teacher. Lozanov emphasizes the importance of the "guru"' (p. 374). Sophrology refers to the study of human consciousness, mental relaxation and pain relief, which was proposed by Alfonos Caycedo, a Colombian neuro-psychiatrist whose work influenced and was influenced by Lozanov's work.

References to Sophrology, yoga and gurus show the extent to which Suggestopedia was based on 'techniques derived from the ancient East' (Bancroft, 1982, p. 373), which imbues what is being done with what can be called the *Mystique of Methods*. This is not a phrase used in language methodology, but has been referred to in other fields, such as Anthropology. For example, in *Research Methods in Anthropology* (2011), Bernard writes that 'There was something rather mystical about the how-to of fieldwork; it seemed inappropriate to make the experience too methodical' (p. vii).

Bancroft gives a detailed description of her use of Suggestopedia in the beginner-level French language classes she taught with students at the University of Toronto in Canada (where, in addition to English, French is the other official language of the country). The lessons started with the teacher reading the lesson text aloud, 'fairly slowly and in a "dramatic" way, i.e., using as many voice levels as appropriate' (1982, p. 377). The teacher then read the lesson text aloud a second time, 'but now in a soft, soothing voice over a background of one or more baroque slow movements' (p. 377). Between the two readings, the students were asked to close their eyes, relax, 'breathe deeply from the abdomen' (p. 378), sit upright and listen to the music.

The third part of the one-hour lesson proceeded much like an Audio-Lingual Methods (ALM) class (see Chapter 6), as the students 'repeated the text sentence by sentence or word group by word group, individually and in chorus, in imitation of the teacher's voice and accent' (p. 377). This kind of activity highlights again the teacher-centredness of Suggestopedia, even though, at first glance, because of its concern for the well-being of the learner, it might appear to be more learner-centred than it actually is. Or, one of the distinctive features of this method may be that it is one of the very few – perhaps the only one – that manages to be both teacher-centred and learner-centred at the same time (depending on how those two terms are defined). For the reading and repeating, short texts are used, grammatical explanations are kept to the minimum, and there is no translation.

One of the problems of the 'overnight success' and the high-speed rise and fall of Suggestopedia was that it went, very quickly, from being an interesting set of possibilities to a commercially marketed product, in the form of *Superlearning*, which is the title of the book by Sheila Ostrander and Lynn

Schroeder, with Nancy Ostrander (1979). These three authors claimed that readers would be able to, among other things, 'Learn language with speed ... Raise your grades and shorten your study hours' and 'Add undreamed-of dimensions to your abilities, using innovative, easy-to-follow techniques *proved in worldwide studies*' (back cover, emphasis added). Inside the book, equally ambitious claims and statements are made: for example, that by using Suggestopedia '1,000 words had been learned in a day ... this system speeds up learning from five to fifty times, increases retention, *requires virtually no effort on the part of the student*' (Ostrander, Schroeder & Ostrander 1979, p. 15, emphasis added). In addition to effortless language learning, according to Ostrander, Schroeder and Ostrander, 'the method appeared to improve health and cure stress-related illnesses' (p. 33). And, citing the work of the creator, they stated: 'In 1977, Lozanov reported some tests showed people capable of absorbing even 3,000 words per day' (p. 35).

Given such hyperbolic claims, it is easy to see why Suggestopedia caught on to the extent that it did. However, this may be a good example of 'too much, too soon', in which the makers and sellers of products promise the consumers far more than the product can deliver, especially within the timeframes promised. The 'Superlearning' hype stopped short of using the word 'magical' to describe the results of this particular method, but this is a good example of what can be called *Method as Magic*. As with the *Mystique of Methods*, *Method as Magic* is not a phrase used in language education, but it is recognized in other fields, such as Cultural Studies (see, for example, Harnad, 2006).

Not only do claims such as 'proved in worldwide studies' appear to have been unsubstantiated, but they were actively challenged. For example, Michael Wagner and Germaine Tilney (1983) published the results of their experiments on 'The effect of "Superlearning Techniques" on the vocabulary acquisition and alpha brainwave production of language learners' (pp. 5–17). During the teaching of 300 words of German vocabulary to 21 students at Florida International University in the USA, Wagner and Tilney used relaxation tapes, made by Superlearning Inc., together with the Superlearning methodology. Wagner and Tilney also used an electroencephalograph to measure brainwave activity, as changes in such activity were claimed as one of the beneficial effects of Suggestopedia, and partly responsible for its success.

Wagner and Tilney concluded that 'the combination of relaxation, special breathing, intonation, and music apparently were not enough to produce "super" results ... it remains to be shown that "Superlearning" really is better than an experienced, successful "traditional" teacher in a "traditional" classroom setting' (p. 16). However, Wagner and Tilney did note that, in the commercial Superlearning packaging of Suggestopedia, marketed and sold by Ostrander, Schroeder and Ostrander (1979), 'Much of Lozanov's technique has been left out of Superlearning' (p. 16), which may have made the study more of an assessment of Superlearning than of Suggestopedia. This is what can happen when markets get hold of methods before they are ready – the 'they' here being learners, teachers, parents and other non-commercial stakeholders in the educational-economic process. This might be called the *Methods Marketplace*, with Suggestopedia as one of the stalls peddling the wares of the methods promoters in the 'marketplace of ideas'.

Another incarnation of Suggestopedia was Suggestive Accelerated Learning and Teaching (SALT), which was reported on in a number of brief and largely anecdotal papers (see, for example, Botha, 1985; Gassner-Roberts, 1986). Some data-based research, using pre- and post-test scores, concluded that 'Teachers will find that suggestopedia is a unique combination of many time-tested techniques (e.g., presenting material in an enthusiastic manner) plus some innovative additions (e.g., passive review with classical music)' (Ramirez, 1986, p. 330). This kind of conclusion highlights the fact that enthusiastic teachers generally engage more successfully with their learners, who then learn more effectively, and the fact that playing some music during a language lesson is something that some teachers have always done (and will always do) – even if they have never heard of Suggestopedia.

An important point here is that there are very few features that are truly unique to one particular method. Therefore, as discussed in Chapter 7, teaching some grammar, and translating some words, does not make it a GTM lesson. Likewise, playing some music, and spending some time making sure that the learners are comfortable before the lesson begins and during the lesson, does not make it a Suggestopedia lesson, any more than having the learners do some listening-and-repeating makes it an ALM lesson (see Chapter 6).

In spite of the failure of Superlearning/SALT to meet the expectations it created, and to keep the promises it made, some positive, data-based results were reported in language classes that used Suggestopedia. For example, Odendaal (2013), working with Afrikaans-speaking students in South Africa, used a number of English language proficiency tests, together with questionnaires. She concluded that 'Suggestopedia seems able to break through the barrier of fossilizations and it enables students to think in the TL [target language/English] and speak with greater confidence and fluency. The findings of the proficiency tests bear this out' (p. 29). In relation to Krashen's work, as mentioned above, Odendaal also concluded that 'Suggestopedia seems to succeed in breaking down the affective filter that impedes language acquisition. Students experience a decrease of tension, an increase in relaxation, an increase in self-confidence and faith in their performance in the TL [target language]' (p. 29). This explicit reference to faith is relatively unusual in the methodological literature, except in relation to the work of Christian educators in ELT, such as Stevick (1990, see below), since faith implies a strong belief in the absence of concrete proof of existence. But, in spite of its conspicuous absence from the mountains of methodological literature, faith does appear to be an important factor in the failure or success of a method, in relation to the extent to which the teachers and the learners believe in the power of the method to enable them to achieve their goals, aims and objectives. This can be called *Method as Messiah*, in terms of 'someone who people believe will save them from trouble or a difficult situation' (*MODE*). I must be clear here that I am not using 'messiah' in relation to any religion, but referring to the notion, which appears to be common in many religions, that someone or something will solve everyone's problems and absolve them of their responsibilities. From this comes the idea that if we could just find the 'right' or the 'best' method, everything would be all right.

One of the other limitations of (De)Suggestopedia is that, apart from test scores gathered for research purposes, assessment of learning outcomes was not felt to be in keeping with the spirit of the methodology, as formal assessment procedures can be stressful. And one of the beliefs about these humanistic and alternative methodologies was that they should stress the learner as little as possible. Although unstressed learners – and unstressed teachers – most likely do perform better than those who are stressed, this position makes it difficult to know how well a method is working, assuming it is working at all. The assumption seemed to be something along the lines of: if the teacher believes that s/he is teaching, and the learners believe that they are learning, then teaching and learning are therefore taking place. Although there may be some truth to this kind of assumption, such assumptions may also appear to be a convenient way of not having to justify claims made by proponents, and not allowing such claims to be examined and explored more critically and rigorously, beyond a faithful belief in the methodology.

A damning review of Suggestopedia, published in the *TESOL Quarterly* by one of the leading linguists of the day, to a large extent marked the end of Suggestopedia's aims and claims to revolutionize language teaching and learning: 'If we have learnt anything at all in the seventies [the 1970s], it is that the art of language teaching will benefit very little from the pseudo-science of suggestology' (Scovel, 1979, p. 265). 'Pseudo-science' is one of the harshest criticisms that can be found in a journal like *TQ*. However, Richards and Rodgers (2001) decided not to 'further belabour the science/nonscience, data/double-talk issues', but instead to 'try to identify and validate those techniques from Suggestopedia that appear effective and that harmonize with other successful techniques in the language teaching inventory' (p. 106). Richards and Rodgers' position on Suggestopedia reiterates another of the recurring themes in this book, which is that all methods have their strengths and weakness, their advantages and limitations. Therefore, to use one method only, based on the belief that it is the 'best' method or the 'one true method', is a mistake, but one that can be avoided by using a range of techniques, methods and approaches, combined in different ways. It is also important that the rationale for these different combinations can be stated clearly and concisely by the teacher, and in some cases, by the learners themselves.

ACTIVITY 8.2

If you have never used Suggestopedia/Desuggestopedia before, do you think you would be interested in trying it out? If so, with whom would you try it, and to teach what?

If you are not interested in trying it out, what reservations or doubts do you have, and how might these be addressed?

Total Physical Response

As we saw with (De)Suggestopedia, in terms of drawing attention and establishing credibility, *where* methodological articles are published can be important as *what* is written. For Suggestopedia, although the Wagner and Tilney (1983) article in *TQ* concluded that so-called 'Superlearning' was really not all that 'super', having an article in *TQ* signalled to the ELT world that Suggestopedia was, at least for a while, being taken seriously. Likewise, when James Asher, then at San José State College in California, USA, published his article on Total Physical Response (TPR) in the 50th volume of the *Modern Language Journal* in 1966, the language teaching world sat up and took notice. Notice, I did not refer to the 'ELT world', because many of these methods, such as Suggestopedia and TPR – and others in this category of what are considered to be humanistic methods (see Earl Stevick's *Humanism in Language Teaching*, 1990) – were not used to teach English as much as they were used to teach other languages to native users of English.

It is also worth noting that, although Asher did describe the principles of TPR a couple of years earlier in his paper titled 'Toward a neo-field theory of behavior' (1964), that paper was published in the *Journal of Humanistic Psychology* and therefore not noticed by language educators at that time. Asher (b. 1929) retired from what was by then San José State University in 1996, but the business of selling TPR has continued. For example, at the tpr-world.com website, TPR 'starter kits' can currently be bought for around 50 US dollars, and TPR 'super starter kits' can be bought for around 70 US dollars.

In his 1966 paper, complete with photographs of students and teachers jumping into the air in response to '*Tobe!*', the Japanese word for 'jump!', Asher was clear that with TPR the focus is on fluency: 'Perhaps one of the most complex tasks in human learning is the problem of how to achieve fluency in a foreign language' (p. 79). Although that is likely to be an overstatement, as there probably are more 'complex tasks in human learning', such statements and such papers may have helped governmental-level decision-makers in countries such as the USA, England, Canada and other English-dominant countries to take the teaching of foreign languages to native users of English more seriously. If so, then whatever the shortcomings of TPR, if it helped countries such as England, America and Australia to take second and foreign language learning more seriously, that would constitute a valid contribution.

Five different sets of experiments are reported by Asher in his 1966 paper, with students being exposed to verbal commands in Japanese and Russian, with pre- and post-testing carried out using instruments such as the Modern Language Aptitude Test, the American College Testing Program and the Otis Intelligence Test. Based on the test results of the first two experiments, Asher tentatively concluded that the use of TPR 'seemed to facilitate the learning of listening skill [sic] for complex foreign utterances' (Asher, 1966, pp. 81–82). The third, fourth and fifth studies were carried out with children (in the second, fourth, sixth and eighth grades) exposed to some spoken Russian and pre- and post-tested using the California Achievement Test. Based on the results of all five sets of experiments, Asher concluded: 'The results suggest that dramatic facilitation in learning listening skill for a second language is related to acting out during retention tests' (p. 84). By 'acting out', Asher meant the physical actions of TPR, such as jumping up and down and running backwards and forwards, and by focusing on listening, we can see one of the main limitations of TPR. It is worth noting that TPR also entailed smaller movements, such as pointing, turning, raising a hand or putting one object on top of, below or next to another.

In the same way as CLT (Chapter 4) proponents mentioned the other language modalities, but CLT nonetheless came to be synonymous with speaking, Asher and other proponents of TPR mentioned the other modalities too, but the focus came to be on listening. Comparing and contrasting CLR and TPR in this way should make it clear that some methodologies are better suited to some modalities than others. However, as we have seen in previous chapters, the tendency has been for methodological proponents, publishers and other purveyors of 'the one true method' to claim that the newest thing can be all things to all teachers and all learners. Instead of doing this, it would be so much more helpful to simply accept and admit what should be the fairly uncontroversial fact that some methods work better for some purposes and in some contexts than others. If we do not embrace that fact, we allow ourselves to be dragged back to the days of bandwagoning, best practices and one-size-fits-all, in which one particular methodology is adopted – or mandated – *to the exclusion of the others.*

ACTIVITY 8.3

Are you in a one-size-fits-all language teaching and learning context or organization? If so, what are some of the limitations of teaching in such a context or organization? Have you been able to compensate for some of these limitations, and if so, how?

Are you in a language teaching and learning context or organization driven by the idea that there are best practices, which are believed to be generally applicable in most or even all contexts? If so, what are some of the constraints of teaching in such a context or organization? Have you been able to compensate for some of these constraints, and if so, how?

In a follow-up paper, Asher and Price (1967) compared the understanding of 'Russian utterances' (p. 1220) by children aged 8, 10 and 14 with college students between the ages of 18 and 21. Based on the results of the experiment, Asher and Price concluded that 'when adults learn a second language under the same conditions as children, the adults are superior' (p. 1225). However, Asher and Price also noted that the comparison may have been 'blurred somewhat because of a selectivity factor for the adults' (p. 1225), because the older students, who were at San José State College, were selected from the top one-third of high school graduates in California at that time. The Russian phrases presented to the learners using TPR included: 'Pick up the pencil, walk to the chair, put down the pencil, and run to the window' (p. 1225), for which the assessment of comprehension is clear – if the learners carry out the commands successfully, they have understood the commands.

And with such four-part commands – pick up, walk, put down, run – the range of scores could be from zero to four.

However, as we can see, TPR is generally confined to orders and instructions, or the language of the imperative mood, which can take an individual up to a certain point in a linguistic interaction. But for the interaction to move to more meaningful communication, within which both parties are equally engaged, rather than one issuing commands and the other following orders, statements need to be made, questions asked and answered, and so on. Therefore, when Asher and Price drew conclusions about 'when adults learn a second language', they were referring to the listening comprehension of a specific and limited subset of the language, that is, imperatives. In a 1969 paper, again with photos of teachers and students, this time squatting when they heard the Japanese word '*kagame*', Asher explained that 'An objective of listening and speaking may be an unrealistic one with the limited time available' (p. 261). Therefore, he suggested that, 'in the first stage of learning, only one of the four language skills be selected. The skill we recommend is listening fluency' (p. 261). The reason, Asher claimed, for a focus on listening was 'because it seems to have positive transfer to the other three skills' (p. 261). This claimed transfer may or may not be the case, but the main reason for the focus on listening in TPR is more likely to be because that is the main language modality that TPR can help to develop, as long as the learner is listening to and 'acting out' commands. The focus on listening may also have been because this is the first language skill developed in the acquisition of our first language.

An example of the limited usefulness of TPR – but one in which TPR can still be useful in language teaching and learning – was provided by Elisabeth Elliott and Lisa Yountchi (2009), who carried out and reported on experiments teaching Russian verbs of motion to learners who are native users of English. According to Elliott and Yountchi, 'Instructors of Russian know all too well that mastering Russian Verbs of Motion (VoM) is a complicated and difficult area of Russian grammar for L-1 English-speaking students' (p. 428). The article appeared in a special issue of *The Slavic and East European Journal* on the 'Teaching and Learning of Russian Verbs of Motion', making this a good example of the 'focused' use of methods such as TPR. This kind of focused use may be called *Niche Methods*, that is, methods that are useful for pedagogically and linguistically (very) specific purposes.

In the same way as there is a long history of Language for Specific Purposes (LSP), and within that, English for Specific Purposes (ESP), we can also think of *Methods for Specific Purposes*. It is important to note that methods such as TPR, (De) Suggestopedia, Community Language Learning (CLL, see below) and the Silent Way (also below) were referred to as 'Designer Methods' by writers such as H. Douglas Brown, according to whom 'the good deal of hoopla about "designer" methods', in the 1970s and early 1980s, was 'symbolic of a profession at least partly caught up in a mad scramble to invent a new method' (2002, p. 11).

TPR was given a new lease on life in the late 1990s with the publication of *Fluency Through TPR Storytelling*, subtitled *Achieving Real Language Acquisition in School* (1997), by Blaine Ray and Contee Seely, a fourth edition of which was published in 2004. That book led to a new acronym, TPRS, for TPR Storytelling. That technique eventually led to a new form of TPRS, Teaching Proficiency Through Reading and Storytelling. It is, then, interesting to see how methods can take on a life of their own (see Chapter 9), in this case, morphing from TPR to TPR Storytelling, then to a TPRS in which there is no mention of 'total', 'physical' or 'response'. According to Liu Ying, working with Chinese students at an aeronautics and astronautics university in China, 'TPRS [Teaching Proficiency Through Reading and Storytelling] combines TPR [Total Physical Response] with language acquisition strategies, and combines vocabulary teaching with that of grammar, reading and writing' (2011, p. 169). Liu also explained that Teaching Proficiency Through Reading and Storytelling is based on three steps: 'in step one the new vocabulary structures to be learned are taught using a combination of translation, gestures, and personalized questions; in step two those structures are used in a spoken class story; and finally, in step three, these same structures are used in a class reading and discussion' (2011, p. 169). It is also worth noting that Liu's is a relatively recent publication, indicating that, in some contexts, some versions of the original TPR are still finding a place in the language classroom.

To return to the original storytelling TPRS, James Davidheiser (2002) reported on teaching German to his students at a university in Tennessee, USA using TPRS. Davidheiser gives a detailed description of what he does as a teacher in his German language TPRS classes: 'On the first day of class I play James Asher's 23-minute video, "Strategy for Second Language Learning", before uttering a word in class. In the introduction Asher himself orients students to TPR; a demonstration of several actual German classes follows. Thereafter I immediately begin with commands' (p. 26). Davidheiser explained that he modelled the commands twice, then had the students repeat them, with a list of 21 lexical items that he 'embedded in commands', which he recycled 'over and over' (p. 27), sometimes to individuals and sometimes to the entire class. (It is worth noting that the 'exclusive' or 'singular' way in which this method is seen by Asher is alluded to in the title of his video, i.e., "strategy" rather than "strategies" for language learning.)

On the second day of class, the teacher reviewed the first day in detail, then added 'four colors, five numbers, the letters of the alphabet, and various objects' (p. 26). On the third day of classes, the teacher introduced 'the accusative article "den", calling it both *maskulin* and *Akkusativobjekt*. In German, I illustrate what a direct object is and then proceed to the next command. On that day I also refine pronunciation by emphasizing that *z* is like *ts*' (p. 27). Approximately every four classes, the teacher quizzed the students briefly 'on a combination of listening comprehension, action, and spelling. Small groups act out the commands to show comprehension and the entire class writes down the commands' (p. 27). Davidheiser, like most proponents of such methods, is very enthusiastic about TPRS – in this case, in the absence of any data, quantitative or qualitative, from the learners – yet with all kinds of benefits claimed. However, even Davidheiser challenges Asher and Ray's advocacy of 'continuing TPR/TPRS into the more advanced levels of language learning' (p. 33), as Davidheiser had 'not always found it advantageous to continue TPRS in second year', because his students preferred 'to move beyond storytelling in the second year' (p. 33). This account, like many such narratives, shows that TPR and TPR Storytelling can be effective with beginner language learners and younger language learners, developing their listening skills for the understanding of basic commands and other imperative instructions. But they may not be as effective with older learners, at higher levels of target language competence, or for developing the other modalities, and when the language learning needs to progress beyond following orders and carrying out commands.

As noted above, TPR is one method in which assessment of learning outcomes can be immediate and concrete: 'Teachers will know immediately whether or not students understand by observing their students' actions. Formal evaluations can be conducted simply by commanding individual students to perform a series of actions' (Larsen-Freeman & Anderson, 2011, p. 111). Although such immediately observable understanding, or lack thereof, may be one of the advantages of TPR, in terms of its limitations, it would not be possible to assess a learner's understanding of even such basic and fundamental greetings as, for example, 'Hello, how are you?' in the target language, as this requires a verbal response, rather than a physical one.

> **ACTIVITY 8.4**
>
> How would you compare and contrast the similarities and the differences between (De)Suggestopedia and the original TPR?
> Are you more inclined to try one of these two methods than the other? If so, which one and why?

Community Language Learning

This method, like the other humanistic approaches to teaching and learning, aims to 'engage the whole person, including the emotions and feelings (the affective realm) as well as linguistic knowledge and behavioral skills' (Richards & Rodgers, 2001, p. 90). And this method, like the other types of humanistic approaches to language teaching and learning, is also based primarily on the work of one particular individual, in this case Charles A. Curran (1913–1978). One of the recurring themes in this chapter, and elsewhere in this book, has been 'methodologies as acts of faith', in relation to how the beliefs of the teachers and the learners influence the likelihood that a particular method will succeed or fail (depending on how these terms are defined). In the case of Community Language Learning (CLL), this relationship between methodologies and faith is more literal, and can be seen more clearly and more directly, as Curran was first a priest, who then later received a Doctorate in Psychology in 1944.

As noted above, although the Christian aspect of CLL featured prominently in the work of Earl Stevick (1974, 1980, 1990), and Christian ELT is the basis of some more recent books (see, for example, Wong, Kristjansson, & Dornyei, 2013), this aspect of CLL is rarely mentioned in most of the mountains of methodological literature. This is perhaps because such a Christian orientation might be at odds with the millions of teachers and learners of English in the world today who follow faiths other than

Christianity. Whatever the reasons for this omission, Christianity has been a recurring feature of CLL. An example is the article by David Smith in the *Journal of Research on Christian Education*, titled 'In Search of the Whole Person: Critical Reflections on Community Language Learning' (1997). In that article, Smith stated that 'Teaching methods in the modern-language classroom are widely assumed to be relatively value-neutral techniques, justified by their pragmatic usefulness' (p. 159), thereby highlighting one of the false assumptions that have been challenged in this book, and elsewhere (see Chapter 3 and Chapter 4), that is, that techniques, approaches and methodologies can be 'value-neutral'. Given the centuries-long history of language teaching and learning, and the fact that Smith's article is just 20 years old, we can see the longevity and the persistence of this particular myth of methodological neutrality – which may still be operating in some contexts today.

In Smith's article, CLL is described as 'the offspring and chief application of Counseling-Learning', which emerged in the 1960s and 1970s from the work of Curran (1960), who was described by Smith as 'a Roman Catholic priest and specialist in psychotherapy' (1997, p. 160). One reason for the relatively short-lived interest in and limited use of CLL could be the fact that 'Curran's educational writings demonstrate little awareness of or interest in mainstream language learning' (Smith, 1997, p. 162), even though Curran's 1976 book was titled *Counseling-Learning in Second Languages*. But, as Richards and Rodgers observed, 'Curran himself wrote little about his theory of language' (2001, p. 91).

The word 'alternative' is defined quite neutrally in *MODE* as 'something that you can choose instead of something else', but being alternative is often seen as taking a position that opposes the current status quo. This kind of opposition can be one important way of moving our thinking and our actions forward, positively and productively. However, the desire to be alternative can sometimes mean that those proposing the alternatives are not as aware as they should be of exactly what it is they are opposing. This appears to have been the case with

CLL. To use an old expression in English, in the wholesale rejection of what is currently being done, those proposing the alternative 'throw the baby out with the bathwater', that is, opposing or discarding everything that was done before, including that which might be helpful and important.

CLL is also a good example of how the political values and cultural values of those who propose particular methods are reflected in the methodologies they are promoting, as two of the four principles of Curran's CLL are 'the democratic ideal' and 'rugged individualism' (Smith, 1997, p. 163), with the latter described by Hirschman (2003) as 'a core American cultural value' (p. 9). In addition to the agenda of those proposing particular methods, gender may also play a role (see, for example, Ensmenger, 2015), as the inventors and promoters of all four of the alternative and humanistic methods discussed in this chapter constitute *The Men Behind the Methods*. However, the view of the language learner in CLL 'as a social, spiritual, cultural, moral, accountable, fallen being with central faith commitments and a responsibility to image [sic] God' (Smith, 1997, p. 179) raises the question of how appropriate such a method would be in non-religious, and in particular non-Christian, language teaching and learning contexts.

In CLL, the communal aspects and the group dynamics, where the language learning 'takes place in the social setting of a group' (La Forge, 1971, p. 55), based on the 'common ground between linguistics and modern group psychology', are the basis for the in-class interaction. There is, then, no notion of independent, autonomous or self-directed language learning in CLL, as everything, by definition, must take place in a group. Although this would suit some learners and some teachers, doing everything in a group limits the language learning and teaching opportunities to the time that everyone is together, at the same time, in the same place.

Paul La Forge (1971), who was a student and a follower of Curran, observed and described a number of CLL experimental lessons taught by Curran himself. The lessons were usually carried out with small numbers of students, partly because they are seated in a circle, rather than in rows, so everyone in the room and in the group can see and be seen by each other. This is good for face-to-face interaction, but limits the number of students in a lesson, making CLL in many countries, such as China, India and elsewhere, where class sizes are generally large, contextually inappropriate. Another important aspect of CLL is the names for the roles of the participants. Rather than 'teachers' and 'learners', the teacher is referred to as a 'counselor' and the students are called 'clients'. Today, 'clients' more commonly refers to 'someone who pays for the services of a professional person' (*MODE*), but in CLL it comes from the therapist–patient model and the medical metaphor, which relates to what can be called a belief in *Methods as Medicine*.

ACTIVITY 8.5

What do you think of the metaphor of Methods as Medicine? Do you think it is a helpful way of thinking about methods? What are some other metaphors or analogies that could be used to think about and talk methods?

According to La Forge, 'When a client wished to say something to the group, he would speak first in his native language, so that everyone in the group could understand. Then the counselor would say the same thing in the target language. The client would then repeat the same thing in the target language' (1971, pp. 54–55). This part of CLL, like TPR, resembles the Audio-Lingual Method (ALM), in terms of the listen-and-repeat patterns. However, in the CLL lesson, 'The clients were free to say anything they desired. Since the responsibility for the conversation and the language learning remained with the clients, the counselor did not initiate or take part in the conversation' (p. 55). This kind of process is very different from TPR (above), in which the learners mainly listen and respond with actions, and ALM (Chapter 5), in which the learners mainly listen and repeat what they have just heard. The role of the teacher-as-counsellor is to be 'supportive and helpful, but only on conditions dictated by the clients, that is, *only when such help and support were asked for*' (p. 55, emphasis added).

This counselling approach to language teaching and learning, in which input from the teacher is only provided when the learner asks for it, may be empowering for some learners. But for learners who are not used to being in such a position – if you do not ask the teacher for help you do not receive any help – this could be stressful. However, such stresses are in contradiction to one of the main espoused beliefs in these kinds of methods, which is the physical and psychological well-being of the learner. Only giving help when it is asked for may work well in clinical counselling situations, in which the counsellor is possibly being careful to avoid interrupting, pre-empting or overly influencing the patient's verbalized stream of consciousness. However, not offering input unless it is explicitly asked for may be an important example of how different therapeutic counselling is from teaching and learning, which appears to be a substantial difference that is rarely discussed in the CLL literature, if at all.

As we saw with the rise of the Audio-Lingual Method (Chapter 5), technologies that are now nearly obsolete, such as compact cassette tape recorders, were making a major impact on the methodologies of the day, as they had only recently become available, affordable and portable. This influence is also seen in CLL, in which audiotape recordings of the small-group interaction are played back to the group during the lesson. The recordings provide a review of the lesson and an opportunity for the participants to reflect on the interaction, with such reflection described as 'An essential part of the CLL' (La Forge, 1971, p. 55). The way the recordings are used is that the 'Sentences in the foreign language are taken from the tape and written out by the *native expert* for the class. Usually, as a result of the direct living experience with the foreign language, students are positively motivated to freely inquire about the language' (p. 55, emphasis added). The reference to 'the native expert' demonstrates how CLL, as did CLT (Chapter 4), has played a central role in the problem of the native user of the target language being considered – *by that fact* – to be the 'best' language teacher, or at least, 'better' than a non-native user-teacher. Sadly, we are still struggling with those issues today, nearly 50 years later. (See, for example, Paikeday, 1985; Doerr, 2009; Mahboob, 2010.)

Unfortunately, the results claimed by proponents of methods such as CLL can be different from those reported by the learners. For example, La Forge (1971) reported that, 'When asked after the session was over, exactly how much they could remember, the clients were able to produce bits and pieces of the foreign languages' (p. 58). These 'bits and pieces' of the target language, such as individual words and short phrases, may be a good starting point for language learning. But, like the imperative commands listened to and acted on in TPR, they can only take the learners to a fairly limited level. Therefore, if methods such as CLL are used as the main method, or the only method, progress will be limited. However, if such methods are used, for example, at the beginner level, with learners who are not concerned with *how* the language works – they just want it *to work* – then methods such as TPR and CLL can be useful starting blocks on which to build.

An example of a situation in which CLL can be useful was provided by Eileen Ariza (2002), who was teaching Spanish to monolingual, English-speaking students, whose families had relocated to Puerto Rico. Ariza describes her four students, all males, as being in difficult personal circumstances at the time of the Spanish language course: 'The common denominator for relocation to Puerto Rico was a crisis, such as a breakup of the family, remarriage of a parent, separation of siblings, fatal motor vehicle accident, or all of the above' (p. 719). This, then, may be a situation in which the therapeutic approach of CLL may be a good fit, especially with such a small class size. By extension, it may also be that these kinds of humanistic and alternative methodologies are well suited to 'at-risk' learners, who have recently experienced traumas of some kind, such as children who have crossed international borders to escape large-scale, long-term wars of the kind in Syria (Lucente & Al Shimale, 2016). In relation to assessment of learning outcomes, although Ariza did not use any formal assessment procedures to avoid stressing the already distressed learners, after an extended period of using CLL, she concluded that 'Over a period of five months, these youngsters progressed from total disdain for Spanish, to taking delight in every new utterance because it served their purpose, the intrinsic desire to communicate. This experience demonstrates what every teacher knows; that is, learning cannot occur until students want to learn' (Ariza, 2002, p. 726).

In conclusion, it is important to note that, like TPR, CLL now means something different. For example, in the UK, and elsewhere in Europe, Community Language Learning refers to COLT, which stands for Community and Lesser Taught Languages (Handley, 2011). In that context, CLL refers to 'languages in use in a society, other than the dominant, official or national language' (McPake et al., 2007, p. 6). These COLTs are not the same as Modern Foreign Languages, which in Europe refers to languages such as French, Spanish and German, whereas COLT usually refers to the first language of immigrant communities, such as those from the Indian subcontinent, Sub-Saharan Africa and elsewhere.

ACTIVITY 8.6

According to Ariza, 'learning cannot occur until students want to learn'. Do you agree with this statement? If so, what can be done to help students who do not want to learn to reach the stage where they do want to learn?

The Silent Way

As with the other methodologies in this group of alternative and/or humanistic approaches to language teaching and learning, there is one particular name associated with the Silent Way, that of Caleb Gattegno (1911–1998), the Egyptian-born mathematics educator, who also turned his attention to language education. However, although Gattegno made the Silent Way widely known, it began with the work of a Belgian primary school teacher, Emile-George Cuisenaire (1891–1975), who used Cuisenaire rods in the 1920s as a tool for teaching mathematics. The rods, which were called by Cuisenaire 'régelettes', are small, brightly coloured pieces of wood or plastic of various regular sizes, which are used to help learners visualize the way numbers work, and to help concretize the abstract relationships between numbers. The use of these kinds of rods can be traced back to the German educator Friedrich Fröbel (1782–1852), who is credited with coining the term 'kindergarten', and the Italian physician and educator Maria Montessori (1870–1952), who established the Montessori Schools and the Montessori Method of educating children. However, it was Gattegno who called the rods 'Cuisenaire', and in 1957 Cuisenaire and Gattegno published a 60-page handbook, *Numbers in Colour: A new method of teaching arithmetic in primary schools*. Gattegno initially focused on mathematics education, with books such as *A Teacher's Introduction to the Cuisenaire-Gattegno Method of Teaching Arithmetic* (1965) and *The Common Sense of Teaching Mathematics* (1974), but he also turned his attention to language, with books such as *In the Beginning There Were No Words: The Universe of Babies* (1973).

This apparent assumption that learning mathematics and learning languages are somehow connected, at the neural level, in the brain may have come from the work of mathematics educators like Brune (1953), who was interested in the symbolic and communicative connections between language and mathematics. Brune saw these connections in terms of the fact that 'words are links in the chain of communication' (p. 160), and that 'mathematical words often represent mental constructs rather than tangibles' (p. 161). Brune also wrote that 'spoken words are symbols' (p. 161) and that 'words represent spoken agreement between people' (p. 161). In discussing Brune's work, Ellerson and Clarkson (1996) pointed out that 'language factors have long been recognized as having an important influence on mathematics learning' (p. 987), and more recent studies have also found that 'half of the genes that affect 12-year-olds' literacy also play a role in their abilities in mathematics' (Sample, 2014, p. 1).

In Gattegno's *In the Beginning*, we can see the influence of the American psychologist Carl Rogers (1902–1987), who worked with Curran, and who is known for popularizing the notion of a 'person-centred approach' to psychotherapy, counselling and education. As Gattegno wrote in *In the Beginning*, 'Whatever one's place of birth, the creed of one's parents, the language one learns, the color of one's skin, the economic level of one's family and community, one asks today to be looked at as a person, *complete at any age* and in most circumstances' (p. 1, emphasis added). This notion of 'complete at any age' may have been a challenge to the work of the Swiss child psychologist Jean Piaget (1896–1980). Piaget is known as one of the founders of Constructivism, which is based on the idea that humans make sense of the world based on the interactions between their experiences and their ideas, rather than on explicit communication of, for example, facts and figures in a formal setting. Piaget's model is based on children passing through four stages – Sensorimotor, Preoperational, Concrete Operational and Formal Operational – after which they could be considered to be 'complete' (Piaget, 1926).

It is important to note here that, although (De)Suggestopedia, TPR, CLL and the Silent Way, based on their person-centredness, are all in the category of humanistic and alternative approaches and methodology, there are some important differences between them. One of the distinguishing features of the

Silent Way is Gattegno's belief that, as he wrote on the last page of *In the Beginning*, 'Each of us has been by far the best teacher each of us has had' (1973, p. 186). From this viewpoint came one of the central principles of the Silent Way, which is the importance of 'subordinating teaching to learning' (p. 186).

As noted earlier, in the consideration of (De)Suggestopedia and TPR, *where* a methodology is discussed can matter as much as *what* is discussed, as the source shows how seriously a methodology is/was being considered by the academic community, even if it is, ultimately, rejected. It is, therefore, important that a review of Gattegno's *Teaching Foreign Languages in Schools: The Silent Way* (1972) was published in the *TESOL Quarterly* in 1974. This book review raises another potentially important factor in the attention that some methodologies receive, which is *who* did the review. In the case of Gattegno's 1972 book, the review, which appeared under the title 'Some Basic Facts About "The Silent Way"', was carried out by Earl Stevick (1923–2013), an influential Christian language educator and a proponent of Communicative Language Teaching (Chapter 4).

Stevick considered himself to be an 'insider', as he started his review by stating a point made above, about some proponents of some language teaching and learning methodologies appearing to have limited knowledge of the field of language education. Stevick also considered CLL and the Silent Way to be similar, in that they both suffered from some of the same shortcomings: 'This is another book by an outsider. Like Curran (1972, reviewed in Stevick, 1973), Caleb Gattegno does language teaching as a by-product and special case of a professional commitment which is broader than language teaching as such. Again like Curran, Gattegno makes almost no mention of those who are conspicuous in the field' (Stevick, 1974, p. 305).

Based on extensive classroom observation of Silent Way language lessons, and Stevick's experience of 150 hours of being taught using the Silent Way, he discussed the five main principles of the methodology, starting with, as noted above, 'Teaching should be subordinated to learning' (Gattegno, 1972, p. 1) and 'Learning is not primarily imitation or drill' (Gattegno, 1972, p. 3). The second principle is the opposite of the Audio-Lingual Method (Chapter 5), as the ALM is based on learners listening to the teacher or to a recording, then repeating what they hear. This second principle compared with the ALM raises the interesting question of how methodologies designed to achieve the same thing, that is, the learning of a second or foreign language, can be based on principles that are not just different, but completely the opposite. Yet, they can both/all be embraced at the same time, by the same people. These contradictions between methodologies are another strong argument for the careful combining of different methodologies, based on a *principled and informed eclecticism*. (See, for example, Boswell, 1972; Olagoke, 1982; Mellow, 2002.)

Gattegno's third principle is that the mind of the individual learner 'equips itself by its own working, trial and error, deliberate experimentation, by suspending judgment and revising conclusions' (Gattegno, 1972, p .4). According to Stevick, that principle affirms the importance of the adult ego-state in the language learning process, and the fourth principle is based on the theory that 'As it works, the mind draws on everything it has already acquired, particularly including its experience of learning its native language' (Stevick, 1974, p. 306). However, based on the differences between first language acquisition and second/foreign language learning, Gattegno was 'content to devise an "artificial" method, rather than trying for a "natural" one' (p. 306). One of the most distinguishing features of the Silent Way, and the reason why it is called that, is the fifth principle, which is based on the idea that 'the teacher must stop interfering with and sidetracking' (p. 306) interaction within the classroom. The teacher, therefore, says as little as possible, using the Cuisenaire rods, hand gestures and pointing to avoid saying anything, unless saying something is unavoidable.

Using silence in this way, the teacher can provide 'knowledge of the language, and a firm overall structure for activity', meeting the learner's need for security and fulfilling 'the role of a Nurturing, or Natural Parent' (p. 360). At the same time, the teacher can avoid 'the constant modeling, prescribing and directing kinds of activity which are typical of the Controlling Parent', which, Stevick believed, 'many teachers seem to believe are inseparable from effective, responsible teaching' (p. 360). This distinctive aspect of the Silent Way may indeed help some students, who might find that their teachers sometimes do get in the way of their learning, as it were. But that aspect could also put considerable pressure on the student to speak, and in the same way as some students may find this to be positive pressure, others may find it to be negative and anxiety-inducing.

ACTIVITY 8.7

How would your students respond if you were to say little or nothing in class? If, for example, one day you lost your voice, would you still be able to teach the lesson, and if so, what are some strategies you would use to teach, when you could not say anything?

This silence of the teacher also raises the recurring question of the appropriateness of different methods in different cultural contexts. For example, Yang Hu and Stacey Fell-Eisenkraft (2003) explored their immigrant Chinese students' perceptions of silence in their language arts classrooms in a school in New York City's Chinatown. Based on their investigation, Hu and Fell-Eisenkraft identified four themes that explained their eighth-grade students' silence: '(1) Silence as a result of being shy; (2) Silence as a result of fear of not having the correct answers; (3) Silence as a result of unfamiliarity with talking to learn; and (4) *Silence as a result of a lack of confidence in speaking the English language*' (2003, p. 55, emphasis added). This last finding highlights how confident learners need to be to speak in another language, in public, in a small group, with such confidence levels needing to be even higher in a Silent Way class. Another example of how silence is perceived in different cultures was written by the Native American author N. Scott Momaday (who was awarded the Pulitzer Prize for Fiction in 1969): 'Silence ... is powerful. It is the dimension in which ordinary and extraordinary events take their proper places. In the [Native American] Indian world, a word is spoken or a song is sung not against, but within the silence. In the telling of a story, there are silences in which words are anticipated or held on to, heard to echo in the still depths of the imagination' (Momaday, 1997, p. 16).

In an interview, Caleb Gattegno stated his beliefs about aspects of learning such as facts and figures, in relation to memorization: 'Rather than make people try to remember what they are told – that is, facts – we let them know that they are retaining, not facts, but systems. We are all equipped with retention, with recognition, and with memory' (Arena, 1980, p. 238). Gattegno also referred to the importance of sensory input, rather than facts and figures, which he believed reduced the effort needed to learn, including learning another language: 'We can hold the energies that reach our systems in the forms of shapes, colors, visual patterns, sounds, melodies, languages, and so on, and without much effort' (Arena, 1980, p. 238), which recalls the use of music in (De)Suggestopedia. In terms of assessment of learning outcomes, although there may be on-going assessment by the teacher of the learners, little formal assessment or testing appears to take place in Silent Way classrooms, to avoid stressing the learners. (See Ariza (2002) in the discussion of CLL above.)

ACTIVITY 8.8

Silence can signify different things. In your classroom, when you ask your students 'Do you understand?' and they say nothing, what are some of the different things that this silence might mean? What are some other strategies you could use for assessing whether or not the students have understood?

Tying Them Together

Some of the recurring themes that connect these four humanistic and alternative methodologies are revealed in an examination of the Silent Way. One of these is the importance of a charismatic leader, championing the new methodological cause. Clifford Prator (1979) referred to this as the problem of the 'New Prophet' in the field of language teaching and learning (p. 6): 'The new [language] teacher will probably also be struck by the highly individualistic tone of much methodological literature. He will note that great prophets have arisen … who have built up large and often blindly enthusiastic groups of followers and who have been able to impose their somewhat closed systems of thought on a generation or more of disciples by their personal prestige and authority' (cited in Varvel, 1979, p. 484). This damning indictment was published in an article titled 'The Cornerstones of Methods' (Prator, 1979, pp. 5–15), aimed specifically at ESL and EFL teachers, and which alludes to the potentially 'cultish' nature of the ways in which some proponents and adherents promote a particular method. The potential influence of religion, especially with reference to Christianity, as discussed above, is another recurring theme highlighted by Prator: 'Unlike the prophets of the Bible, however, these spokesmen of the profession have developed no coherent body of doctrine; indeed their dominant ideas are to a considerable extent *mutually exclusive*' (Prator, 1979, p. 6, cited in Varvel, 1979, p. 484, emphasis added).

It may be that religious belief systems can positively enhance the language teaching and learning experience – as long as the teachers and the learners share the same belief system as the creators of the methodology. However, if such belief systems are not shared, this could be a potentially important barrier, as Terry Varvel explained in a *TESOL Quarterly* article titled 'The Silent Way: Panacea or Pipedream?' (1979, pp. 483–494): 'Unfortunately, the religious fervor that many, especially new, disciples of the Silent Way display tends to lessen the positive reactions of those first encountering the Silent Way' (p. 484). Varvel also noted 'the religious tone that permeates ... the use of words like "inspiration", "enlightenment", "spiritual energy", "the spirit of the Silent Way", "inner motivation" and others like them' (p. 484) used by proponents to describe the theory and the practice of the Silent Way.

A third recurring theme that emerges from a careful consideration of these methods is what Prator referred to as 'dominant ideas are to a considerable extent mutually exclusive' (see above). This mutual exclusiveness, in which methodologies cannot peacefully and positively co-exist, may be related to the Christian belief that 'We know that there is only one God' (1 Corinthians, 8:6), which recalls the notion of the 'One True Method'. This notion also relates to the idea of a 'panacea', as 'something that people think will solve all their problems' or 'a medicine that can cure any illness' (*MODE*).

Another reason for this mutual exclusiveness, according to Varvel (1979), is the fact that 'Silent Way advocates deplore anything but total immersion in the system, inferring that anything else would taint or corrupt. Thus, to think of the Silent Way as a method that could equally co-exist with or be subordinate to another methodology in the same classroom, used only part of the time, is apparent heresy' (p. 493). Notions of 'tainting' or 'corrupting' strongly imply deeply held beliefs about the 'purity' of a methodology. Such beliefs may relate to notions about the 'purity' of languages and cultures, which are unhelpful and even troubling because, as Varvel concluded, 'However, I believe the greatest strength of the Silent Way lies in its use as part of an eclectic approach by the average teacher' (p. 493). This is a point which has been made throughout this book, in relation to, as noted above, a *principled and informed eclecticism*.

Suggested Readings

Humanising Language Teaching is a freely available UK-based online journal, which can be accessed at http://www.hltmag.co.uk/index.htm. *HLT* has been published since 1999, with an emphasis on humanistic methods, and contains articles on many of the methodologies mentioned in this book.

In Diane Larsen-Freeman and Marti Anderson's *Techniques and Principles in Language Teaching* (2011), there are chapters on the Silent Way (Chapter 5, pp. 51–69), Desuggestopedia (Chapter 6, pp. 71–84), CLL (Chapter 7, pp. 85–101) and TPR (Chapter 8, pp. 103–114).

In Jack Richards and Theodore Rodgers' *Approaches and Methods in Language Teaching* (2014), there are chapters on TPR (Chapter 5, pp. 73–80), the Silent Way (Chapter 6, pp. 81–89), CLL (Chapter 7, pp. 90–99) and Suggestopedia (Chapter 8, pp. 100–107).

CHAPTER 9
Where Do We Go From Here?

> Before you read this last chapter, think about the following questions:
>
> - What are some of the main points that you will remember, some time after you have finished reading this book?
> - What are some of the main points made in this book that you have *agreed* with?
> - What are some of the main points made in this book that you have *disagreed* with?

Introduction and Overview

In this concluding chapter, I make a number of statements, which may be considered controversial, and which I hope will be challenged by some of my colleagues, as that is how our knowledge bases grow and move forward. As the discussion of some of the methodologies presented in this book has shown, when almost everyone has agreed that a particular method was 'all good' – or that it was 'all bad' – those are the times when we stopped making progress, when we stopped advancing and went back to 'bandwagoning' (see Chapter 1), or back to scapegoating (see Chapter 7).

I should also add that this final chapter is more experiential than the others in this book. Of the five books in the *ALLC* series (so far), this is the only one that refers to more than 250 works published over a period of more than 100 years. That might seem somewhat excessive for a relatively slim volume like this, but as I have made a number of challenging statements throughout this book, those positions needed to be especially well researched. Another reason for such extensive referencing is that one of the goals of this *ALLC* series is to help bridge the still-big gap between the day-to-day realities of classroom teachers and language learners and the published work of university-based professional researchers, applying for employment, promotion and tenure. Therefore, to bridge that gap between language teaching and applied linguistics, it helps to refer to as much of the literature as possible, from both fields.

This chapter is still, like the rest of the chapters, extensively researched and referenced, but it is based more on my experiences than on the literature, so there will be more statements in this chapter that reflect my opinion, rather than what the literature tells us. The experiences that have shaped those opinions include more than 20 years in the field of ELT and TESOL, working with tens of thousands of teachers in dozens of countries. In particular, my year as the 50th President of the TESOL International Association (2015–2016), together with my years as President-Elect (2014–2015) and Past President (2016–2017), gave me a unique opportunity to travel hundreds of thousands of miles, to hear from teachers all over the world, and to sit in their classrooms. I am profoundly grateful to the language teachers and learners in Europe, Asia, Africa and the Middle East, as well as those in North, South and Central America, for teaching me about, and for showing me, what it really means to be a language educator in today's conflict-torn world.

The main concluding claims I will make here are that:

i. We have yet to go beyond paying lip service to the Centrality of Context, to fully acknowledging that *where* we do our teaching and learning is at least as important as the who, what, when, how and why of what we do.
ii. We still have a lot to learn about how languages are learned.
iii. We are not in a 'post methods condition'. As we are past that, we are now 'post post methods'.

iv. Methods still matter.
v. And as long as teaching and learning matter, methods will continue to matter.

The Context of Language Teaching and How Languages Are Learned

In spite of a number of popular and helpful books, such as *How Languages Are Learned* (2013) by Patsy Lightbown and Nina Spada, which is now in its fourth edition, having been first published 20 years earlier in 1993, it appears that we still have much to learn about how languages are learned. This may not sound like a particularly controversial claim to language teachers who have been in language classrooms for many years, and who have seen claims and counter-claims, fads and fashions come and go. However, for those people and those publishers who have claimed to know, definitively, how languages are learned, this will be an unwelcome statement, and one that may be highly contested by those who have a vested academic and economic interest in claiming that we now know all we need to know about how languages are learned.

In the same way as the principles of a number of methodologies appear to confuse – or at least, not to distinguish clearly between – L1 acquisition and the learning of other languages, we seem to have confused the massive amounts of work published on how languages are *taught* with the assumption that we know how languages are *learned*. What we have produced is millions of published pages of research about how languages are *taught*, which is certainly an impressive volume. But the fact is that all of those pages and all of those studies have not been able to answer the question: How are languages *learned*? I should add that 40 years of published studies on second language acquisition (SLA) (see, for example, the journal *Studies in Second Language Acquisition*, published since 1979) have revealed a great deal about SLA. But we still have some way to go, not least because 40 years is not a long time in the history of a disciplinary field of knowledge.

After summarizing, in one chapter, 40 published studies on language teaching and learning, Lightbown and Spada conclude that 'there is still much work to be done' (p. 195). This supports my second claim, above, and raises the question of 'How much is enough?' in relation to the amount of research that needs to be done, and the number of studies that need to be published, before we can answer the question: How are second and foreign languages learned? Based on the 40 studies, from which Lightbown and Spada derive six 'proposals for second and foreign language teaching' (p. 153), they also conclude that 'it seems evident that proposals representing an almost exclusive focus on form or those representing an almost exclusive focus on meaning alone can not be recommended' (p. 195). A number of points stand out here, one of which is the fact that an exclusive focus on any one thing, to the exclusion of everything else, is unlikely to be successful and unlikely to achieve the goals set, or to produce the intended outcomes, *in any endeavour*. At most, some partial success may be possible with such an exclusive focus. That is why, throughout this book, I have reiterated the importance of language teachers and learners using more than one approach or method in their language lessons and classes. This is something that most effective language teachers do anyway, regardless of whether or not they have read any of the thousands of studies or millions of pages on language teaching and learning.

The second point in relation to Lightbown and Spada's conclusion above is that after citing, summarizing and referring to hundreds of published studies, they offer tentative proposals, rather than possible answers to the question of how languages are learned. This is a wise move, as we still do not know the answer, but a more accurate title for a book in this area could be something like: *How Some Aspects of Some Languages Are Learned by Some Learners in Some Contexts*. Needless to say, book publishers are highly unlikely to allow such titles, which is entirely understandable, as that kind of accurate and honest titling is unlikely to lead to substantial book sales!

In assessing the six proposals, Lightbown and Spada state that 'Approaches that provide attention to form within communicative and content-based interaction receive the most support from classroom research' (p. 195). However, they also note that, 'in throwing out contrastive analysis, feedback on error, and metalinguistic explanations and guidance, the "communicative revolution" may have gone too far' (p. 195), which is a point made in this book (see Chapter 4). These kinds of Confounding Contradictions or Conflicting Conclusions (see recurring references, in this book, to Kramsch's 'dubious dichotomies') have acerbated the polarizing tensions caused by proponents of certain methodologies claiming to have found 'the one true method' to the exclusion of others, rather than simply accepting and admitting that some aspects of some methods work better with some learners in some contexts. As Lightbown and Spada put it, 'it is not necessary *to choose* between form-based and meaning-based instruction. Rather the challenge is *to find the best balance* between these two orientations' (p. 197, emphasis added). For me, 'orientations' is an effective and helpful way of avoiding dichotomous positioning, and instead looking for continua rather than dichotomies. Also, the reference to 'balance' relates to the notion of informed and principled eclecticism, as part of the methodological balancing act that takes place in every language teaching and learning class.

How Languages Are Learned has been a very popular book, and one that I believe has helped many language teachers around the world understand more about how some students learn some languages in some contexts. However, one of the limitations of such books is their limited reference to local contexts. For example, in his review of the fourth edition of *How Languages Are Learned*, McDonough (2014) notes that 'it is a little odd that very little "practitioner research", i.e. research by teachers on and in their own classrooms, is included' (p. 90). It may be that Lightbown and Spada did not intend their book to take into account 'practitioner research', but a greater concern is expressed by McDonough, as he believes that the lack of reference to such research may be 'a consequence of the tension between the search for general principles of language learning and the need for *relevance to local contexts*' (p. 90, emphasis added). That comment from McDonough highlights one of the main themes of this book, which is the fact that how languages are taught in one context depends to a great extent on the characteristics of that context, such as the language learning opportunities and limitations therein. It may, then, be a logical extension to say that how languages are learned is also context-dependent, which is one reason why the question of how languages are learned cannot be answered without adding the caveat that 'it depends – *on where*'.

In a review of the first edition of *How Languages Are Learned* (1993), Angell (1995) noted some of the other recurring themes of that book, which include 'the fundamental gap between classroom practitioners on the one hand and theoreticians and researchers on the other' (p. 268). Hopefully, after the last 20 years or so, that gap is not as wide now as it was then – but I believe it is still far from being bridged. Angell also refers to the 'ever expanding variety and sheer mass of second language research' (p. 268), as well as 'the occasionally arcane and often hermetic discourses of language research' (p. 269), that is, the sometimes obscure and detached language of research. All of these problems have been referred to, as recurring themes, in the previous chapters of this book.

We still have much to learn about how languages are learned, in spite of more than a century of published research on this topic, the thousands of studies, and the millions of pages produced. However, it is also important to note that, in addition to knowing a tremendous amount about how languages are *taught*, we also have a much clearer idea these days of how languages are *not* learned. For example, we know that being surrounded by a foreign language can make no difference at all. That fact was brought home to me many times during my first stint working in Hong Kong, from 1995 to 2000, during its last years as the far-flung Asian jewel in the slipping crown of the British Empire. I lost count of the number of expats from England who had spent *their entire professional lives in language education* in Hong Kong, who were not only not embarrassed by not being able to speak a word of Cantonese after 20 years or more of living there – they were actually proud of that fact, in a kind of defiant Rule Britannia, the-Sun-never-sets-on-the-Empire sort of way! So much for immersion ...

Many of the reasons for not being able to answer the question about how languages are learned can be related to the idea of Confounding Contradictions or Conflicting Conclusions, introduced above. For example, although there is general acceptance that every learner is unique, and that every teacher is unique, and we therefore reject the notion of one-size-fits-all, we are still being sold the seductive idea that there may still be, somewhere out there, 'the one true method'. We are 'only' human. So, try as we may to resist the lure of shiny new textbooks (full of high-resolution photographs of happy multi-coloured children in festive costumes) that claim to be based on the latest, greatest methodological innovation, we are still susceptible to the idea that we/they have, finally, found *the* methodology that will do the trick.

A related Confounding Contradiction or Conflicting Conclusion is our intellectual understanding that, because every learner and every teacher is unique, every context and every class must also therefore be unique. Yet this understanding does not stop us from continuing to talk about and promote 'Best Practices'. For example, in 2016, the TESOL International Association started publishing a monthly blog on 'ELT Best Practices'. We justify the continued use of 'best practices' by saying that we understand that there is, of course, no practice that can be best in all places, for all teachers and learners. However, we are conveniently ignoring the fact that we naturally focus on the word 'best' and its clear connotations of 'the person or thing that is the most ... effective, of the highest quality etc.' (*MODE*).

Another one of these Contradictions and Conclusions is the commitment to learner-centred language teaching, and adapting to the learning styles of our learners. However, if those learners prefer not to say anything, and prefer the Grammar Translation Method – for example, because speaking is not tested in the exams, and passing those exams is their main purpose for knowing the target language – some teachers may still feel the desire to put their students into small groups and get them to talk about things using CLT. That may be especially the case if the teachers have limited grammatical knowledge of the target language they are teaching – or 'facilitating' instead of teaching – as native users of that language (see Chapter 4). Another way of thinking about these Contradictions and Conclusions is the gap between the Rhetoric and the Reality, which may relate to 'the fundamental gap between classroom practitioners on the one hand and theoreticians and researchers on the other', as noted above (Angell, 1995, p. 268). There are, of course, different ways of defining 'practitioner research', but for me, the research at the rhetorical end of the continuum is about language, that is, how language works, whereas the research at the classroom-reality end of the continuum is about how second/foreign languages are taught, in relation to how they might be learned.

ACTIVITY 9.1

Do you agree or disagree with the claim: 'We still have a lot to learn about how languages are learned'? If you agree, why do you think that is the case? If you disagree, how would you rephrase the claim?

The *Claimed* Demise and the Death of Methods

According to Kumaravadivelu (2006), research carried out in the previous 20 years 'revealed four interrelated facts' (p. 166), on which he based his claim that Methods are moribund. The first fact is that 'Teachers who claim to follow a particular method do not conform to its theoretical principles and classroom procedures at all' (p. 166). As I have highlighted in previous chapters, one of the main reasons for this lack of conformity is the lack of effective initial teacher training and education, followed by a lack of on-going teacher professional development (see, for example, Freeman, 1989 and Richards, 2003). This is not the fault of the teachers, and it may not be the fault of the method itself. However, it might be the fault of, for example, the proponents of methods who do not make it clear exactly how a method works (see Chapter 8), or the fault of governments who impose methods without adequate support (see Chapters 3 and 4). For most of the teachers I have worked with, in many different countries and contexts, if they were given the time and the opportunity to fully understand how a particular method works, they would welcome the chance to deepen their understanding. They realize that such an understanding will help them to teach more effectively, benefitting both themselves and their learners, making it a 'win-win' situation.

Kumaravadivelu's second and third facts are that 'teachers who claim to follow different methods often use the same classroom procedures' and that 'teachers who claim to follow the same method often use different procedures' (2006, p. 166). However, as Larsen-Freeman pointed out back in 1986, 'a given technique may well be associated with more than one method' (p. xii) (see Chapter 2). She also went on to note that the reason for this overlap is that 'If two methods share certain principles, then the techniques that are the application of these principles could well be appropriate for both methods' (p. xii). And Larsen-Freeman concluded that 'a particular technique may be compatible with more than one method, depending on the way in which the technique is used' (p. xii). (Although Kumaravadivelu referred to 'procedures' and Larsen-Freeman to 'techniques', the difference between the two is not clear.)

If a narrower perspective of teachers, teaching and learning is taken, conformity to theoretical principles is key. However, this is at odds with the idea that teaching should be a creative endeavour. This does not mean that teachers should 'make it up as they go along', adding this and that willy-nilly, carelessly and without planning. To use the metaphor of 'recipe' (see, for example, de Zwart's description of 'Recipes as Postcolonial Metaphors', 2005), if the chef just throws in ingredients randomly, then the result will be a hotchpotch, that is, 'a collection of things that do not belong together or have been put together carelessly' (*MODE*). However, if each different ingredient is added with knowledge and experience of how adding them, in different combinations, will affect the resulting overall flavours and textures, then this kind of planned, purposeful and deliberate culinary creativity, based on knowledge, skills and experience, will result in positive outcomes. The same applies to planning language lessons, courses and programs.

The fourth reason for rejecting the idea of methods given by Kumaravadivelu was that 'teachers develop and follow in their classroom a carefully crafted sequence of activities not necessarily associated with any particular method' (2006, p. 166). This fourth reason is in line with the notion of teachers creatively crafting their teaching and learning. However, like the previous three, it is not, for me, a particularly compelling reason to reject the idea of methodologies. The fact that different activities, like different techniques, can be associated with different methods (as Larsen-Freeman pointed out) may be a positive reflection of teachers' and learners' creativity, rather than a criticism of methods.

Based on these four reasons, Kumaravadivelu concluded that 'teachers seem to be convinced that no *single* theory of learning and no single method of teaching will help them confront the challenges of everyday teaching' (p. 166, emphasis added). For me, this lack of singularity is a very good thing, as teachers who rely on a single theory or a single method are narrowing themselves and their teaching, as well as their learners' learning. No caring, competent and committed teacher would knowingly and deliberately do that, unless s/he had no choice, which may be the case in some contexts.

Methods *Still* Matter: Or, 'Reports of My Death Have Been Greatly Exaggerated'

The fact that we still have much to discover about language learning makes methodologies all the more important, not less so, as each teaching approach or method can help us learn more about how language learning takes place. However, in the same way as some methods have come and gone – and in some cases, may be coming back – the notion that language teachers and learners are 'post methods' was also popular for some time, even to the extent of announcing the death of methods. This premature pronouncement turned out to be a similar kind of confusion as that which led to the *New York Journal*, on 2 June 1897, publishing the obituary of the American writer Mark Twain (1835–1910), *while he was still alive*. (The source of the confusion appears to have been that Twain's cousin, who had the same family name, was seriously ill in London at that time, which led Mark Twain to declare, with typical brevity, wit and charm: 'The report of my death was an exaggeration.') In relation to methods coming and going, and sometimes coming back, it may also be the case that it is some of the techniques, principles and procedures of certain methodologies that make a comeback, rather than a full-blown resurrection, as we saw with the GTM.

A different kind of confusion led writers such as H. D. Brown to propose, in the same year as the first edition of *How Languages*

Are Learned was published, a 'Requiem for Methods' (1993). 'Requiem' refers to 'a Christian ceremony in which people pray for someone who has died' or 'a piece of music that can be performed as part of this ceremony' (*MODE*), so again we can see the recurring religious references. Brown picked up on this theme in his later work, 'as we lay to rest the methods that have become familiar to us in recent decades' (2002, p. 11), asking the question: 'Why are methods no longer the milestones of our language teaching journey through time?' (p. 10), and listing 'four possible causes of demise' (p. 10).

According to Brown, the first of the four causes of death is: 'Methods are too prescriptive, assuming too much about a context before the context has even been identified' (p. 10). As all of the chapters in this book have shown, I wholeheartedly agree with highlighting the importance of the context. However, it seems unfair to blame the method itself, when it is the *way* in which the method is promoted, regardless of the context, that is at fault, rather than the method itself. And, as we have seen, a great deal of the blame for the application of contextually inappropriate methodologies can often be laid at the feet of those who gain – economically, academically or in some other way – from the widespread use of a particular method, whether or not it is appropriate within a particular context. As methods are non-human abstractions and not sentient beings, they cannot make assumptions about anything – for that, we need researchers, universities, academic journals, textbook publishing companies, governments, and other people, organizations and institutions with vested interests.

Brown uses Community Language Learning as an example of the second of his four causes of death, which is that, 'Generally, methods are quite distinctive at the early, beginning stages of a language course and rather indistinguishable from each other at later stages' (p. 10). Again, it is difficult for me to see how this blurring of distinctions over time renders the whole notion of methods moribund. Certainly, there is a degree of overlap between most methods, but that is to be expected, as they are all supposed to be trying to achieve the same thing, that is, the teaching and learning of a target language. Also, some methodologies, such as TBLT, have grown out of earlier methodologies, such as CLT, which will therefore naturally lead to a high degree of similarity.

The third cause of death, according to Brown, relates to the notion of what is 'best': 'It was once thought that methods could be empirically tested by scientific quantification to determine which one is "best". We have now discovered that something as artful and intuitive as language pedagogy cannot ever be so clearly verified by empirical validation' (p. 10). Again, as noted above and as previous chapters in this book have shown, I fully agree that the whole notion of 'best', in relation to teaching and learning, is unfortunate and unhelpful. However, this third misdiagnosed cause of death seems to be a problem of applying 'the scientific method' to language teachers and learners, as though they were experimental subjects in a laboratory (see Chapter 2), not necessarily a flaw in the methodology itself. Also, the use of 'intuitive' here seems to imply that teachers should rely on their intuition, that is, their 'ability to know or understand something through your feelings, rather than by considering facts or evidence' (*MODE*). This appeal to intuition adds two new pairs to Kramsch's 'dubious dichotomies' – Art versus Science, and Feelings versus Facts. We need Art *and* Science, Facts *and* Feelings, to make sense of the world around us. Therefore, we should not be required to choose between one and the other.

Brown's fourth and final cause of death relates to the postcolonial politics of ELT, as methods are 'laden with ... the quasi-political or mercenary agendas of their proponents' (p. 10), in which methods are 'the creations of the powerful "centre" [which] become vehicles of a "linguistic imperialism" ... targeting the disempowered periphery' (p. 10). Once again, much as I agree with that position, I hope that the creations are not being blamed for the actions of their creators, as we know that there is nothing in the world that is 'man-made' – including methodologies – that cannot be used for evil as well as for good, or vice versa. For example, every vaccine developed as a cure can be turned into a bioweapon of mass destruction; all pieces of military hardware can be used to start wars just as easily as they can be used to keep the peace.

As a way of issuing the 'last rites' to the end of the life of Methods, Brown draws on the work of Nunan (1991), who wrote that: 'It has been realized that there never was and probably never will be a method for all' (p. 228, quoted in Brown, 2002, p. 10). However, all that line from Nunan does is reiterate the fact that there is no 'best' method, which is very different from claiming that the whole idea of methods is – or should be – dead and buried. Methods are not dead. For better or worse, they are very much alive and kicking. What would be more helpful, I believe, than the premature pronouncement of their demise would be to (re-)examine methodologies in the light of what is and is not working, depending on where and when, with whom and why the language teaching and learning is taking place.

ACTIVITY 9.2

How do you respond to Brown's claims that methods are 'laden with ... the quasi-political or mercenary agendas of their proponents', and that methods are 'the creations of the powerful "centre" [which] become vehicles of a "linguistic imperialism" ... targeting the disempowered periphery'?

Do you consider yourself and/or your students to be on what Brown calls 'the disempowered periphery'? If so, how does that positioning shape what you do and how you do it in your language classes?

Why Methods Still Matter

The public proclamations of the Death of Methods were incorrect, and to call the proclamations 'premature' (as they were with Mark Twain) is to suggest that the whole notion of Methods will one day die, which seems unlikely. As long as second and foreign languages are learned, different ways in which they can be taught will continue. There are many reasons for this methodological longevity, some of which were given by Larsen-Freeman and Anderson (2011), including the idea that methods 'serve as a foil for reflection that can aid teachers in bringing to conscious awareness the thinking that underlies their actions' (p. xi) and 'by becoming clear on where they stand (Clarke, 2003), teachers can choose to teach differently from the way they were taught' (p. xi).

The first of Larsen-Freeman and Anderson's reasons, in which methods can be 'a foil for reflection', relates to the idea of teachers as reflective practitioners (see, for example, Farrell, 2009), and to the idea of informed and principled eclecticism, in which teachers selectively adapt and combine complementary aspects of different methodologies, as discussed in previous chapters in this book. The second reason given by Larsen-Freeman and Anderson, which is about teachers teaching differently from the ways in which they were taught, explains why a significant number of teachers struggle to employ some methods in their context. This is due not only to inadequate teacher training and professional development, and important contextual differences between the context in which the method was developed and the one to which it has been exported, but also to differences between the way a teacher was taught and how s/he is required to teach now. This may be a considerable gap that needs to be bridged. Reflective practice, together with comprehensive initial teacher training and on-going professional development support, can help build and maintain such bridges (Farrell, 2009).

The third reason given by Larsen-Freeman and Anderson is that 'A knowledge of methods is part of the knowledge base of teaching. With it, teachers join a community of practice' (p. xii). A great deal has been written and said about Communities of Practice (CoPs) over the last 25 years, from the early, anthropological work of Jean Lave and Etienne Wenger (1991) to books such as David Barton and Karen Tusting's *Beyond Communities of Practice: Language Power and Social Context* (2005). More recent books combine notions of teachers as reflective practitioners and CoPs: for example, *Reflecting in Communities of Practice* (Curtis, Lebo, Cividanes, & Carter, 2013). An important part of CoPs is the existence of a shared language that can be used by members to communicate thoughts, ideas and so on among each other. In terms of teaching, an essential function of that language is to enable methodological discussions of what teachers and learners do – and do not do – in and out of class.

The fourth and fifth reasons given by Larsen-Freeman and Anderson are that, by being members of CoPs and professional discourse communities, 'teachers may find their own conceptions of how teaching leads to learning being challenged' and that 'a knowledge of methods helps to expand a teacher's repertoire of techniques' (p. xii). The fourth reason highlights the taken-for-granted but highly problematic notion that 'teaching leads to learning' or that 'learning is the result of teaching'. This is not necessarily the case, as many of us have seen language lessons in which the students appear to be learning *in spite of* the teacher and their teaching, rather than *because of* them.

One of the keys to understanding such situations is to look at possible causes for teaching not leading to learning, which may lie in a disconnect between the method being used and the context. There may be other disconnects as well, such as between the teacher and the students, between the textbook and the target language, and so on. My point here is that a broad and deep knowledge of methodologies enables teachers to know more about what is and is not happening in their classrooms.

ACTIVITY 9.3

If you are familiar with the idea of teachers as reflective practitioners, what does 'reflective practice' mean to you? And if you consider yourself to be a reflective practitioner, how do you engage in that kind of practice?

The Future of Methods

In 1984, in an article on 'The Secret Life of Methods', Richards concluded: 'We have seen that the field of methods in language teaching has been revitalized by different theories concerning the nature of language, by new theories concerning the central process of language acquisition, by innovative proposals for syllabus development and the design of instructional systems, as well as by the use of a variety of novel practices, techniques, and procedures in the language classroom' (p. 21). I agree with this statement, as all of the developments Richards referred to have continued in the 30-plus years since he drew his conclusion; theories have continued to be developed, as have practices, procedures and techniques. It cannot be argued that things within the worlds of language teaching and learning have stood still since 1984, making Richards' statement as true today as it was then.

As I have noted elsewhere (see Brown, 2014), 'instead of ignoring the obvious ironies of treating "post-methods" as though we've finally hit the methodological mother lode, I would like to propose that we set "post-methods" aside, as another useful phase (and/or phrase) in the discussion, but one that is over – and that we're now "post post-methods"' (p. 60). As the 50th President of the TESOL International Association (2015–2016), which is the world's largest international association of language educators, I travelled hundreds of thousands of miles, meeting language teachers in dozens of countries. As

I listened to them talk about what they do in their language lessons, and as I observed while in their classrooms, it was clear that they are all using methods, of one kind or another. Or, at the very least, they are using practices, procedures and techniques from one or more methods, which they were combining in meaningful and effective ways, based on their local, contextualized knowledge, skills and understanding.

Therefore, when some researchers wrote about our field being 'beyond methods' and claimed that we were in some sort of 'post-method condition' (Kumaravadivelu, 1994, 2003, 2006), they were, I believe, mistaken (Curtis, 2016a). The whole notion of being in a 'post-methods condition' made it sound as though we were recovering from an illness, or waking up in a hospital after an operation to remove our 'methods' gland, which, like our appendix, was found to have no purpose. Importantly, the discourse of the most recent publications in this area hardly mention 'post-method' at all (Kumaravadivelu, 2016), but instead focus on the 'post-colonial' positioning of ELT in relation to the NNEST–NEST debate (discussed earlier in this book). In this re-formulated/re-packaged argument (see Kumaravadivelu, 2006), methods are discussed primarily in terms of the imperial forces of oppression, from places like England and America, in which methods are 'the most crucial and consequential area where hegemonic forces find it necessary and beneficial to exercise the greatest control, because method functions as an operating principle shaping all other aspects of language education' (Kumaravadivelu, 2016, p. 73). Interestingly, and perhaps somewhat ironically, this statement highlights the tremendous importance of methods, which might be seen as running counter to the idea that we are, in any way, 'beyond methods'.

As the chapters in this book have shown (see, for example, the section on 'The Dark Side of ELT' in Chapter 4), I believe strongly that methodologies need to be seen in relation to their colonial origins, in contrast to their current contexts of use, and that we need to move beyond any notion of any methodology being 'context neutral' or 'context independent'. However, to suggest that a good way to move forward, past colonial methodological origins, is to claim that we are 'beyond methods' is not, for me, a particularly persuasive argument. And to propose 'microstrategies' such as 'Maximize learning opportunities' (Kumaravadivelu, 2003, p. 39) is to simply describe what I see all good teachers doing all the time. However, some of the microstrategies helpfully highlight the importance of knowing and showing 'how language usage and use are shaped by linguistic, extralinguistic, situational, and extrasituational contexts' (p. 39).

A more positive and productive way of moving forward would be to critically consider some of the methodological entities identified in the previous chapter (Chapter 8), such as the *Mystique of Methods*, *Methods and Magic*, the *Methods Marketplace* and *Methods as Messiah*. We could also critically consider ideas such as *Niche Methods* and *Methods for Specific Purposes* as well as *Methods as Medicine*. In this way, instead of claiming that we have somehow moved past methods, we could look at methodologies as necessary and integral, but complex and complicated, parts of how we can more fully and more deeply understand what teachers and learners in language classrooms do, and why and how they do it in those ways and not others. That kind of understanding is, after all, the shared goal of all of us who have chosen to be language teachers and language learners.

ACTIVITY 9.4

With reference to the last line, above, why did you become (or why do you want to become) a language teacher? What kind of language teacher are you now, and how will you use what you have learned in this book in your daily classroom language teaching and learning lessons?

Suggested Readings

As noted above, *How Languages Are Learned* (2013, fourth edition) by Patsy Lightbown and Nina Spada summarizes a great deal of research on Second Language Learning (SLL), with chapters on individual differences in SLL, explaining SLL, observing learning and teaching in the SL classroom, SLL in the classroom, and popular ideas about language learning revisited.

The teachingenglish.org.uk website has a short article titled 'The Future of Language Teaching' (2014) by David Petrie, based on a hypothetical case study of a language learner in the year 2034. https://www.teachingenglish.org.uk/blogs/david-petrie/future-language-teaching-%E2%80%93-a-case-study-2034

In terms of a specific context, in an officially bilingual country, a thorough and detailed report came out of a symposium in 2015 on 'Future Directions for Language Education in Ontario', which was held at the Ontario Institute for Studies in Education. The 60-page report is freely available at https://www.oise.utoronto.ca/ctlsa/UserFiles/File/Symposium_program_Final.pdf

Glossary

Dear Reader: It is important to note that this is not your typical book-end glossary, as perfectly good standard definitions of most of the terms below already exist elsewhere. Therefore, this glossary is more of a reflection/ expression of my own feelings about different aspects of our field. As such, this glossary includes some neologisms created just for you!

alternative When used in phrases such as 'alternative methods/ methodologies', 'alternative' means 'created as a challenge to the existing and accepted ways of doing things'. 'Alternative' here also indicates that the method is being used by a relatively small number of teachers and learners.

anti-methods The 'anti-methods movement' was formed by people who were opposed to the whole notion of methods and methodologies, who felt that all methods were, by definition, bad for teaching and learning. The movement eventually faded away, only to be replaced by the 'post-methods movement' (see **post-methods**).

appropriateness The notion of 'appropriateness' has emerged as an alternative to concepts such as 'authenticity' (see **authentic materials**), and to a lesser extent as an alternative to 'accuracy'. Rather than talking about how authentic the language input is, or about how accurate the language output is, we can, instead, focus on how contextually appropriate the input and the output are.

assessment For the purposes of this book, 'assessment' refers to in-class assessment, including the ways in which teachers check the understanding of their learners during the lesson. As such, 'assessment' as it is used in this book can refer to a wide range of in-class interactions, ranging from the teacher asking whether the learners have any questions to impromptu quizzes.

authentic materials (See **appropriateness**.) Here, 'authentic' refers to materials that were not created specifically for language teaching and learning, for example, a French-language newspaper read in a country where the majority of inhabitants speak French as their first language. It is possible that too much time has been spent on deciding how 'authentic' the materials are, or are not, or should be.

bandwagon(ing) The use of 'bandwagon' here refers to the thoughtless adoption of ways of doing things, and ways of thinking, that are mainly being adopted based on the logical fallacy that 'if everyone else is doing it, it must be good'. It may be considered to be the professional equivalent of 'peer pressure' among teenagers and other less mature groups.

causal As opposed to 'correlational'. When one thing is the result of/caused by something else, the relationship is causal. If something is correlated with something else, they are connected, but one thing does not necessarily cause the other thing to happen. For example, although we may assume that learning is the direct result of teaching – that teaching causes learning to take place – the relationship is likely to be more correlational than causal. Please note that these are entirely non-statistical uses of 'causal' and 'correlational'.

communicarians This word was created for this book. The word comes from 'Unitarian', which is a branch/brand of Christianity. 'Communicarian' refers to those teachers who cling to Communicative Language Teaching (CLT) as though it were a religious belief system. Teachers belonging to this particular pedagogical faith are fundamentally opposed to grammarians.

competencies 'Skills' and 'competencies' are often used interchangeably, but they are not quite the same thing. 'Skills' usually refers to someone's ability to complete a specific task successfully; for example, how to correctly conjugate a verb. However, 'competencies' refers to a broader collection of knowledge, skills and understanding; for example, how to use different greetings in different situations appropriately and effectively.

continuum As opposed to 'dichotomy'. For many reasons, some of which go back to the way the human brain was first formed, humans have a tendency to see the world in terms of, for example, black *or* white, good *or* bad, and so on: too much A *or* B; too little A *and* B. Few things in life are that clear-cut, as it often depends on the situation/context. Accepting that (almost) all things (ourselves included) can be located at different points along a continuum, at different times, can help us avoid this unfortunate tendency to dichotomize and to polarize.

correlational See **causal**.

deductive 'Deductive reasoning' is sometimes called 'top down reasoning', in which a conclusion is arrived at based on previous statements. The classic example, given by the Greek philosopher Socrates, is: 1. All men are mortal. 2. Socrates is a man. 3. Therefore, Socrates is mortal. In deductive language teaching, the teacher presents the student with items from the target language, which the student then practises until mastery occurs.

dichotomy See **continuum**.

English-dominant country The adjectival phrase 'English-speaking country' was always of limited descriptive value, as there is no notion of how many people in a country need to be able to say how many words of English for it to be considered an 'English-speaking country'. However, the phrase was used for a long time, and can still be heard and seen today. 'English-dominant' is less vague, and refers to any country where English is used by the majority of the population in their daily communications. 'English-dominant' also alludes to the historical dominance of countries such as the UK and the USA in world affairs.

evaluation (See **assessment**.) The process of observing and measuring something, such as language output, to determine its 'value', in terms of how effectively language output communicates the intended meaning of the speaker or the writer. Evaluation is often based on comparison, for example, with a pre-determined standard or level. Like 'summative assessment', evaluation often takes place later in the process, whereas 'formative assessment' takes place throughout the process.

facilitation In its more general sense, 'to facilitate' means 'to help make something happen'. 'Facilitation' is sometimes used as though it were a more learner-centred approach to teaching; for example, "Oh, I don't teach. I facilitate." However, this kind of statement is sometimes used as an excuse for not being able to teach due to lack of training.

form 'Form' has many meanings, but in this book 'form' refers to 'language forms', in terms of the grammatical structures of the language. In terms of grammar and vocabulary, the grammatical form of the word relates to what the word looks like, whereas the grammatical function relates to what the word does. Grammatical forms often relate to 'parts of speech', such as nouns, adjectives, verbs and so on, whereas grammatical functions often relate to grammatical tenses and other ways in which meaning is communicated.

globalization During the 2016 US Presidential Elections, more than 60 million Americans appeared to have voted against, among other things, globalization, which promised prosperity for all, based on the world's markets being seamlessly interconnected in mutually beneficial ways. This did not happen, possibly leading to the beginning of the end of globalization, and a return to nationalism, which would have major implications for language teaching and learning.

humanistic 'Humanism' rejects the belief that our lives are dictated or controlled by beings such as gods, and puts the emphasis instead on humans being fully responsible for their own thoughts, words and actions, without any divine intervention. 'Humanistic methods/methodologies' tried to tap into humanism by focusing on things like the emotional well-being of the learner, and making sure the learners felt safe, secure and comfortable.

inductive As opposed to **deductive**. 'Inductive reasoning' is sometimes called 'bottom up reasoning'. In inductive language teaching, instead of going from the generalization or rule to the specific example or activity, which is deductive, students are given examples or engage in activities that illustrate the generalization or rule. This is thought to be a less teacher-centred and more learner-centred approach, based on language learners 'noticing' how the target language works.

informed eclecticism To be eclectic is to combine different features of, in this case, methodologies, in ways that maximize the opportunities and minimize the limitations of the methodologies. *Informed* eclecticism entails being able to articulate clearly and concisely the basis for the methodological, combinatory choices made.

IRF Initiation-Response-Feedback. 'IRF' refers to a pattern or sequence of interaction between the teacher and the learners. The teacher initiates the interaction, then the learner responds, then the teacher gives feedback on the learner's response. IRF has been criticized for being too teacher-centred, as it is initiated, and to some extent controlled, by the teacher.

language labs Full name: language laboratories. In traditional language labs, learners sit in cubicles, usually separated from one another, wearing headphones with microphones. The learners often listen and repeat, in the style of the Audio-Lingual Method (ALM), after which they can play back the recording of their spoken target language production.

learner-centredness An important part of moving away from traditional teacher-centred teaching towards more humanistic approaches (see **humanistic**), in which the well-being of the learner was a central concern. However, a 'shared centre', in which the teacher is sometimes leading and the learners following – and other times vice versa – may be a more balanced approach.

learning outcomes Two key questions here are: As a result of the teaching and learning that took place, what can the learners do now that they could not do before? Or: As a result, what do the learners know now that they did not know before? The questions may also be expressed in terms of what the learners can do *more effectively* now, or what the learners know *more about* than they did before.

LEEP Learning English for Examination Purposes (McNaught and Curtis, 2008). This idea helps to answer the question: When is a language not a language? The answer: When all communicative intent has been stripped away, leaving only what is necessary to pass the international, local or provincial large-scale, standardized language examinations.

meaning (See **form**.) One example of dichotomous thinking (see **continuum** and **dichotomy**) has been 'form-focused' versus 'meaning-focused'. However, the connections between form and function make it difficult to separate one from the other. This relates to and also applies to the dichotomous thinking regarding 'accuracy' versus 'fluency'.

minority language education A minority language is, as the name implies, a language spoken by a population that is in the minority in a particular place. The goal of minority language education is to avoid language communities losing their first language(s) as a result of being immersed in what is, for them, a foreign language environment.

mother tongue The more accurate, more technical term for this is L1 or 'first language'. 'Mother tongue' was used for a long time to refer to someone's L1, until it was pointed out that societies were changing, and not everyone was raised by their mother any more.

native users This phrase was my less-than-successful attempt to stop everyone always referring to 'native speakers' of a language, as this privileges one modality over the others, and helped give rise to the 'native speaker myth' in language education, especially in English Language Teaching.

pattern practice This kind of practice was especially prevalent in the Grammar Translation Method (GTM), in which students were required to repeat and reproduce a grammatical structure, often many times, which was thought to lead to learning of that structure. Sometimes that worked, but often it didn't.

pendulumic This word was created for this book. It comes from 'pendulum' and describes the unhelpful swinging from one set of thoughts and actions to another, often with relatively little time for thought in between. (See **bandwagoning**.)

pluralistic A pluralist is someone who (like me) believes that societies and civilizations are better and stronger when a wide range of different types of people, beliefs and so on exist within those societies and civilizations. Applying this to teaching and learning means that teachers who can selectively and deliberately draw on a wide range of different methodologies can be more effective educators.

post-methods (See **anti-methods**.) Like the 'anti-methods movement', the 'post-methods movement' was formed by people (mostly professional academics) who claimed to want to liberate teachers and learners from 'the tyranny of methods'. And like the 'anti-methods movement' before it, the 'post-methods movement' also faded away, when a focus on pedagogy was found to be more helpful to teachers and learners than a focus on politics.

prescribed In this book, 'to prescribe' something is the opposite of 'to describe' something. The former is based on telling people how something should be (or should be done), whereas the latter is based on describing how something actually is done. Language analysis and language teaching are thought to have moved away from a more prescriptive approach to a more descriptive one.

real world One of my pet peeves! Unfortunately, the 'real world' is often contrasted with the classroom. However, for teachers and learners, classrooms are as real as it gets! I assume that those writers who refer to the 'real world' – making it sound like some ethereal, other-worldly realm – really mean 'out of class' as opposed to 'in class', which is a valid distinction.

Reform Movement There have been a number of such movements, but in language education the Reform Movement started at the end of the nineteenth century, with calls for major changes to the way that languages were being taught. The Reform Movement was generally against the GTM, with a focus on speaking, and moving away from reading and writing.

scaffold The original meaning of 'scaffold' referred to temporary support structures that workers could stand on while building a permanent structure such as a house. In language education, 'scaffold' came to mean the way in which the support initially provided by the teacher is carefully and gradually removed, with the goal of enabling the learner to eventually be independent and self-directing.

translanguaging This appears to be the most recent incarnation of earlier 'isms', such as bilingualism and multilingualism, as well as a re-packaging of earlier work on code-mixing and code-switching. Translanguaging may turn out to have some similarities to the 'post-methods movement', in that the main focus appears to be on the politics of language education rather than the pedagogy.

References

Adamson, B. (2005). Fashions in language teaching methodology. In A. Davies & C. Elder (Eds.), *The handbook of applied linguistics* (pp. 604–622). Oxford, UK: Blackwell Publishing.

Angell, J. (1995). Review of 'How languages are learned', first edition. *The Modern Language Journal, 79*(2), 268–269.

Anthony, E. M. (1963). Approach, method, and technique. *ELT Journal, XVII*(2), 63–67.

Arena, J. (Interviewer) & Gattegno, C. (Interviewee). (1980). Profiles: An interview with Caleb Gattegno [Interview transcript]. *Intervention in School and Clinic, 16*(2), 235–238.

Ariza, E. N. (2002). Resurrecting 'old' language learning methods to reduce anxiety for new language learners: Community language learning to the rescue. *Bilingual Research Journal, 26*(3), 717–728.

Asher, J. J. (1964). Toward a neo-field theory of behavior. *Journal of Humanistic Psychology, 4*(2), 85–94.

Asher, J. J. (1966). The learning strategy of the total physical response: A review. *The Modern Language Journal, 50*(2), 79–84.

Asher, J. J. (1969). The total physical response technique of learning. *Journal of Special Education, 3*(3), 253–262.

Asher, J. J., & Price, B. S. (1967). The learning strategy of the total physical response: Some age differences. *Child Development, 38*(4), 1219–1227.

Assalahi, H. M. (2013). Why is the grammar-translation method still alive in the Arab world? Teachers' beliefs and its implications for EFL teacher education. *Theory and Practice in Language Studies, 3*(4), 589–599.

Babayiğit, S. (2015). The dimensions of written expression: Language group and gender differences. *Learning and Instruction, 35*, 33–41.

Bachman, L. F. (2002). Some reflections on task-based language performance assessment. *Language Testing, 19*(4), 453–476.

Bailey, K. M. (2005). *Practical English language teaching: Speaking*. New York: McGraw-Hill.

Bancroft, W. J. (1982). Suggestopedia, sophrology and the traditional foreign language class. *Foreign Language Annals, 15*(5), 373–379.

Bartolome, L. (1994). Beyond the methods fetish – toward a humanizing pedagogy. *Harvard Educational Review, 64*(2), 173–194.

Barton, D. & Tusting, K. (2005). *Beyond communities of practice: Language power and social context*. New York, NY: Cambridge University Press.

Bayley, S. (1998). The direct method and modern language teaching in England 1880–1918. *History of Education, 27*(1), 39–57.

Belchamber, R. (2007). The advantages of communicative language teaching. *The Internet TESL journal, 13*(2), 1–4.

Bell, D. M. (2007). Do teachers think that methods are dead? *ELT Journal, 61*(2), 135–143.

Bennett, J. M., & Bennett, M. J. (2004). Developing intercultural sensitivity: An integrative approach to global and domestic diversity. In D. Landis, J. Bennett & M. Bennett (Eds.), *Handbook of intercultural training* (pp. 147–165). Thousand Oaks, CA: SAGE.

Bernard, H. R. (2011). *Research methods in anthropology: Qualitative and quantitative approaches* (5th ed.). Lanham, MD: AltaMira Press.

Berns, M. (1990). *Contexts of competence: Social and cultural considerations in communicative language teaching*. New York, NY: Plenum Press.

Bishop, R., & Berryman, M. (2006). *Culture speaks: Cultural relationships and classroom learning*. Wellington: Huia Publishers.

Boswell, R. E. (1972). Toward a new eclecticism in modern-language teaching. *Foreign Language Annals, 6*(2), 237–246.

Botha, L. (1985). An analysis of SALT in practice. *Per Linguam : A Journal of Language Learning, 1*(1), 7–8.

Bovée, A. (1919). Teaching vocabulary by the Direct Method. *The Modern Language Journal, 4*(2), 63–72.

Bowen, T. Teaching approaches: The communicative classroom. *onestopenglish*. Retrieved December 1, 2016 from http://www.onestopenglish.com/methodology/methodology/teaching-approaches/teaching-approaches-the-communicative-classroom/146489.article

Boyd, R. (2008, February 7). Do people only use 10 percent of their brains? What's the matter with only exploiting a portion of our gray matter? *Scientific American*. Retrieved December 1, 2016 from http://www.scientificamerican.com/article/do-people-only-use-10-percent-of-their-brains/

Breen, M. (1987). Learner contribution to task design. In C. Candlin & D. Murphy (Eds.), *Language learning tasks* (pp. 23–46). London: Prentice Hall.

Brindley, G. (1994). Task-centred assessment in language learning: The promise and the challenge. In N. Bird, P. Falvey, A. Tsui, D. Allison, and A. McNeill (Eds.), *Language and learning: Papers presented at the Annual International Language in Education Conference* (Hong Kong, 1993) (pp. 73–94). Hong Kong: Hong Kong Education Department.

Brindley, G., & Slatyer, H. (2002). Exploring task difficulty in ESL listening assessment. *Language Testing, 19*(4), 369–394.

Brinton, D., Snow, M. A., & Wesche, M. B. (1989). Content-based second language instruction. Boston: Heinle & Heinle Publishers.

Brito, I., Lima, A., & Auerbach, E. (2004). The logic of nonstandard teaching: A course in Cape Verdean language, culture and history. In B. Norton & K. Toohey (Eds.), *Critical pedagogies and language learning* (pp. 181–200). Cambridge: Cambridge University Press.

Brooks, F. B., & Donato, R. (1994). Vygotskyan approaches to understanding foreign language learner discourse during communicative tasks. *Hispania, 77*(2), 262–274.

Brown, H. D. (1993). Requiem for Methods. *Journal of Intensive English Studies, 7*, 1–12.

Brown, H. D. (2002). English language teaching in the 'post-methods' era. In J. C. Richards & W. A. Renandya (Eds.), *Methodology in language teaching: An anthology of current practice* (pp. 9–18). New York, NY: Cambridge University Press.

Brown, J. (2014). An interview with incoming TESOL President, Andy Curtis, Part 2. *TESL Ontario Contact, 40*(4), pp. 55–60.

Brune, I. H. (1953). Language in mathematics. In H. F. Fehr (Ed.), *The learning of mathematics: Its theory and practice* (pp. 156–191). Washington, DC: The National Council of Teachers of Mathematics.

Butler, Y. G. (2011). The implementation of communicative and task-based language teaching in the Asia-pacific region. *Annual Review of Applied Linguistics, 31*, 36–57.

Butler, Y. G., & Zeng, W. (2015). Young learners' interactional development in task-based paired-assessment in their first and foreign languages: A case of English learners in China. *Education 3-13, 43*(3), 292–321.

Bygate, M. (Ed.). (2015). *Domains and directions in the development of TBLT: A decade of plenaries from the international conference.* Amsterdam, the Netherlands: John Benjamins Publishing.

Byram, M., & Grundy, P. (2002). Context and culture in language teaching and learning. *Language, Culture and Curriculum, 15*(3), 193–195.

Byrnes, H. (2002). The role of task and task-based assessment in a content-oriented collegiate foreign language curriculum. *Language Testing, 19*(4), 419–437.

Calvert, M., & Sheen, Y. (2015). Task-based language learning and teaching: An action-research study. *Language Teaching Research, 19*(2), 226–244.

Cambridge Advanced Learner's Dictionary. http://dictionary.cambridge.org/

Cammarata, L. (Ed.). (2016). *Content-based foreign language teaching: Curriculum and pedagogy for developing advanced thinking and literacy skills.* New York: Routledge.

Cammarata, L., Tedick, D. J., & Osborne, T. A. (2016). Content-based instruction and curricular reforms goals: Issues and goals. In L. Cammarata (Ed.), *Content-based foreign language teaching: Curriculum and pedagogy for developing advanced thinking and literacy skills* (pp. 1–21). New York: Routledge.

Canagarajah, A. S. 1999. *Resisting linguistic imperialism in English teaching.* Oxford, UK: Oxford University Press.

Canagarajah, S. (2011). Codemeshing in academic writing: Identifying teachable strategies of translanguaging. *The Modern Language Journal, 95*(3), 401–417.

Canale, M. (1983). From communicative competence to communicative language pedagogy. In J. C. Richards & R. W. Schmidt (Eds.), *Language and communication* (pp. 2–27). London, England: Longman.

Canale, M., & Swain, M. (1980). Theoretical bases of communicative approaches to second language teaching and testing. *Applied Linguistics, 1*(1), 1–47.

Carroll, L. (1872). *Through the looking-glass.* London: Macmillan.

Celce-Murcia, M. (1991). Grammar pedagogy in second and foreign language teaching. *TESOL Quarterly, 25*, 459–480.

Celce-Murcia, M., Dörnyei, Z., & Thurrell, S. (1997). Direct approaches in L2 instruction: A turning point in communicative language teaching? *TESOL Quarterly, 31*(1), 141–152.

Celce-Murcia, M., & Olshtain, E. (2000). *Discourse and context in language teaching: A guide for language teachers.* New York: Cambridge University Press.

Chastain, K. D., & Woerdehoff, F. J. (1968). A methodological study comparing the audio-lingual habit theory and the cognitive code-learning theory. *The Modern Language Journal, 52*(5), 268–279.

Cheng, L., & Fox, J. (2017). *Assessment in the language classroom: Teachers supporting student learning.* Basingstoke, England: Palgrave Macmillan.

Chomsky, N. (1957). *Syntactic structures.* Berlin, Germany: Moulton.

Clarke, M. A. (1982). On bandwagons, tyranny, and common sense. *TESOL Quarterly, 16*(4), 437–448.

Coyle, D. (2007). Content and language integrated learning: Towards a connected research agenda for CLIL pedagogies. *International Journal of Bilingual Education and Bilingualism, 10*(5), 543–562.

Crawford, J. & Reyes, S. A. (2015). *The trouble with SIOP®: How a behaviorist framework, flawed research, and clever marketing have come to define – and diminish – sheltered instruction.* Portland, OR: Institute for Language & Education Policy.

Creese, A. & Blackledge, A. (2010). Translanguaging in the bilingual classroom: A pedagogy for learning and teaching? *The Modern Language Journal, 94*(1), 103–115.

Cuisenaire, G., & Gattegno, C. (1957). *Numbers in colour; a new method of teaching the processes of arithmetic to all levels of the primary school.* London: Heinemann Educational Books.

Cummins, J. (1981). *Bilingualism and minority-language children.* Toronto: OISE Press.

Cummins, J. (2015). How to reverse a legacy of exclusion? Identifying high-impact educational responses. *Language and Education, 29*(3), 272–279.

Curran, A. (1960). The concept of sin and guilt in psychotherapy. *Journal of Counseling Psychology, 7*(3), 192–197.

Curran, C. A. (1976). *Counseling-learning in second languages.* Chicago: Apple River Press.

Curtain, H., & Haas, M. (1995). *Integrating foreign language and content instruction in Grade K-8* (ERIC Digest EDO-FL-95-07). Washington, DC: ERIC Clearinghouse on Languages and Linguistics. Retrieved December 1, 2016, from ERIC database (ED381018), http://files.eric.ed.gov/fulltext/ED381018.pdf

Curtis, A. (2012). Doing more with less: Using film in English language teaching and learning in China. *Research on English Education,* 英语教育研究, *1*(1), 1–10.

Curtis, A. (2013). Book review of 'Testing the untestable in language education' (2010) by A. Paran & L. Sercu. *Language Testing, 30*(4), 557–560.

Curtis, A. (2016a). Looking in the Mirror at 50. Presidential keynote, presented at the *TESOL International Association 50th Annual Convention,* Baltimore, USA, 6 April.

Curtis, A. (2016b). Series Editor. *ELT In Context.* Alexandria, VA: TESOL Press.

Curtis, A. (2016c). Engagement in an Age of Distraction. Opening plenary presented at the *7th International ETAI Conference,* Ashkelon, Israel, 4 July.

Curtis, D., Lebo, D., Cividanes, W., & Carter, M. (2013). *Reflecting in communities of practice: A workbook for early childhood educators.* St. Paul, MN: Redleaf Press.

Czura, A. (2016). Major field of study and student teachers' views on intercultural communicative competence. *Language and Intercultural Communication, 16*(1), 83–98.

Daniel, S. M., & Conlin, L. (2015). Shifting attention back to students within the sheltered instruction observation protocol. *TESOL Quarterly, (49)*1, 169–187.

Davidheiser, J. (2002). Teaching German with TPRS (Total Physical Response Storytelling). *Die Unterrichtspraxis/Teaching German, 35*(1), 25–35.

Davison, C. (2004). The contradictory culture of teacher-based assessment: ESL teacher assessment practices in Australian and Hong Kong secondary schools. *Language Testing, 21*(3), 305–334.

Davison, C. (2007). Views from the chalkface: English language school-based assessment in Hong Kong. *Language Assessment Quarterly, 4*(1), 37–68 de Zwart, M. L. (2005). White sauce and Chinese chews: Recipes as postcolonial metaphors. In S. Carter, L. Erickson, P. Roome & C. Smith (Eds.), *Unsettled pasts: Reconceiving the west through women's history* (pp. 129–147). Calgary, AB: University of Calgary Press.

Dhority, L. (1991). *The ACT approach: The use of suggestion for integrative learning*. Amsterdam: Gordon and Breach Science Publishers.

Doerr, N. M. (Ed.). (2009). *The native speaker concept: Ethnographic investigations of native speaker effects*. Berlin: Mouton de Gruyter.

Dornyei, Z., & Schmidt, R. (Eds.). (2001). *Motivation and second language acquisition*. Honolulu, Hawaii: University of Hawaii Press.

Douglas, S. R., & Kim, M. (2015). Task-based language teaching and English for academic purposes: An investigation into instructor perceptions and practice in the Canadian context. *TESL Canada Journal, 31*(8), 1–22.

Duranti, A., & Goodwin, C. (Eds.). (1992). *Rethinking context: Language as an interactive phenomenon*. New York: Cambridge University Press.

East, M. (2012). *Task-based language teaching from the teachers' perspective: Insights from New Zealand*. Amsterdam, the Netherlands: John Benjamins Publishing.

Edwards, A. D., & Westgate, D. P. G. (1994). *Investigating classroom talk* (revised and extended 2nd ed.). London: Falmer Press.

Elder, C., Iwashita, N., & McNamara, T. (2002). Estimating the difficulty of oral proficiency tasks: What does the test-taker have to offer? *Language Testing, 19*(4), 347–368.

Ellerson, N. F., & Clarkson, P. C. (1996). Language factors in mathematics teaching and learning. In A. J. Bishop, K. Clements, C. Keitel, J. Kilpatrick, & C. Laborde (Eds.), *International handbook of mathematics education* (pp. 987–1033). Dordrecht, the Netherlands: Kluwer Academic Publishers.

Elliot, A. M., Thomas, C., Joynes, E. S., Hewett, W. T., de Sumichrast, F. C., Lodeman, A., ... von Jagemann, H. C. G. (1893). *Methods of teaching modern languages: Papers on the value and on methods of modern language instruction*. Boston: D. C. Heath.

Elliott, E., & Yountchi, L. (2009). Total physical response and Russian multi-and unidirectional verbs of motion: A case study in acquisition. *Slavic and East European Journal, 53*(3), 428–450.

Ellis, R. (Ed.). (1987). *Second language acquisition in context*. Englewood Cliffs, NJ: Prentice-Hall International.

Ellis, R. (2003). *Task-based language learning and teaching*. Oxford: Oxford University Press.

Ellis, R., & Roberts, C. (1987). Two approaches for investigating second language acquisition. In R. Ellis (Ed.) *Second language acquisition in context* (pp. 3–29). Englewood Cliffs, NJ: Prentice-Hall International.

Ensmenger, N. (2015). 'Beards, sandals, and other signs of rugged individualism': Masculine culture within the computing professions. *Osiris, 30*(1), 38–65.

ETS. (no date). TOEFL. Retrieved December 1, 2016 from www.ets.org/toefl/ibt/about

Farooq, M. U. (2015). Creating a communicative language teaching environment for improving students' communicative competence at EFL/EAP university level. *International Education Studies, 8*(4), 179–191.

Farrell, T. S. C. (2009). Critical reflection in a TESL course: Mapping conceptual change. *ELT Journal, 63*(3): 221–229.

Freeman, D. (1989). Teacher training, development, and decision making: A model of teaching and related strategies for language teacher education. *TESOL Quarterly, 23*(1), 27–45.

Freire, P. (1980). *Pedagogy of the oppressed*. London, UK: Bloomsbury.

Fries, C. C. (1945). *Teaching and learning English as a foreign language*. Ann Arbor, MI: University of Michigan Press.

Fries, C. C. (1952). *The structure of English: An introduction to the construction of English sentences*. New York, NY: Harcourt Brace.

Fries, C. C. (1963). *Linguistics and reading*. New York, NY: Holt, Rinehart and Winston.

Gaffield-Vile, N. (1996). Content-based second language instruction at the tertiary level. *ELT Journal, 50*(2), 108–114.

García, O., & Wei, L. (2014). *Translanguaging: Language, bilingualism and education*. Basingstoke, England: Palgrave Macmillan.

Garner, M., & Borg, E. (2005). An ecological perspective on content-based instruction. *Journal of English for Academic Purposes, 4*(2), 119–134.

Gassner-Roberts, G. (1986). Some personal observations of SALT, suggestopedia and other accelerative learning methods in Japan and Europe. *Per Linguam: A Journal of Language Learning, 2*(1), 7–15.

Gattegno, C. (1965). *A teacher's introduction to the Cuisenaire-Gattegno method of teaching arithmetic*. Reading, UK: Educational Explorers.

Gattegno, C. (1972). *Teaching foreign languages in schools: The silent way* (2nd ed.). New York: Educational Solutions.

Gattegno, C. (1973). *In the beginning there were no words: The universe of babies*. New York: Educational Solutions.

Gattegno, C. (1974). *The common sense of teaching mathematics*. New York: Educational Solutions.

Germain, C. (1993). Évolution *de l'enseignement des langues: 5000 ans d'histoire*. Paris: CLE International.

Goodnough, K. (2008). Dealing with messiness and uncertainty in practitioner research: The nature of participatory action research. *Canadian Journal of Education/Revue Canadienne De l'*Éducation, *31*(2), 431–458.

Greenwood, J. (1985). Bangalore revisited: A reluctant complaint. *ELT Journal, 39*(4), 268–273.

Griffiths, C., & Parr, J. M. (2001). Language-learning strategies: Theory and perception. *ELT Journal, 55*(3), 247–254.

Halliday, M. A. K. (1991). The notion of 'context' in language education. In T. Le and M. McCausland (Eds.) *Language education: International developments. Proceedings of the international conference* (pp. 4–26). Ho Chi Min City, Vietnam.

Hamilton, T. E. (1966). The audio-lingual method in the university: Fad or panacea? *Hispania, 49*(3), 434–440.

Handley, S. (2011). Promoting community language learning in the United Kingdom. *Language Learning Journal, 39*(2), 149–162.

Hannan, D. (1966). Common sense and the direct method in language teaching. *The Phi Delta Kappan, 47*(7), 359–360.

Hardman, J., & A-Rahman, N. (2014). Teachers and the implementation of a new English curriculum in Malaysia. *Language, Culture and Curriculum, 27*(3), 260–277.

Harnad, S. (2006). Creativity: Methods or magic? *Hungarian Studies, 20*(1), 163–177.

Harper, D. (no date). *Online Etymological Dictionary*. www.etymonline.com

Haugen, E. (1972). *The ecology of language*. Stanford, CA: Stanford University Press.

Hermann, A. (2015). Translingual writing: From process to product? Globalizing written English in the second language. Indiana

Teachers of English to Speakers of Other Languages Journal, 13(1), 1–15.

Hiep, P. H. (2007). Communicative language teaching: Unity within diversity. *ELT Journal, 61*(3), 193–201.

Hirschman, E. C. (2003). Men, dogs, guns, and cars: The semiotics of rugged individualism. *Journal of Advertising, 32*(1), 9–22.

Holliday, A. (1994). *Appropriate methodology and social context.* Cambridge: Cambridge University Press.

Howatt, A. P. R. (1984). *A history of English language teaching.* Oxford: Oxford University Press.

Hu, G. W. (2005). Contextual influences on instructional practices: A Chinese case for an ecological approach to ELT. *TESOL Quarterly, 39*(4) 635–660.

Hu, Y., & Fell-Eisenkraft, S. (2003). Immigrant Chinese students' use of silence in the language arts classroom: Perceptions, reflections, and actions. *Teaching & Learning, 17*(2), 55–65.

Hyland, K., & Hamp-Lyons, L. (2002). EAP: Issues and directions. *Journal of English for Academic Purposes, 1*(1), 1–12.

Hymes, D. H. (1972). On communicative competence. In J. B. Pride & J. Holmes (Eds.), *Sociolinguistics: Selected readings* (pp. 269–293). Harmondsworth: Penguin.

IELTS. (no date). www.ielts.org/what-is-ielts/ielts-introduction

İlın, G., İnözü, J., & Yumru, H. (2007). Teachers' and learners' perceptions of tasks: Objectives and outcomes. *Journal of Theory and Practice in Education, 3*(1), 60–68.

Jansma, K. (1991). Review of Content-Based Second Language Instruction, by D. M. Brinton, M. A. Snow, & M. B. Wesche. *The French Review, 64*(4), 730–731.

Jin, L., & Cortazzi, M. (Eds). *Researching Chinese learners: Skills, perceptions and intercultural adaptations.* Basingstoke, England: Palgrave Macmillan.

Jobrack, B. (2011). *Tyranny of the textbook: An insider exposes how educational materials undermine reforms.* Lanham, MD: Rowman & Littlefield Publishers.

Kashif, S. A., & Sajjad, H. H. (2015). *Tasked based language learning and teaching.* Saarbrücken, Germany: Lambert Academic Publishing.

Kasper, L. F. (1997). The impact of content-based instructional programs on the academic progress of ESL students. *English for Specific Purposes, 16*(4), 309–320.

Kelly, L. (1969). *25 centuries of language teaching*. New York: Newbury House.

Kramsch, C. J. (1993). *Context and culture in language teaching*. Oxford: Oxford University Press.

Krashen, S. D. (1982). *Principles and practice in second language acquisition*. New York, NY: Pergamon.

Kumaravadivelu, B. (1994). The postmethod condition: (E)merging strategies for second/foreign language teaching. *TESOL Quarterly, 28*(1), 27–48.

Kumaravadivelu, B. (2003). *Beyond methods: Macrostrategies for language teaching*. New Haven, CT: Yale University Press.

Kumaravadivelu, B. (2006). *Understanding language teaching: From method to postmethod*. Mahwah, NJ: Lawrence Erlbaum Associates.

Kumaravadivelu, B. (2016). The decolonial option in English teaching: Can the subaltern act? *TESOL Quarterly, 50*(1), 66–85.

La Forge, P. G. (1971). Community language learning: A pilot study. Language Learning, 21(1), 45–61.

Lado, R. (1957). *Linguistics across cultures: Applied linguistics for language teachers*. Ann Arbor, MI: University of Michigan Press.

Lange, D. (1990). A blueprint for a teacher development program. In J. C. Richards & D. Nunan (Eds.), *Second language teacher education* (pp. 245–268). New York, NY: Cambridge University Press.

Larsen-Freeman, D. (1986). *Techniques and principles in language teaching*. New York: Oxford University Press.

Larsen-Freeman, D. (2000). *Techniques and principles in language teaching* (2nd ed.). New York: Oxford University Press.

Larsen-Freeman, D., & Anderson, M. (2011). *Techniques and principles in language teaching* (3rd ed.). Oxford: Oxford University Press.

Lasagabaster, D. & García, O. (2014). Translanguaging: towards a dynamic model of bilingualism. Culture and Education, 26(3), 557–564.

Lave, J., & Wenger, E. (1991). *Situated learning: Legitimate peripheral participation*. Cambridge, England: Cambridge University Press.

Lightbown, P., & Spada, N. (2013). *How languages are learned* (4th ed.). Oxford, England: Oxford University Press.

Lightfoot, L. (2005). Grammar lessons 'don't help children to write'. The Telegraph. Retrieved December 1, 2016 from http://www.telegraph.co.uk/news/uknews/1481496/Grammar-lessons-dont-help-children-to-write.html

Littlewood, W. (2004). The task-based approach: Some questions and suggestions. *ELT Journal, 58*(4), 319–326.

Liu, Y. (2011). Introduction of TPRS and its implications for Chinese college English teaching. *International Journal of Arts & Sciences, 4*(10), 169–175.

Lo, Y. Y. (2014a). Collaboration between L2 and content subject teachers in CBI: Contrasting beliefs and attitudes. *RELC Journal, 45*(2), 181–196.

Lo, Y. Y. (2014b). L2 learning opportunities in different academic subjects in content-based instruction – evidence in favour of 'conventional wisdom'. *Language and Education, 28*(2), 141–160.

Long, M. H. (1985). A role for instruction in second language acquisition: Task-based language teaching. In K. Hyltenstam & M. Pienemann (Eds.), *Modelling and Assessing in Second Language Acquisition* (pp. 77–99). Bristol, UK: Multilingual Matters.

Long, M. (2015). *Second language acquisition and task-based language teaching*. Hoboken, NJ: Wiley-Blackwell.

Lozanov, G. (1975a). Suggestopedia in primary schools. *Suggestology and Suggestopedia, 1*(2), 1–14.

Lozanov, G. (1975b). The suggestological theory of communication and instruction. *Suggestology and Suggestopedia, 1*(3), 1–13.

Lozanov, G. (1978). *Suggestology and outlines of suggestopedy*. New York, NY: Gordon and Breach.

Lu, S., & Ares, N. (2015). Liberation or oppression? – Western TESOL pedagogies in China. *Educational Studies, 51*(2), 112–128.

Lucente, A., & Al Shimale, Z. (2016). Syria's civil war. Retrieved December 1, 2016 from http://www.aljazeera.com/topics/country/syria.html

Luongo-Orlando, K. (2003). *Authentic assessment: Designing performance-based tasks*. Markham, Ont: Pembroke Publishers.

Lyons, J. (1977). *Semantics, Volume 1 and Volume 2*. Cambridge, UK: Cambridge University Press.

Macedo, D. (1994). Preface. In P. McLaren & C. Lankshear (Eds.), *Conscientization and resistance* (pp. 1–8). New York, NY: Routledge.

Macmillan Online Dictionary of English. www.macmillandictionary.com

Magrath, D. (2016, August 12). Interference patterns: Applying linguistic theory to lesson production. *TESOL English Language Bulletin.* Retrieved December 1, 2016 from http://exclusive.multibriefs.com/content/interference-patterns-applying-linguistic-theory-to-lesson-production/education

Mahboob, A. (2006). Confessions of an *enraced* TESOL professional. In A. Curtis & M. Romney (Eds.), *Color, Race and English Language Teaching: Shades of meaning* (pp. 173–188). Mahwah, NJ: Lawrence Earlbaum.

Mahboob, A. (Ed.). (2010). *The NNEST lens: Non native English speakers in TESOL.* Newcastle upon Tyne, UK: Cambridge Scholars Publishing.

Mart, C. T. (2013). The direct-method: A good start to teach oral language. *International Journal of Academic Research in Business and Social Sciences, 3*(11), 182–184.

McDonough, S. (2014). Review of 'How languages are learned', fourth edition. *Modern English Teacher, 23*(1), 88–90.

McNaught, C., & Curtis, A. (2009). Using policy initiatives to support both learning enhancement and language enhancement at a Hong Kong university. In T. Coverdale-Jones & P. Rastall (Eds.), *Internationalising the university: The Chinese context* (pp. 85–104). Hampshire, UK: Palgrave Macmillan.

McPake, J., Tinsley, T., Broeder, P., Mijares, L., Latomaa, S., & Martynuik, W. (2007). Valuing all languages in Europe. Graz, Austria: European Centre for Modern Language.

Meddings, L., & Thornbury, S. (2010). *Teaching unplugged: Dogme in English language teaching.* Guildford, England: Delta Publishing.

Mellow, J. D. (2002). Toward principled eclecticism in language teaching: The two-dimensional model and the centring principle. *TESL-EJ, 5*(4), 1–18.

Mislevy, R. J., Steinberg, L. S., & Almond, R. G. (2002). Design and analysis in task-based language assessment. *Language Testing, 19*(4), 477–496.

Mohan, B. (1986). *Language and content.* Reading, MA: Addison Wesley.

Momaday, N. C. (1997). *The man made of words: Essays, stories, passages.* New York, NY: St Martin's Press.

Musumeci, D. (1996). Teacher-learner negotiation in content-based instruction: Communication at cross-purposes? *Applied Linguistics, 17*(3), 286–325.

Norman, G. (2010). Likert scales, levels of measurement and the 'laws' of statistics. *Advances in Health Sciences Education, 15*(5), 625–632.

Norris, J. M., Brown, J. D., Hudson, T. D., & Bonk, W. (2002). Examinee abilities and task difficulty in task-based second language performance assessment. *Language Testing, 19*(4), 395–418.

Norton, B., & Toohey, K. (Eds.) (2004). *Critical pedagogies and language learning*. Cambridge: Cambridge University Press.

Nunan, D. (1991). *Language teaching methodology: A textbook for teachers*. New York, NY: Prentice-Hall.

Nunan, D. (2004). *Tasked-based language teaching*. Cambridge: Cambridge University Press.

Oak, H. (2010). *Exploring EFL reading instruction in high school classrooms in Korea: The pedagogic life of the grammar translation method*. Saarbrücken, Germany: VDM Publishing.

Odendaal, M. S. (2013). Raising achievement levels by means of suggestopedia. *Per Linguam: A Journal of Language Learning, 3*(2), 22–30.

Ogilvie, G., & Dunn, W. (2010). Taking teacher education to task: Exploring the role of teacher education in promoting the utilization of task-based language teaching. *Language Teaching Research, 14*(2), 161–181.

Olagoke, D. O. (1982). Eclecticism in theoretical approaches to the teaching of foreign languages. *System, 10*(2), 171–178.

Ostrander, S., & Schroeder, L., with Ostrander, N. (1979). *Superlearning*. London, England: Souvenir Press.

Ouyang, H. (2000). One-way ticket: A story of an innovative teacher in mainland China. *Anthropology & Education Quarterly, 31*(4), 397–425.

Paikeday, T. M. (1985). *The native speaker is dead: An informal discussion of a linguistic myth with Noam Chomsky and other linguists, philosophers, psychologists and lexicographers*. Toronto, Canada: Paikeday Publishing.

Pearce, D. G. (1987). Spatial patterns of package tourism in Europe. *Annals of Tourism Research, 14*(2), 183–201.

Peters, M. O. (1934). An experimental comparison of grammar-translation method and direct method in the teaching of French. *The Modern Language Journal, 18*(8), 528–542.

Phillipson, R. H. L. (1992). *Linguistic imperialism.* Oxford, UK: Oxford University Press.

Phillipson, R. H. L. (Ed.). (2000). *Rights to language.* Mahwah, NJ: Lawrence Erlbaum.

Piaget, J. (1926). *The language and thought of the child.* London: Routledge & Kegan Paul.

Prabhu, N. S. (1987). *Second language pedagogy.* Oxford, UK: Oxford University Press.

Prabhu, N. S. (1990). There is no best method – why? *TESOL Quarterly, 24*(2), 161–176.

Pratchett, T. (2010). *I shall wear midnight.* New York, NY: Harper.

Prator, C. H. (1979). The cornerstones of methods. In M. Celce-Murcia & L. McIntosh (Eds.), *Teaching English as a second or foreign language* (pp. 5–15). Rowley, Massachusetts: Newbury House Publishers.

Prichard, A., & Taylor, J. (1978). Suggestopedia for the disadvantaged reader. *Intervention in School and Clinic, 14*(1), 81–90.

Pulgram, E. (Ed.). (1954). *Applied linguistics in language teaching.* Washington, DC: Georgetown University Press.

Ramirez, S. Z. (1986). The effects of Suggestopedia in teaching English vocabulary to Spanish-dominant Chicano third graders. *The Elementary School Journal, 86*(3), 325–333.

Ray, B., & Seely, C. (1997). *Fluency through TPR storytelling: Achieving real language acquisition in school.* Berkeley, CA: Command Performance Language Institute.

Renner, C. E. (1996). *Enriching learners' language production through content-based instruction.* Madena, Italy: National Conference on Lingua e Nuova Didattica. Retrieved December 1, 2016 from ERIC database. (ED411694). http://files.eric.ed.gov/fulltext/ED411694.pdf

Richards, J. C. (1984). The secret life of methods. *TESOL Quarterly, 18*(1), 7–23.

Richards, J. C. (1985). *The context of language teaching.* New York, NY: Cambridge University Press.

Richards, J. C. (2003). *Beyond training: Perspectives on language teacher education.* New York, NY: Cambridge University Press.

Richards, J. C. (2006). *Communicative language teaching today.* New York: Cambridge University Press.

Richards, J. C., & Renandya, W. A. (Eds.). (2002). *Methodology in language teaching: An anthology of current practice*. New York, NY: Cambridge University Press.

Richards, J. C., & Rodgers, T. S. (1986). *Approaches and methods in language teaching: A description and analysis*. New York: Cambridge University Press.

Richards, J. C., & Rodgers, T. S. (2001). *Approaches and methods in language teaching* (2nd ed.). New York: Cambridge University Press.

Richards, J. C., & Rodgers, T. S. (2014). *Approaches and methods in language teaching* (3rd ed.). New York: Cambridge University Press.

Risager, K. (2005). Foreword. In L. Sercu (Ed.), *Foreign language teachers and intercultural competence: An international investigation* (pp. vii–ix). Bristol, UK: Multilingual Matters.

Rivers, W. M. (1968). *Teaching foreign-language skills*. Chicago: University of Chicago Press.

Roberts, C., & Simonot, M. (1987). 'This is my life': How language acquisition is interactionally accomplished. In R. Ellis (Ed.), *Second language acquisition in context* (pp. 133–148). Englewood Cliffs, NJ: Prentice-Hall International.

Rodgers, D. M. (2006). Developing content and form: Encouraging evidence from Italian content-based instruction. *The Modern Language Journal, 90*(3), 373–386.

Rodgers, T. S. (2001). *Language Teaching Methodology (ERIC Issue Paper)*. Washington, DC: ERIC Clearinghouse on Languages and Linguistics. Retrieved December 1, 2016 from ERIC database. (ED459628). http://files.eric.ed.gov/fulltext/ED459628.pdf

Sample, I. (2014, July 8). Genes that influence children's reading skills also affect their maths. *The Guardian*. Retrieved December 1, 2016 from https://www.theguardian.com/science/2014/jul/08/genes-children-reading-maths-literacy-mathematics

Satilmis, Y., Yakup, D., Selim, G., & Aybarsha, I. (2015). Teaching concepts of natural sciences to foreigners through content-based instruction: The adjunct model. *English Language Teaching, 8*(3), 97–103.

Savignon, S. J. (1972). *Communicative competence: An experiment in foreign language teaching*. Philadelphia, PA: Center for Curriculum Development.

Savignon, S. J. (2007). Beyond communicative language teaching: What's ahead? *Journal of Pragmatics, 39*(1), 207–220.

Schleppegrell, M. J., Achugar, M., & Oteiza, T. (2004). The grammar of history: Enhancing content-based instruction through a functional focus on language. *TESOL Quarterly, 38*(1), 67–93.

Scovel, T. 1979. Review of Suggestology and outlines of Suggestopedy by George Lozanov. *TESOL Quarterly, 13*(2), 255–266.

Selivan, L. (2016). *Seventh International ETAI Conference Program Book*. Ashkelon, Israel, 4–6 July 2016.

Shawer, S. (2013). Preparing adult educators: The need to develop communicative language teaching skills in college-level instructors. *Journal of Literacy Research, 45*(4), 431–464.

Shintani, N. (2016). *Input-based tasks in foreign language instruction for young learners*. Amsterdam, the Netherlands: John Benjamins.

Short, D. J., & Echevarria, J. (1999). *The sheltered instruction observation protocol: A tool for teacher-researcher collaboration and professional development*. Santa Cruz, CA: Center for Research on Education, Diversity, and Excellence.

Shrum, J. L., & Glisan, E. W. (2010). *Teacher's handbook: Contextualized language instruction*. Boston, MA: Heinle Cengage Learning.

Sidis, B. (1919). *The psychology of suggestion: A research into the subconscious nature of man and society*. New York, NY: Appleton and Company.

Skehan, P. (1998). Task-based instruction. *Annual Review of Applied Linguistics, 18*, 268–286.

Skinner, B. F. (1953) *The possibility of a science of human behavior*. New York, NY: The Free House.

Smith, D. (1997). In search of the whole person: Critical reflections on community language learning. *Journal of Research on Christian Education, 6*(2), 159–181.

Song, B. (2006). Content-based ESL instruction: Long-term effects and outcomes. *English for Specific Purposes, 25*(4), 420–437.

Spiteri, D. (2010). Back to the classroom: Lessons learnt by a teacher educator. *Studying Teacher Education, 6*(2), 131–141.

Stern, H. H. (1983). *Fundamental concepts of language teaching*. Oxford: Oxford University Press.

Stevick, E. W. (1974). Some basic facts about 'the silent way'. [Review of Teaching Foreign Languages in Schools: The Silent Way, by C. Gattegno]. *TESOL Quarterly, 8*(3), 305–314.

Stevick, E. W. (1980). *Teaching languages: A way and ways*. Rowley, MA: Newbury House Publishers.

Stevick, E. W. (1990). *Humanism in language teaching: A critical perspective*. New York, NY: Oxford University Press.

Tang, H., Chiou, J., & Jarsaillon, O. (2015). Efficacy of task-based learning in a Chinese EFL classroom: A case study. *English Language Teaching, 8*(5), 168–176.

The Telegraph. 2005, January 17. Is grammar necessary? Retrieved December 1, 2016 from http://www.telegraph.co.uk/news/1481523/Your-view-Is-grammar-necessary.html

Thomas, M., & Reinders, H. (2012). *Task-based language learning and teaching with technology*. London: Bloomsbury Academic.

Thormann, W. E. (1969). The Audio-Lingual Method in the past: 'Anti-grammar' in seventeenth century France. *The Modern Language Journal, 53*(5), 327–329.

Thornbury, S. (1998). Comments on Marianne Celce-Murcia, Zoltan Dornyei, and Sarah Thurrell's 'Direct approaches in L2 instruction: A turning point in communicative language teaching?': A reader reacts. *TESOL Quarterly, 32*(1), 109–116.

Tudor, I. (1996). *Learner-centredness as language education*. Cambridge: Cambridge University Press.

Ur, P. (2013). Language-teaching method revisited. *ELT Journal, 67*(4), 468–474.

van den Branden, K. (Ed.). (2006). *Task-based language education: From theory to practice*. Cambridge: Cambridge University Press.

van den Branden, K., Bygate, M., & Norris, J. M. (Eds.). (2009). *Task-based language teaching: A reader*. Amsterdam, the Netherlands: John Benjamins Publishing.

van den Branden, K., Depauw, V., & Gysen, S. (2002). A computerized task-based test of second language Dutch for vocational training purposes. *Language Testing, 19*(4), 438–452.

van Lier, L. (1988). *The classroom and the language learner: Ethnology and the second language classroom research*. New York, NY: Longman.

Varvel, T. (1979). The silent way: Panacea or pipedream? *TESOL Quarterly, 13*(4), 483–494.

Wade, P. (2015). The native speaker teacher and the issue of equality. *TEFL Equity Advocates*. Retrieved December 1, 2016 from https://teflequityadvocates.com/2015/11/19/the-native-speaker-teacher-and-the-issue-of-equality-by-phil-wade/

Wagner, M. J., & Tilney, G. (1983). The effect of 'superlearning techniques' on the vocabulary acquisition and alpha brainwave production of language learners. *TESOL Quarterly, 17*(1), 5–17.

Waldrop, J. B., & Bowdon, M. A. (Eds.). (2016). *Best practices for flipping the college classroom*. New York, NY: Routledge.

Wang, L., Qian, Y., Scott, M. R., Chen, G., & Soong, F. K. (2012). Computer-assisted audiovisual language learning. *Computer, 45*(6), 38–47.

Watanabe, Y. (1996). Does grammar translation come from the entrance examination? Preliminary findings from classroom-based research. *Language Testing, 13*(3), 318–333.

Wheeler, G. (2013). *Language teaching through the ages*. New York: Routledge.

Willis, D., & Willis, J. (2007). *Doing task-based teaching*. Oxford: Oxford University Press.

Willis, J. (1996). *A framework for task-based learning*. Harlow, England: Longman.

Wong, M. S., Kristjansson, C., & Dornyei, Z. (2013). *Christian faith and English language teaching and learning: Research on interrelationship of religion and ELT*. New York: Routledge.

Wong, T. (2015, June 5). China's gaokao: High stakes for national exam. *BBC News*. Retrieved December 1, 2016 from http://www.bbc.com/news/world-asia-china-33059635

Xu, Z. (2013). Globalization, culture and ELT materials: A focus on China. *Multilingual Education, 3*(1), 1–19.

Zheng, X., & Borg, S. (2014). Task-based learning and teaching in China: Secondary school teachers' beliefs and practices. *Language Teaching Research, 18*(2), 205–221.

Index

Accuracy, 23, 24, 26, 79, 80, 83, 85, 153, 156
Anti-grammar, 127, 140
Anti-methods, 2, 4, 15, 16, 17, 18, 127
Applied linguists, 24, 59, 97, 141
Appropriate/ness, 25, 26, 47, 53, 60, 74, 79, 80, 111, 145, 205
Authentic/ity, 70, 81, 120

Bandwagon/ing, vii, 5, 6, 7, 59, 138, 150, 173, 194
Best fit, 75
Best method, 58, 64, 75, 127, 141, 169, 170, 207
Best practice, 64, 75, 141, 173, 200

Cape Verde, 21, 32, 37, 38
China, 25, 34, 45, 64, 69, 89, 92, 97, 98, 175, 189
Choice/s, 10, 14, 24, 36
Christian/ity, 168, 178, 179, 180, 187, 191, 192, 205
Circular, 1, 9, 12, 18
Colonial, 16, 34, 211, 212
Communicative competence, 73, 75, 76, 77, 78, 93, 100, 101
Community/ies of practice, 14, 209
Confidence, 63, 135, 142, 168, 190

Continuum, 64, 76, 79, 82, 83, 112, 156, 201
Control, 22, 56, 62, 63, 64, 65, 136, 155, 156, 189
Counselling, 182
Culture, 21, 25, 27, 28, 32, 33, 34, 98, 190, 193
Cyclical, 1, 9, 12, 18, 131

Death, xi, 52, 202, 204, 205, 206, 208
Dichotomy, 27, 64, 156
Doctrine, 44, 130, 191

Economic(s), 30, 74, 95, 97, 107, 109, 121, 155, 156, 167, 186, 196, 205
England, 94, 95, 127, 128, 148
English as a Foreign Language (EFL), 27, 31, 94, 99, 102, 109, 123, 154, 156, 191
English as a Second Language (ESL), 27, 31, 109, 123, 191
English as the Medium of Instruction (EMI), 111, 120, 121
English-dominant country/ies, 27, 111, 145, 171
English for Academic Purposes (EAP), 55, 85, 111, 112, 119, 121

English for Specific Purposes
(ESP), 111, 121, 175
English for Vocational Purposes
(EVP), 111
Experiment/al, 26, 33, 112, 139,
140, 162, 166, 172, 173, 174,
188, 206

Facilitate, 57, 63, 83, 112,
153, 172
Fads, 127, 138, 196
Faith, 44, 160, 168, 178, 180
Fashions, 18, 105, 129, 131, 196
Fluency, 79, 80, 83, 84, 85, 86,
168, 171, 174, 175
French, 112, 128, 151, 165

Games, 61, 62, 80, 82, 87, 88
Governments, 33, 45, 139, 148,
150, 202

History, vii; xi; xiii; 1, 2, 3, 4, 5,
8, 9, 10, 12, 16, 17, 19, 37, 38,
58, 79, 96, 106, 108, 112, 127,
139, 141, 175, 179, 197
Human subjects, 26, 33

IELTS (International Language
Testing System), 89, 124
Immersion, 108, 112, 123, 129,
192, 200
Informed eclecticism, xiii; 2,
10, 14, 17, 67, 188, 193,
198, 208
Interaction, 23, 27, 28, 29, 30,
36, 50, 56, 57, 63, 69, 81, 85,
111, 119, 136, 174, 180, 181,
182, 186, 188, 198
Italian, 108, 118

Laboratory/ies, 26, 139, 206
Language Acquisition, 14, 22, 27,
44, 76, 80, 108, 119, 138, 140,
153, 168, 174, 175, 188, 196, 210
Languages for Specific Purposes
(LSP), 90, 175
LEEP (Learning English for
Examination Purposes), 89
Linear, 1, 9, 12, 18, 149, 150

Magic(al), 159, 166, 212
Marketplace, 111, 159, 167, 212
Mathematics, 185, 186
Medicine, 5, 98, 160, 181,
192, 212
Medium of instruction, 37,
112, 113
Messiah, 98, 159, 169, 212
Messy/Messiness, 12, 47
Methods for Specific Purposes,
160, 212
Modern Language Journal,
138, 171
Music, 163, 165, 167, 168, 190
Mystique, 159, 164, 166, 212

Native speakers, viii; xi; 76, 110
Native users, 28, 76, 81, 93, 94,
95, 96, 110, 134, 201
Neo-colonialism, 98
Niche methods, 160, 175, 212
Non-native user, 93, 96, 110,
121, 134, 183
Non-linear, 9, 18, 149

One-size-fits-all, 17, 60, 130,
173, 200
One true method, 170, 172, 192,
198, 200

Organic, x, xi, 35

Panacea, 138, 192
Paradigm, 17, 26, 75, 76, 129
Politics/political, 7, 30, 32, 33, 60, 74, 97, 105, 107, 109, 120, 129, 161, 180, 206
Post-colonial, 74, 96, 203, 206, 211
Post-methods, ix, 1, 2, 4, 15, 16, 18, 195, 204, 206, 210, 211
Post post-methods, ix, 195, 210
Publishers, 49, 59, 174, 196, 198

Real World, 42, 48, 50, 51, 71, 134, 143, 170,
Reform Movement, 127, 128

Self-esteem, 163, 164
Spanish, 183, 184
Storytelling, 175, 176, 177
Student Talk Time (STT), 84
Syllabus, 82, 210

Teacher Talk Time (TTT), 84
TESOL Quarterly, 169, 170, 187, 192
TESOL International Association, 200, 210
Textbook publishers, 49, 148
TOEFL (Test of English as a Foreign language), 89
Tourism, 94, 95
Translanguaging, 6, 7
Trust, 56, 64

www.ingramcontent.com/pod-product-compliance
Lightning Source LLC
Chambersburg PA
CBHW071822300426
44116CB00009B/1400